FREE TO LOVE

Margaret Gill, MB, BS, MRCS, LRCP was born in Edinburgh and trained as a doctor at St Bartholomew's Hospital in London. She worked in the fields of child health and family planning before specializing in psychosexual medicine, in which she is involved in training other doctors.

Dr Gill is a part-time member of staff at the Acorn Healing Trust in Hampshire, and a visiting lecturer at All Nations College in Hertfordshire. She is married to Mike and they have two grown-up daughters.

HANDBOOKS OF PASTORAL CARE

SERIES EDITOR: MARLENE COHEN

FREE TO LOVE
Sexuality and Pastoral Care

MARGARET GILL

HarperCollins*Publishers*

HarperCollins*Publishers*
77-85 Fulham Palace Road,
Hammersmith, London W6 8JB

First published in Great Britain in 1994
by HarperCollins*Publishers*
1 3 5 7 9 10 8 6 4 2

A catalogue record for this book
is available from the British Library

ISBN 0 551 02789-4

Typeset by Harper Phototypesetters Limited,
Northampton, England
Printed and bound in Great Britain by
HarperCollinsManufacturing Glasgow

To Eric, my father
and Mike, my husband;
the two men closest to me
who have taught me so much
about the many dimensions of sexuality.
I thank them for their love.

ACKNOWLEDGEMENTS

Thanks are due to the following for permission to quote copyright material: Cairns Publications, from *Pleasure, Pain And Passion* and *Good Fruits* by the Revd James Cotter; Darton, Longman and Todd, from *Living Love* by Ruth Burrows; Pan Macmillan Ltd, from *Later Poems* by R. S. Thomas; Gill & Macmillan, Dublin, from *Prayers of Life* by Michel Quoist.

CONTENTS

Many years ago Joy, my wife, and I were invited to attend a large summer conference for a Christian community so that I could give a series of talks to the young people present on 'relationships'. There seemed to be quite a buzz amongst the young, and not so young, as sexual themes and practicalities were addressed and, subsequently, spilled over into 'table-talk' and wider discussion. One mother of small children took Joy aside and earnestly enquired, 'Is your husband an expert on sex?' Joy, her mind awash with a kaleidoscope of intimate memories, assured the woman that I was!

Free to Love is written by a fellow-doctor who is a real expert on sex. Trained by the Institute of Psychosexual Medicine, Dr Margaret Gill has years of experience at the coal-face of human sexual need. Her expertise, though, is not limited to identifying and advising men and women on the physical aspects of their intimate relating. Her remit is a wider one, and that is expressed clearly in this beautifully written book, where sexuality is celebrated as integral to our humanity and, indeed, to our spirituality.

Free to Love, in its enquiry into sexuality and pastoral care, offers a rich resource for all Christian carers, counsellors and listeners – since all godly caring needs to be aware of the sexual dimension of human life, whether explicit, affective or genital. Through careful reasoning, sharply-etched case-histories, apt quotations, and a warm and compassionate sharing of our own story, Margaret Gill takes us on a journey that explores the heights and depths of sex, both within our inner worlds and in its richly varied manifestations. We can pin-point three characteristics of this exploration: *practicality*, *sensitivity* and *spirituality*.

Practicality. Although this book is not solely a 'how to do it' manual (Margaret Gill rightly points out that we cannot simply read our way to effective counselling), it is full of practical wisdom for the pastoral carer. Principles that are applicable to all counselling are given a particular weight amidst the complexities and taboos of sexual themes. Margaret Gill writes with great perception on, for example, the need in counselling sexual partners to listen carefully to the relationship, to what is going on between the two individuals. She investigates, too, the nuances of non-verbal communication in matters of sex, the way the body is often more articulate than the tongue, and the importance of beginnings and endings in the pastoral encounter. Many counsellors and carers can feel out of their depth in the waters of sexual reality. Whether they have plunged in fully alert, or strayed unwittingly into the danger zone, Margaret Gill offers much wise advice on the rescue operation of careful listening, on the essential nature of competent supervision and on the need to discern when we should seek professional help beyond our skills.

Sensitivity. It is one thing to be practical, it is another to be sensitive to the delicate, deeply felt, and often strongly defended, nature of sexual matters. *Free to Love* demonstrates a compassionate sensitivity in the face of a wide range of issues and everyday human realities that are shunned and left unexamined by many Christians. There is a caring and courageous tackling of, for instance, questions of headship within marriage, the nature and value of same-sex friendships, the expression of sexuality in celibacy, the constructive and destructive aspects of fantasy, the taboo subject of masturbation and the need for support and understanding at the surgical loss of a sexual organ, such as the breast or the womb. None of these areas are examined lightly. Margaret Gill has given of herself as she has wrestled, for example, with the attempt to do justice to the Scriptures within the tantalizing debate on male and female roles in marriage and in the deep pastoral dilemmas of homosexuality - where, at the end of an especially perceptive chapter, she declares the struggle she had had to be true to what she believes 'about our holy and compassionate God and about biblical teaching.'

Spirituality. Towards the end of the book, Margaret Gill quotes Philip Sheldrake's dictum that spirituality is 'theology on two feet' and it is the earthed nature of her spiritual perspective that undergirds her exploration of human sexuality and its pastoral care. Beginning at the beginning, she grounds her venture in the sexual imagery of creation itself, as the earth is 'impregnated with the energy of God'.

Throughout her unfolding argument I felt, time and time again, that I stood on holy ground, as the God-ordained interweaving of humanity, sexuality and 'bipedal' theology is proclaimed. The book's climax (the imagery of sex is never far away!) comes in the final chapter on 'Sexuality and Spirituality' where an earlier refrain, that of the incarnated Christ, is amplified powerfully and movingly. The humanity of Jesus, comprising the integration of sexuality and spirituality, is our model for living. Margaret Gill challenges us all, pastors and pastored, carers and cared for, when she writes of the One who trusts himself to his creation:

If God can take such risks, can we not begin to trust our bodies as containers of the incarnate God and as 'temples' of the Holy Spirit? We can demonstrate something of God's grace and truth in our bodily sexuality *or* we can tell lies with it. What we cannot do is keep it silent - however much we might like to think we can.

ROGER HURDING

SERIES INTRODUCTION

The demand for pastoral care and counselling in churches has increased to record levels and every indication is that this trend will continue to accelerate. Some churches are fortunate to have ready access to professionally trained and qualified counsellors, but in most situations this onerous task falls to pastors.

Some pastors* are naturally gifted for the ministry of counselling. Some receive training before ordination and then seek to extend this as opportunity permits through the years. Others have the task of counselling thrust upon them. Most seem to feel some sustained demand, internal or external, to be competent in the field. This series aims to address some of the gaps frequently left in theological training. It is intended to offer support to those entrusted with responsibility for the care and well-being of others.

Comparative studies of healing agencies were pioneered in the United States. As long as thirty years ago The Joint Commission on Mental Illness reported that 42 per cent of 2,460 people canvassed would go first to the clergy with any mental health problem.

Of course there may be reasons other than overtly religious for a preference for clergy counselling. There may seem less stigma in seeing a pastor than a psychiatrist. Also, viewing a problem as a primarily spiritual matter may preclude taking some degree of

---

*The term 'pastor' is used generically here, to include all who have a recognized pastoral role within a local church or Christian community.

responsibility for it and for examining its depths. And, of course, clergy visits are cheaper! Unfortunately, there can be the additional reason that parishioners feel an inappropriate right of access to their pastor's time and skills. God's availability at all times is sometimes confused with ours, as is divine omniscience.

Being a front-line mental health worker can put a pastor under enormous and inappropriate strain. Counselling is becoming the primary time consumer in an increasing number of parish ministries.

Feeling unsafe and inadequate in any situation inevitably produces some form of self-protective behaviour, unless we can admit our inadequacy while retaining self-respect. Religious professionals who are under pressure to function as counsellors but know their skills and knowledge to be in other areas may understandably take refuge in various defences, even dogmatism. The term 'religious professional' is more familiar in some countries than in others. The clerical profession actually preceded all others, in status and in time. 'But what are we professional *at*?' can be a difficult question to answer. This is especially so when clergy are driven to believe that anything short of multi-competence will let God down.

Pastors may feel obliged not to appear inadequate in the area of counselling because of their confidence that the Bible contains the answer to every human need. And it does, conceptually. The difficulty is not with the Bible nor with the pastor's knowledge of the Bible. Neither of these should be in question. The concern is whether pastors have the additional ability of a clinician. Naming a counselling problem correctly – not the presenting problem but the real, underlying issues and their components – is a refined specialism. Making a faulty diagnosis, especially when God and biblical authority are somehow implicated, is the cause of much damage. Clinical terminology can be applied almost at random but with a surprising degree of assurance. Understanding the Bible, and understanding the complexities of clinical practice, are not one and the same skill. In 1985 a comparative study was conducted into the ability of 112 clergy to recognize 13 signs of suicidal tendencies.

(Reported in the *Journal of Psychology and Theology*, 1989, Vol 17, No 2.) It was found that clergy were unable to recognize these signs any better than educated lay people and substantially less well than other mental health workers. This is no necessary reflection on the clergy. Why should they be expected to have this professional ability? Considering them culpable would only be just if they were to assume, or to allow an assumption to go unchecked, that their skills were identical to those of other caring professionals.

One pressure is that graduates of some theological colleges have actually been taught that ordination will confer counselling skills. 'We must insist upon the idea that every man who has been called of God into the ministry has been given the basic gifts for . . . counselling' (Jay Adams, *The Christian Counsellor's Manual*, 1973, Presbyterian and Reformed Publishing Company; Part One, Page 20).

Equating a ministry calling with being a gifted counsellor could be seen to involve some leaping assumptions. These are becoming more apparent as we distinguish what we used to call 'the ministry' from God's calling of *all* believers into ministry. As more work is done on what we mean by 'ordination' more clergy can be released into those areas of ministry for which they are clearly gifted and suited.

Belief that counselling skills are divinely bestowed in conjunction with a ministry 'call' will probably not issue in the purchase of this series of handbooks! Other pastors who believe or fear that neither counselling nor any other skills can be taken for granted, are possibly conducting their ministries under some heavy burdens. This series is written with a concern to address these burdens and to redress some erroneous equations that relate to them. Each author has extensive experience in some avenue of ministry and is also trained and experienced in some aspect of counselling.

These Handbooks of Pastoral Care are designed to aid pastors in assessing the needs of those who come to them for help. The more accurately this assessment can be made the more confident that pastor can be about the form of ministry that is required in each instance. Sometimes pastors will decide to refer the matter

elsewhere, but on other occasions there can be a prayerful
assurance in retaining the counselling role within their own
ministry.

Marlene Cohen
Oxford, March 1994

SEXUALITY IN SCRIPTURE

Before writing this chapter I was discussing the subject with a friend. She is an experienced nun living in community and I have just celebrated my Silver Wedding. Two very different women you might think. Both of us could say we are fulfilled women – in measure, at least. As we talked together our different experiences seemed to mesh, to complement each other in our search for what is creative and life-giving in our God-given sexuality with all its varied expressions. We had much in common, our sexual feelings, our womanliness, our creativity, our need to nurture and a certain independence of spirit. We just had differing ways of fulfilling these aspects of our sexuality – my friend within her community, I within my family, both of us in the wider world of caring and teaching as well as writing.

As we considered sexuality in the context of Scripture we acknowledged that there is little direct reference to it in the Bible. Apart from the beautiful and erotic poetry in the Song of Songs. (Most of the material is to do with prohibitions or rules.) But there is much about the creativity of God, about the nature of his love and about the priorities for loving relationships which Jesus showed in his life and ministry, and Paul makes reference to in some of his teaching. (I will come back to Paul's teaching in later chapters.) These speak volumes about the principles undergirding the use we make of our gift of sexuality and how we help others struggling with what can feel to be an unwieldy and, sometimes, an unwanted gift! So I asked my friend 'where shall I start?' 'Start at the beginning,' she said, 'start with Genesis,' and I took her advice.

Sexuality created

In Genesis chapter 1 we see God at work 'in the beginning' as creator, as life-giver. The dark, 'formless', motionless earth is 'hovered' over by the Spirit of God. This 'hovering' is a kind of 'vibrating' or 'trembling'[1]. The only movement or energy is God's energy working on the earth's receptive void. Can it be an accident that this picture of the moment of creation has such similarities with the climax of the sexual act with all its potential for creation? And perhaps not only in human beings. I have been told that the mating of dragonflies involves a huge effort of energy as the male hovers over the female to impregnate her. At any rate, out of the earth impregnated with the energy of God and under his direct will and word, creation evolves. First the elements, then the plants, then the creatures. Finally the high point: humankind, created male and female in the image of God.

What does it mean to be created 'in God's likeness'? Psalm 8 puts it this way:

> You made him a little lower than the heavenly beings and crowned him with glory and honour (v5).

To be made in God's image is a glorious thing.

Irenaeus, writing in the second century, said that 'The glory of God is a human being who is fully alive'. Sexuality should be a part of us that is fully alive and vibrant - not a sleeping snake within us which must never be let out!

All aspects of masculinity and femininity can be found in the Godhead, and we reflect this in our human sexuality. God can be both father and mother, sustainer and nurturer, strength and gentleness. With our modern understanding of the masculine and feminine attributes in each one of us we can see how these complement each other, not only in male-female relationships but in same sex friendships and within the same person. The wide variety in the balance of these in each individual contributes to their uniqueness. Some of the most 'whole' men I have known have been unafraid to own the gentler side of their nature as well as their strength, to weep at times and to show their sensitivity. Similarly I greatly value and respect those women I know who, whilst losing none of their 'softness', can also have about them a strength, determination and cutting edge worthy of any man! We fit people into stereotypes and strait jackets at our peril.

Our sexuality reflects, too, God's capacity for relationship, for intimacy. The mystery of the Trinity speaks of relationship at the very heart of God. He is also concerned with every detail of his created world:

> Are not two sparrows sold for a penny? Yet not one of them will fall to the ground apart from the will of your Father. And even the very hairs of your head are numbered (Matthew 10:29-30).

God did not create us for 'aloneness' – for a state of self-reliant independence – but for relationships. Our sexuality is inextricably bound up with our capacity to give and receive love, to complement and supplement each other. This is a far wider concept than genital sexuality, though it includes it, for it embraces our whole personality.

The picture in Genesis 2 of Eve being created as a person who was like Adam ('bone of my bone and flesh of my flesh' was his joyous recognition of his helper), is a picture of the need in every human being for intimacy. Our sexuality is a 'space' for the 'other' – God *and* man. A space created within us, drawing us, like a vacuum seeking to be filled, into relationship. Notice that at this stage in creation there is no hint of a suggestion of anyone 'second class' in Adam's welcome of Eve – only of an equal but different person.

Ecclesiastes makes a very good case for the first kind of relatedness:

Two are better than one, because they have a good return
for their work.
If one falls down, his friend can help him up.
But pity the man who falls and has no one to help him up!
Also, if two lie down together, they will keep warm.
But how can one keep warm alone? (Ecclesiastes 4:9-11).

And Jim Cotter puts it this way: 'May you say of each person who
is part of your life, however fleetingly, I need you in order to be
myself.'[2]

In our physical bodies as well as in other ways our sexuality
reflects God's capacity for creativity. Although he made some
creatures with both male and female organs in the same body, he
chose to make us either male or female. No one has the capacity
to reproduce alone, although artificial insemination techniques can
get quite close to divorcing a woman from her child's father! She
may not even know who he is.

There is no sense in Genesis 1 that only our *spirit* is made in God's
image. Our whole person is created this way – body, mind and spirit.
Much Christian thinking has split off the body as inferior, sinful
and lustful; unlike the spirit which is seen as superior. There is no
evidence in the creation narrative for this. As Ezekiel puts it:

You were the model of perfection,
full of wisdom and perfect in beauty (Ezekiel 28:12).

And Paul:

For we are God's workmanship, created in Christ Jesus to do
good works, which God prepared in advance for us to do
(Ephesians 2:10).

The inclusion of the Song of Songs in the Old Testament gives us
some beautiful, erotic and very physical poetry and cannot be said
to be only an allegory of love between man and God – though it
may well be that too. The whole book sparkles with the delights

of physical sexuality as God created it to be.

> Let him kiss me with the kisses of his mouth – for your love
> is more delightful than wine (1:2).

> My lover is to me a sachet of myrrh resting between my
> breasts (1:13).

> Your two breasts are like two fawns . . . (4:5).

> Many waters cannot quench love; rivers cannot wash it away
> (8:7).

Society today can be in danger of ruling out physical intimacy for
certain categories of people. A single woman, for example, can
easily go to the home of a family and cuddle and play with the
children; whereas gentle intimate touch with the adults, of either
sex, may produce strongly negative reactions, being interpreted
either as lesbianism or a threat to the marriage. Celibate Roman
Catholic priests, too, may have very little physical touch if they
have to live alone. By virtue of their office they are isolated to
some extent from those they serve. No wonder some find it too
much to live that way and opt out into marriage or other sexual
relationships.

Our sexuality, as God created it, can be likened to a multi-faceted
diamond, its light reaching out in many directions and its centre
reflecting the intimacy which is at the very heart of God.

Sexuality fallen

A few days ago I was listening to a young woman who was struggling
to build a life with her new husband and was dogged by a constant
sense of guilt and self doubt. To a few people only had she revealed
the cause – years of sexual abuse by her father who had threatened
her with family break-up if she should ever tell. Even now she is
filled with shame and horror at the thought of what was hidden

ever coming to light within her family. What a far cry from sexuality as God created it!

Genesis 3 puts into narrative form some of the truths about man's disobedience to God and its consequences in the present. Eating of the tree of good and evil gave Adam and Eve knowledge that they were quite unable to cope with. From being 'naked and not ashamed' they became all too aware of their sexuality and its potential for evil as well as good. They covered their bodies with fig leaves and hid themselves from God. Shame and fear took the place of joy and confidence.

> When Adam and Eve broke with the Companion,
> they were immediately ill at ease with themselves as bodies,
> they were ashamed.
> And the shame bred lust
> (it was not the other way round).
> Then, consumed by desires that were no longer recognizable
> as the desire for God,
> their (and our) sexuality went out of control –
> or became sternly controlled.[3]

Not everyone views the story of the fall in this way, some see it as a sort of glorious rebellion. Ann Loades in her book *Searching for Lost Coins* quotes a nineteenth century feminist addressing a meeting in 1832:

> The tyrant God, Necessity, said to the subject man: 'Of the tree of the knowledge of good and evil thou shalt not eat'. Sweet and fair liberty stepped in . . . spurned the order . . . of the tyrant, 'She took of the fruit thereof and did eat, and gave also to her husband with her, and he did eat.' Do you not, with one voice exclaim, well done woman! LIBERTY FOR EVER! If that was a fall, sirs, it was a glorious fall, and such a fall as is now wanted . . . I will be such an Eve, so bright a picture of Liberty![4]

Whilst the feminists among us may have more than a sneaking admiration for Eve's independence, there can be little doubt about the consequences of sexuality out of control (rape, abuse, prostitution, for example). For each one of us the reality is that there are aspects of our sexuality of which we are ashamed and which we keep hidden, not only from others but also from ourselves, in denial and repression.

'If we attempt to repress our sexuality by refusing to or fearing to accept it, then it will break out in various undesirable, ugly ways such as jealousy, moodiness, withdrawal, domination, ruthless oppression, materialism, passive docility, crushes, unhealthy dependence, etc.'[5]

Another way of dealing with unacceptable aspects of our sexuality is to split off the undesirable part and idealize its opposite. Again and again, both in Christian and secular culture, we come across images which illustrate this. The 'fairy godmother' and the 'wicked stepmother' are very familiar stereotypes which allow us to split off what we dislike in the one person (mother). We can then love the good mother and hate the bad one because they are no longer the same person. The 'handsome prince' and the 'ugly beast' would serve the same function in a man.

Sexually, the tension between what is felt to be good and bad in the same woman may be split into the stereotypes of 'Madonna' and 'whore'. She (or her partner) may idealize the pure, virginal, spiritual 'Madonna' and banish the 'whore', who is seen as too physical, earthy and profligate. In fact, these different facets need each other if they are not to become distortions. They both contribute to the whole woman. To deny them is to remain sexually fragmented. To attempt to integrate them appropriately can lead to greater wholeness. In pastoral care the temptation can be to collude with such splitting, especially if we have not done our own work of integration.

We live, as Christians, with that tension in our sexuality, as in our whole humanity, with its potential for life-giving intimacy or life-denying violence. We can either begin the painful work towards integration or remain fragmented. Either way the longings of our unfulfilled sexuality can, for all of us, create, at times, an aching loneliness.

THE WORD

A pen appeared, and the god said:
'Write what it is to be
man.' And my hand hovered
long over the bare page,

until there, like footprints
of the lost traveller, letters
took shape on the page's
blankness, and I spelled out

the word 'lonely'. And my hand moved
to erase it: but the voices
of all those waiting at life's
window cried out loud: 'It is true.'

R. S. THOMAS[6]

Sexuality redeemed

Fortunately, God the creator is also God the redeemer. Before we leave the early chapters of Genesis we get some glimpses of that. In spite of the consequences to Adam and Eve of their disobedience (Adam's toil for his livelihood and Eve's pain in childbirth) God makes them 'garments of skin'. Gently and compassionately he covers their nakedness. He has not given them up but is redeeming his fallen people. As Bonhoeffer puts it: 'That means he accepts men as those who are fallen. He does not compromize them in their nakedness before each other, but he himself covers them. God's activity keeps pace with man.'[7]

There are some important principles here, I think, for the way we deal with ourselves as sexual people and with those we seek to help. Gentleness and compassion rather than judgement are needed, and a right respect, even reverence, for each other's privacy, shame and hiddeness. After all, God was able to say to Israel:

Fear not, for I have redeemed you;
I have called you by name; you are mine.

. . . you are precious and honoured in my sight,
and. . .I love you. (Isaiah 43:1,4).

So what of the young woman who had been abused? How can we see God at work in her struggle with her sexuality? Although, as far as I know, she has no Christian faith, I think we can see the redemptive power of God at work in the way her young husband is faithfully trying, under difficult circumstances, to 'cover' her nakedness and vulnerability after such abuse with his loving touch and with his commitment to her. Slowly, she is beginning to receive loving sexual contact without guilt and recoil. To me this portrays something of God's commitment and sacrifice in his hurting world.

The sexuality of Jesus

The redemption of sexuality, as of humanity as a whole, finds its focus and completion in the life, death and resurrection of Christ. The gospels tell us some important things about the sexuality of Jesus and the redemptive power of his encounters with men and women.

Nowhere in the New Testament do we see more of the nature of Jesus' remarkable ease in his human sexual body than in his individual dealings with women. Women were able to talk with him, touch him, follow him, love him. And he received them, not as an asexual person, but fully aware of their sexuality and his own. Not violating, exploiting or condemning them, but responding to them as unique individuals and meeting some of their deepest needs. No wonder they loved him!

Think of the story in Luke 7 of the woman who had 'led a life of sin'. She was a prostitute. Possibly she was Mary Magdalen. Jesus was reclining at table in the house of Simon the Pharisee. The woman stood at his feet. Her warm tears fell on him. She could not approach him directly, face to face, because she was a woman and because of her lifestyle. She came, therefore, to his feet. Feet that were hot, dusty and unwashed, but at least exposed to receive her tears. This woman was used to touching men erotically. She wiped Jesus' feet with her hair, kissed them and poured on perfume, her touch no less erotic than with other men, but this time offered in deep repentance and love. Something about Jesus allowed her to release her sexuality to him with all her sadness and longings, and trust that this man would receive her and understand.

Simon the Pharisee watched and criticized the sexual nature of the encounter. Perhaps a wave of jealousy went through him and was quickly suppressed. His thoughts were condemnatory and Jesus 'heard' them. He responded first to Simon; but spoke also, indirectly, to the woman at his feet, saying he heard both her need for forgiveness and the love that was in her reaching out to him. Then he spoke directly to her - forgiving and releasing her, telling her to go in peace.

Simon was clearly not at ease with his sexuality, with its darker aspects. He needed to blame and condemn this prostitute and had she approached him she would, no doubt, have been forcibly pushed away. Jesus, in contrast, did not need to react that way. He could receive the sexual and sensual aspects of this woman because he was at ease with those parts of himself - and in control of them. Repressed sexuality expresses itself in distance, denial or exploitation. Integrated sexuality expresses itself in an ability to receive another as a sexual person, to give them space, but with a freedom to choose a right response: one which will not dishonour or do violence either to oneself or to the other.

There are other examples, too, of Jesus' attitude to and love for women, whose position in society in his day was very vulnerable and at times desperate. They could be divorced for the slightest misdemeanour, and widows and orphans often had no means of support at all. A far cry, we may think, from today. But although the position of women has changed greatly, we only have to look as far as the current arguments following on the ordination of women to see examples, right in the centre of the Christian church, of able and gifted women being treated as 'second class citizens' by virtue of their sex. Conversely, we don't have to look much further than the 'Andy Capp' figures of the North for examples of women dominating men! There is in each of us the potential for distortion of our sexuality out of fear and prejudice. Some of this may not change this side of heaven – but we can begin with ourselves.

> May the oppressor and the victim in each of us begin by turning face to face.[8]

Jesus was fully aware of these distortions and yet not bound by them. When the woman taken in adultery was brought to him (John 8) with the question about whether she should be stoned, he quietly confronted the teachers of the law and Pharisees with their sins. 'If any one of you is without sin, let him be the first to throw a stone at her.' Jesus had no need to side with them against her, joining in their denial of their own adulterous thoughts or actions, or to avoid the issue by a discussion about the law of Moses. He went straight to the point.

Imagine what a profound effect this man must have had on a frightened, exposed woman in fear of her life. 'Neither do I condemn you. Go now and leave your life of sin.' I would love to know what happened next, but we are not told. Whilst this is not made explicit in the gospel, I think this woman must have walked away with her sexuality somehow still intact when it could have been crushed forever – and with much to think about as to how she used it in the future. Personal contacts with Jesus never crush a person, but always redeem and bring hope. They leave a 'larger' person, potentially at least, not a diminished one.

One final example: Jesus' meeting with the Samaritan woman at the well near Sychar (John 4). Tired and weary, Jesus sat down to rest by the well whilst his disciples went for food. When the Samaritan woman appeared he could quite easily have hidden himself behind the conventions of the day and remained silent, resting. Not Jesus. He reached out to this needy woman, cutting through the conventions which said that Jews do not talk to Samaritans and men do not talk to women alone. He discussed with her her dissatisfaction with her life, her search for meaning. He put his finger on her irregular sexual situation in such a way that she felt recognized and understood, not threatened or condemned. Finally, he revealed himself to her as the Messiah, the one who could give her 'living water' in her dry, parched life.

Jesus, it seems, was at ease with women, as with men. He was not afraid of touch, with or without a sexual content. Fully human, fully sexual, and with a deep integrity of being, he could relate to people as they really were, in all their need and vulnerability – as if, with him, they could at last begin to be 'naked and not ashamed'.

Perhaps Jesus' attitude to women is the more remarkable because it was in contrast to so much of the prevailing attitudes of the day. That he was at ease with men is possibly less remarkable but we do have glimpses of the degree of love his disciples had for him as they spent day after day in his company. Peter, in particular, the rough fisherman, declared his love for Jesus in ways which might well have earned him ridicule from a group of 'macho' men today. It seems, too, that Jesus could have special same-sex friendships and physical touch within the wider circle of his group of disciples and friends. References to 'the disciple whom Jesus loved' (John 13:23 and 21:20) who was reclining next to him at the last supper and who leaned against him to speak to him, indicate an ease with same-sex intimacy which is also a sign of rounded sexuality. Apparently this did not cause any dis-ease or comment amongst the twelve, so it was not uncomfortably exclusive as such friendships can be if possessive. It is not commented on, just accepted as part of the love relationships of Jesus.

These examples and others give us, I think, glimpses into the wholeness and wholesomeness of Jesus' sexuality. Sometimes he can be portrayed as 'asexual' or 'above' such earthy things because he was celibate. Celibacy can be as creative a response to sexuality as can marriage - it does not need to deny it. Jesus struggled through puberty with its unpredictable sexual urges and he knew what it was to be aroused - to have erections. How else could he relate so understandingly to the sexuality of others?

> For this reason he had to be made like his brothers in every way, in order that he might become a merciful and faithful high priest in service to God, and that he might make atonement for the sins of the people. Because he himself suffered when he was tempted, he is able to help those who are being tempted (Hebrews 2:17-18).

However, Jesus' sexual desires were ordered rather than disordered. They did not just well up out of a chaos of thinking and feeling. Sexual desire doesn't begin in the genitals but in the head and heart. For Jesus, his sexuality was governed by true love and respect for women - presumably fuelled by his relationship with his mother - and so his first reaction to another was not one of lust but of deep love. This is very different from the fear of women seen sometimes in a man who has not really separated from his mother. We do not worship an 'asexual' Lord, but one whose sexuality was a real and full part of his humanity. As pastors and counsellors our sexuality needs to be real and available, in appropriate ways, in our care for others. We do not care as asexual people! Becoming more at ease with our sexuality may be a slow process. We can take courage from the fact that Jesus is not only our model but our greatest resource.

God's covenant love

Over the years I have had some odd looks and critical questions from Christians about my psychosexual work. One lady who did some temporary housework for me and saw my range of sexual books said to a mutual friend, 'Margaret looks such a *nice* person, doesn't she? You'd never think, to look at her, that she does what she does!' There is a fine line between listening to people in a non-judgemental way and being so tolerant of anything sexual that, in effect, anything goes – provided it 'does you good'.

I have to confess to having a great deal more sympathy and feeling for those struggling with an extra-marital affair or gay or lesbian relationship than the ones who are rather proud of never being unfaithful but manage to complain that for 30 years of marriage their partner has 'never really satisfied them'. It has always seemed to me that there is more reality in struggle and failure than in a search for 'satisfaction'. Some Christians (and others) may find this hard to understand. Others go much further than I am able to in their love for society's 'misfits'. But I don't find any inconsistency with the kind of love that God shows his people in the Old Testament, or Jesus shows in the New.

It seems to me that God is never portrayed as a God for whom 'anything goes' – his holiness and righteousness never waver. Indeed, because God's love is always holy, there must be boundaries and restraints to it. He cannot, by definition, love the 'unholy' in us. But he shows amazing forgiveness and understanding of his people's sins and in spite of his anger with them goes to great lengths to woo them back into loving relationship with him. It is as if he never stops yearning for the 'unholy' in us to be made whole.

There are some very moving examples of God's covenant love for his people in the Old Testament. He is fully committed to them 'to the end of time'. Time and again in the Psalms we read of his faithfulness and loving kindness in spite of his people turning away:

> If his (David's) sons forsake my law
> and do not follow my statutes,
> if they violate my decrees
> and fail to keep my commands,
> I will punish their sin with the rod,
> their iniquity with flogging;
> but I will not take my love from him
> nor will I ever betray my faithfulness. (Psalm 89:30-33)

The relationship of Hosea the prophet with his adulterous wife mirrors that of God with his adulterous people. God draws his people back to him as a husband wooing his wife.

> Therefore I am now going to allure her;
> I will lead her into the desert
> and speak tenderly to her. (Hosea 2:14)
> I will betroth you to me for ever;
> I will betroth you to me in righteousness and justice,
> in love and compassion.
> I will betroth you in faithfulness,
> and you will acknowledge the Lord. (Hosea 2:19,20)

God tells Hosea to go and show his love to his wife who is 'loved by another'. He says to him 'Love her as the Lord loves the Israelites, though they turn to other gods'. Hosea writes 'So I bought her for fifteen shekels of silver and about a homer and a lethek of barley. Then I told her, 'You are to live with me many days; you must not be a prostitute or be intimate with any man, and I will live with you' (3:2,3).

This covenant love has about it an unconditional givenness to the other, irrespective of return. Someone once said to me, speaking of her experience of her mother's love, 'Oh yes, she gave me her love, but it was on elastic.' Most of us, if we are honest, love without 'elastic' very rarely, but if we receive even a tiny bit of unconditional loving ourselves it can go a long way.

When I was in my teens we lived in an old, fairly large house in a Midlands city where my father was a busy GP. I was the eldest by six years and had quite a bit of homework to do. We had two sitting rooms, one a family room with a TV in it watched by my brother and sister (as often as they could!), the other a smarter one with a piano and more elegant furniture (or so I thought) which my parents kept mainly for their guests. I loved being allowed into that other room, so it was a special treat when one evening my mother said I could go in there to do my homework. I spread out my books on a lovely little wooden coffee table near the fire and proceeded to luxuriate in my privilege. Imagine my horror, about half an hour later, when I felt the edge of the table, to find that the varnish on it had overheated and bubbled all over. I had put it too near the fire! Trembling, I went to tell my mother. She was not pleased. 'Wait till your father comes home' was her way of stalling on the punishment for my carelessness. I waited. Eventually Dad returned from his busy day. After his supper (we never told him anything of importance until he had eaten!), he was told of my accident. I watched his face. He was always so careful of things and hated seeing them spoilt or broken. He looked at me. Gently he said 'I think you've had enough punishment Moy' (my nickname in the family). 'We will get the table seen to. Just be more careful next time.' I hugged him. Not only was it over but I was to be allowed a 'next time'! A trivial incident perhaps, but his love, understanding and forgiveness went deep – such that I can still weep as I think of it.

Covenant love involves sacrifice. Ultimately Jesus' love led him to sacrifice his life on the cross. Other lesser sacrifices may speak to us of this kind of loving. When Jesus, their Lord and Master, washed his disciples' feet he showed them 'how much he loved them' (John 13). Laying down any status to which he might have laid claim, he took the servant role and tended their feet, washing and drying them as his had been washed and dried by the prostitute in Simon's house.

At an Easter houseparty recently we were offered the chance to take part in a footwashing as part of a Eucharist on Maundy Thursday. Somewhat nervously I removed my shoes and waited for my turn. I moved forward and sat in the chair, both feet in the bowl of water. Silently, and with loving eloquence, the warden of the community (whom I hardly knew) washed and dried my feet. Part of me wanted to hold back – perhaps my feet smelt, I was embarrassed about my corns! Part of me, on feeling the tenderness with which I was touched, could well have said with Peter 'not only my feet, but my hands and head as well'.

Footwashing and sacrifice come in many guises. Van Gogh, a painter with a strong faith in God as well as a man tortured by mental illness, lived for a while with Sien, the poor, low-born woman who, when pregnant, posed for his beautiful drawing 'Sorrow'. He married her and gave her a home with her children even though he lost many friends and acquaintances through his association with her. When, eventually, he had to leave her he defended her with the words 'She has never seen what is good, so how can she be good?'[9] Writing to his brother Theo in 1883, he said of her 'I often think with melancholy of that poor woman and the children, if only they were provided for; Oh, it is the woman's own fault, one might say, and it would be true, but I am afraid her misfortunes will prove greater than her offence'.[10]

I have tried to draw out some threads of the way our sexuality can be seen from a biblical and Christian perspective. This has been, in no way, theologically comprehensive. It would take a whole book and a competent theologian to do that. Some may well disagree with my viewpoints, but they may serve as a background to the way we consider our pastoral care of those with sexual difficulties and the place of our own sexuality in that caring relationship. They form a set of principles for our loving relationships as sexual people and as Christians. Above all perhaps they may encourage us to trust and to hope as they point to a God who works constantly through his Holy Spirit to redeem his fallen world and to bring healing to our brokenness. Trusting ourselves and our hurting sexuality to him will not be easy, but it could be life-transforming.

> Say yes to a love
> that will drag you through the depths
> scour your emotions
> scar and heal your heart
> and lift you to the skies.

Thank God the Gospel has a lot of pelvis in it.

JIM COTTER.[11]

EMBRACING OUR SEXUALITY

Embrace this frail flesh of ours with love[1]

Bill and Sarah had come a long way during our sessions in under-standing themselves and each other, their sexual likes and dislikes, anxieties and fears. There was a feeling of mutual gain in our times together although, in the nature of such counselling, I had shared very little of my life with them directly. Now it was time to review our work and say goodbye for the present. Towards the end Sarah quietly volunteered that as she had seen the way Bill had talked with me and how I had gently drawn him out she had realized that she could be quite 'rough' with him in her own anxiety, and had often failed to enable him to share himself with her in depth. She had learnt something important, she said, as she listened to us talking. At one level I was glad, aware of the truth of this, for Bill had had little if any opportunity to share his feelings before and was apprehensive at first. It had been a joy to see him come alive in this way. I was glad, too, that Sarah had learnt something for herself and had not felt excluded or in any way diminished. But there was something else going on in me – an echo of myself in Sarah's word 'rough'. It caused me to reflect on those times when, in my own preoccupation and anxiety, I, too, can be 'rough' with another's sexual fellings.

The more we come close to others in the area of sexuality and intimacy the more we come face to face with ourselves, our own fears and anxieties, our own 'hidden' places. We can choose to look further at these, to grow in understanding and a certain 'spaciousness' in who we are sexually, or we can shut off this kind of reflection firmly and barricade ourselves in with fixed ideas of 'right' and 'wrong'. These may or may not be theologically correct, but, used in this way, they serve to keep us protected from the discomfort of facing our own 'no go' areas.

In her beautiful book *A Tree Full of Angels*, Sr Macrina Wiederkehr explores the theme of coming home to ourselves. She quotes a dream in which she is running from a fierce buffalo with a group of friends. They take shelter in an old house, the buffalo pawing the ground outside. In her dream, Macrina knows that she has to walk towards the buffalo, look it in the face, touch it and invite it into the house. She wakes up with her hand on the door, trying to find the courage to go out to the buffalo. She says: 'That buffalo was my life with all its fears. I had to face it and embrace it'.[2]

The unexplored parts of our sexuality are often full of fears – fears of finding out how unloving we are, fears of our own self-centredness, fears of unwanted attractions – to fantasy, pornography, to the same sex (and sometimes to the opposite sex) and of our own unattractiveness. 'How could anyone love me if they knew what I was really like?' is a heart cry of many of us and relates to our sexuality as well as to the rest of us.

If we are to have the space for others to share their sexual fears with us, it seems to me that we must touch our 'buffalo' and slowly learn to embrace more and more of our sexual frailty, with love. This is a lifelong process and we can only do it as God gives strength and insight and with the help of our lovers, friends and counsellors. Our starting point as Christians is, I think, to learn to see ourselves as God sees us. It is only as we begin to experience his loving gaze on us, directly and through the accepting love of others, that we can bear to look with him into some of the darker recesses of our sexuality.

Many of us find it hard even to begin to see ourselves with God's eyes in a true sense – our life experience may have emphasized our weaknesses and given us little encouragement to value our potential and our worth. We may have learnt that to acknowledge our good points is to be seen as bragging or arrogant. We should perhaps brush off any encouragement or praise, however true it might be. Even more seriously, we project on to God some of the values we have learnt and our image of him is then distorted into a critical God who pounces on our wrongdoings and values us only for our achievements. The gaze of such a God is far from encouraging. No wonder we avoid it!

God's 'gaze' on us takes in the elements of creation, fall and redemption that we looked at in chapter 1. Undergirding all that, it is permeated with his covenant love for his people. As he looks at us, he sees first our potential, our essential created goodness. 'God saw all that he had made and it was very good' (Genesis 1:31). He also sees our reality, our fallenness – not as the whole story, but as part of it. God is a God of truth, not denial, and those of us who have well-meaning friends who try to deny that we are as we are, know how unhelpful that is to our growth. God's gaze looks beyond that reality to the possibility of redemption as he embraces us in his unremitting compassion, flowing from his longing to draw us closer to him in loving relationship. Perhaps as we open ourselves to glimpses of this love we can dare to begin to be at home with our sexuality, with parts of our thinking and feeling that we have pushed away in fear or never even recognized as 'me' rather than 'other'. To be on this journey ourselves is vital if we are to be 'at home' to others on the way.

Some years ago I went to a workshop on 'creative writing' at a holiday houseparty. We were invited to respond to Psalm 139. I got no further than the first four verses before I felt I wanted to run from God's knowing gaze!

> O Lord you have searched me and you know me.
> You know when I sit and when I rise;
> you perceive my thoughts from afar.
> You discern my going out and my lying down;
> you are familiar with all my ways.
> Before a word is on my tongue you know it completely.
> O Lord. (Psalm 139:1-4)

Out of the feeling of wanting to hide from God's knowledge of me came the following thoughts. These allowed me to move from a place of rather arrogantly and defensively trying to control what he might see (what *I* thought acceptable!) to a place of being at home with him. I still have to repeat the journey almost daily.

Where am I now?

Where am I now?
Do you know, God? Are you looking?
What do you see?
I will choose what to show you.

You may see that I am tall and slim and wearing
pretty colours.
Do you approve?
You made me so. You gave me eyes to see your
coloured world.
I have done nothing except look at it and love
your colour. I offer it to you.

You may see that I use words with pleasure and
some skill. I am proud of that.
Do you like my words?
You are the WORD. You spoke within the Trinity
with love and we were born.
You gave me words. I offer them to you.

You may hear that I love you. In this place and
at this time I long to praise you. Prayer comes
readily.
Do you like what you hear?
You are my love. You loved me into being
and in love you call me to you.
I offer you *your* love.

I will share some thoughts with you, Lord.
I think a lot about how others *ought* to be -
it would be easier to love the family if they
were not so awkward and selfish.
Easier for *me*.
If you thought that of me, I could not begin to
come near to you.
Your thoughts are of your created image in me.
Clear, life-giving, affirming thoughts.
I hear them, and in hearing, think them too.

God, look deep into me. Show me what you see.
Suddenly I want you to go deep.
I do not fear your searching, knowing love.
Beyond my feeble choices lies your image.
I choose now to ask to see it.

AT SCARGILL, 1986.

Becoming what we are - influences on our journey

Developmental influences

In our work of training Christian Listeners in the Acorn Christian Healing Trust, my colleagues and I have often reflected rather ruefully on the fact that our courses always seem to attract far more women than men. We long to include more men as listeners, knowing that they have much to offer; but as so often in pastoral care, women seem to be drawn to the work more readily. In fact, in some churches, pastoral care can still be regarded as 'women's work'.

In my medical work in the Institute of Psychosexual Medicine the same pattern holds true. Yet in similar disciplines such as psychiatry, men and women seem to be equally represented. Perhaps this is because psychiatry offers a range of more varied disciplines within it. It would seem that work which involves being in touch with and listening to feelings is generally easier for women to adapt to and learn than for most men. Having said that, some of the men who have chosen this kind of work, in medicine or in pastoral care, are among the best listeners I know.

Roy McCloughry has said that 'many men are inarticulate emotionally'[3] and much research would seem to confirm that.[4] Certainly in the many couples I have met and tried to help, this difference has been evident again and again. 'Men's neglect of emotional expression causes great frustration in their relationships with women and isolation from the possibility of intimacy with other men.'[5] I have long wondered why this should be so, when neither social conditioning nor biological differences seem to give an adequate explanation for the widespread difference between the sexes.

Dr Lillian Rubin, in her helpful and very readable book *Intimate Strangers*, draws on her own research and that of others to offer one explanation in terms of the developmental changes that men and women have to make in their first five years. Although this is only one way of looking at these differences, I find it a very helpful and enlightening perspective. Dr Rubin suggests that the root of the difficulty lies in the pain of the disruption of early gender identification with the mother that the baby boy has to make in order to establish his male gender identity. This pain is experienced at a time when the infant has little language in which to express it and therefore remains largely inarticulate and repressed.

In the first few months of life (provided there is continuity with a mother figure) the loved infant has a sense of perfect unity with his mother or primary carer. In the perception of the infant the two are one. Gradually the task of separation begins, the finding of the infant's own identity in terms of his 'ego boundaries' – those personal boundaries which separate self from the rest of the world – and his gender. 'This, in a large part, is what a child's separation struggle is all about – a struggle that is different for boys and for girls just because it's a woman who has mothered them.'[6] At this stage, father is still experienced as a much more peripheral figure to the infant in his internal world, even if he is present and caringly involved with his child.

Whereas a girl can retain her sense of sexual identification with mother, a boy has to find a way of distancing himself from empathy with her femaleness. He finds himself gently pushed away from her by the fact that she treats him differently, saying in effect 'you are not like me, you are male'. He must withdraw from the person to whom he has formed his first and deepest attachment in both physical and psychic terms, and form another attachment to a father figure who until now has been more remote, if present at all. To protect himself from some of the pain of this disruption of his internal world, he develops defences in terms of strong ego boundaries, barriers that separate self from other and to some extent from his own inner feeling world, so that he will not have to experience such a loss of a loved figure again. When the process is disturbed by actual separation from mother, or by the absence of a father on whom to model his new sexual identity, he may cut off his feelings almost entirely in order to cope. Even with a father present, the masculine role model he is offered can often contribute to further denial of feelings, especially of vulnerability and fear, as his father passes on to him *his* way of coping and his learned view of masculinity.

Just at the time when the little boy is learning to suppress his emotions he begins to focus his sexual identity on his penis as the most obvious and distinctive evidence of his maleness. Erotic feelings towards mother are aroused by virtue of her different sexuality. So his genital sexuality develops whilst his other feelings are being, in measure, cut off.

> One effect of this process is that a man's sense of identity is at once more rigid and more closely tied to genital potency and performance than that of a woman. . . . It also means that men tend to make love in order to get in touch with what they feel, whereas most women prefer to be in touch with their feelings before wanting to make love.[7]

But what of the girl's developmental struggle? So far it may seem
that the boy has all the difficulties. The harder part for the girl can
be the formation of firm ego boundaries, a clear distinction
between herself as a person and her mother – and later between
herself and others. This tendency to have more 'permeable'
boundaries than a man, a sense of continuity between herself and
others, can create the facility of empathy with another's feelings.
It can also make it difficult for some women to be appropriately
separate. They can become over-involved with another's pain and
whereas a man may tend to be rather too detached, a woman can
lack the ability to stand back sufficiently. Both are responses which
need to be adapted in order to relate well in a sexual relationship
or in a pastoral one. Possibly women have been somewhat quicker
in recent years to take on board the more 'masculine' attributes
of detachment and rationality, perhaps spurred on by the feminist
movement. For men to learn to be in touch with their 'softer'
feelings of vulnerability and fear may be a slower process.

This is necessarily an over-simplified view of male/female development. The reality is not so black and white. It is made up of many
shades of grey, taking into account differing temperament
preferences as well as some of the influences we will look at later
in this chapter. Some may disagree with it, but it can help to shed
light on differences between men and women. It can help us to see
why, if feelings have to be denied by men at such an early stage, it
is far easier for them as adults to express themselves in action rather
than translate their feelings into words. Hence needs for closeness
and relatedness can become displaced into workaholism, an
emphasis on problem solving and rationalism, obsession with
physical fitness or with cars, alcoholism, and so on. The damage this
can do to a man's experience of his humanity and to his relationships
is immense. Until recently it had gone largely unexamined by many
Christian men who, with their partners, assumed that the traditional
roles were entirely biblical and that to attempt change was to go
against God's created plan. 'Not showing weakness, regarding
others as competitors and being ambitious are not helpful in a
relationship where intimacy and self disclosure are expected.'[8]

We can see many examples of unhelpful denial of feelings in the world of business and commerce, as well as in other spheres. In 1990 my husband was made redundant with the small tele-communications research team he led. They worked in the research labs of a large multinational company. The news came as a devastating shock to which we reacted very differently. I wept a great deal in the first few hours (not typical of me) experiencing feelings of loss and fear. Later these gave way to anger, a certain protectiveness of my husband and a determination to look ahead in practical ways. My husband was stoical though shocked. He entered quickly into discussions with his (all male) team – not about how they felt, but about what they could do. His feelings only gradually came to light with patient listening over several weeks. After a month he received a letter saying that there was no further need for the team to be redundant as sufficient savings had been made. I will never forget the only sentence which contained a feeling word: it said 'We are sorry for any concern caused'. What understatement! I felt deeply for those without loving friends to hear them and faith in a God to whom no one is 'redundant'.

Our developmental gifts as men and women can create expect-ations of ourselves and others which are hard, if not impossible to fulfil, particularly when our usual ways of functioning are under stress. It can be helpful to understand some of the patterns that have made us what we are, so that we do not remain 'stuck' in our sexuality but move forward with more realistic goals. Some of us are deeply wounded in these areas and have a longer journey to make, some of which may not be made this side of heaven, but as we reflect on our own sexual development, perhaps there are aspects we would be more ready to bring under God's compassionate gaze in prayer. For, as a friend said to me as I was discussing this with her, 'God is in the business of change'.

Family and life experiences

We may take on board roles or beliefs similar to those of our parents, or we may react differently to them, even go deliberately in an opposite direction. Not long ago I was with a group of students, inviting them to look at models of sexuality they had taken on from their parent figures, often unconsciously. To help them to do so, I suggested they draw a little 'profile' of each parent (or significant male or female adult in their childhood) and reflect on it prayerfully. Not wanting to ask of them what I was not willing to do myself, I drew my own parents.

Dad, 6ft. 2in., elegantly dressed, always careful to close the bathroom door when he was washing, was, none the less affectionate and generous with his hugs. He earned the money for the family and did the accounts. Mum, 5ft. 2in., was the practical carer. Less concerned with clothes, but always well presented, she was not a very physical person, at least as I saw her. She kept house, washed, cooked and generally looked after Dad's and the family's needs. She was not always, I felt, as fulfilled as she might have been (though this, I hasten to add, is only my perspective).

So, what sexual roles did I assume from my parents? The man should be tall, the woman dainty. (Not good news as I am 5ft. 7in. and take size 8 in shoes!) The man earns the salary, the woman keeps house and is, in measure, unfulfilled. (This created in me a determination never to be 'just a housewife' and led to my being slow to take a real pride and pleasure in the domestic side of cooking and caring. This is coming now, after 25 years!) Physicality, especially sexual relating, is a fairly private affair, and it is the man's job to initiate. (Again, not necessarily good news in a marriage to someone with different expectations.)

These are personal examples of some of the roles we may take on from our parents. If we are aware of them and able to make conscious choices, either to behave similarly or in a different way, that is fine. But mostly we are only dimly aware of how they affect us, and some time spent in reflection on them could be helpful.

From our earliest days we are exposed to a variety of family 'scripts' or 'mottoes', some of which help to mould us as sexual people. Different family members will react differently to these messages, but some will go deep and we may be living our lives by them without even realizing we are doing so.

Gail's parents were, she said, 'very enlightened' sexually. She was one of five brothers and sisters. Sex was often the topic of conversation around the dinner table. Consequently, Gail's view of sexuality was of something open and available, easily talked about and potentially fulfilling. Alan, her husband, was an only child. Sex was rarely, if ever, mentioned. Most of what he learned about it was through furtive and inaccurate conversations with his young male companions. His view of sexuality was of something secret, potentially embarrassing and somewhat shameful. He did not have very high hopes for himself. Gail breezed into marriage with her 'anything goes' attitude and expected Alan to respond with ease. He found this expectation overwhelming and exposing and withdrew into impotence and loss of desire. There was much work to be done in hearing and appreciating the other's family experience before they could establish their sexual relationship again, this time seeing some of their differences as potentially enriching.

Some family mottoes or phrases can stay with us into adulthood and bear examining: 'Silly girl!', for example, can lead to a feeling of contempt for softness, tears, or even for playfulness, in boys or in girls. 'We have no secrets in our family!' can create an impression that to have a need for privacy, physical or emotional, is to deny a sexual partner something they have a right to, rather than being a request for a loving respect for the other's need for space in relationship.

The adolescent years (and beyond!) are times when faltering attempts at relationships with the same and opposite sex from within a rapidly changing and disturbing body are likely to generate some, if not many, experiences of rejection and failure. These may incapacitate us well into adulthood. Comparisons are rife - as young men compare the size of their penises and the amount of hair on their chests, young women are anxiously comparing the size and shape of their breasts, hips and thighs! At this sensitive and vulnerable stage it can take only one insensitive remark to scar us deeply. Conversely, a word of encouragement can be worth its weight in gold.

It takes courage to move on - to pick ourselves up again after rejection and to rebuild our sexual confidence. We can either let these experiences stop us from trying again and turn us into bitter men and women or we can embrace them and become 'at home' in our hurting places in such a way as to become available to those who need to be heard as they struggle with their sexual identity.

Kevin, a single Christian man in his early 40s, had not been to church for nearly seven years. He had been deeply hurt by his rejection by his ex-wife, had formed a fulfilling homosexual relationship for a short while with a friend who also left him, and, since then, had lived with a profound and crippling sense of guilt, shame and unacceptability to others and to God. One day, after much painful sharing, he said to me 'I can tell you what is true, not what I think you want me to say.' A simple statement and due far more to Kevin's integrity than to anything I had done; but it found in me an echo of a longing that it should be increasingly true of Christ's church, for it speaks, I am sure, of the way in which he receives us.

Cultural influences

The way I relate as a sexual person will depend, to some extent, on my cultural experience and world view. Some common British proverbs which have migrated to Australia and the States tend to emphasize the cultural norm of the stiff upper lip and denial of feelings, especially the more vulnerable ones. 'Big boys don't cry.' How glad I am to know, among my male friends, some 'big boys' who do cry when it is appropriate. They hold responsible jobs and some are quite 'macho' in their appearance and fitness. But they do not think it weak to cry, at times, when they and others close to them are hurting. I value their vulnerability as well as their strength.

'When the going gets tough, the tough get tougher.' This was quoted to me by a young man who was struggling hard to survive a broken marriage and the care of his young son. He needed to give himself permission to feel without the sense that to do so was, in some way, 'weakness'. 'Laugh and the world laughs with you, cry and you cry alone.' So many of our proverbs encourage us to be strong, resilient, work hard and keep any signs of weakness hidden from general view. (So different from the Latin temperament where men are far more free in owning and expressing emotions.) At first sight these would seem to apply more to the men in our society than the women, who could be permitted a tear or two on account of their sex. But think what this does to the relationship between the sexes. How many women, wanting to pour out their hearts to the man they love, and finding these feelings dismissed as 'weak' or 'trivial' turn inwards in depression or share themselves more readily with a female friend.

How hard we have to work at understanding these subtle influences on us in order to be the complementary men and women God intended us to be! How very different are the cultural 'norms' from God's words, 'My power is made perfect in weakness' (2 Corinthians 12:9).

Other countries and cultures can challenge our acceptance of our norms and prompt us to review our sexual attitudes. Differences in sexual practices (Jewish times of uncleanliness, Roman Catholic restrictions on contraception) and marital practices (polygamy, arranged marriages) can challenge our own attitudes. We might otherwise take for granted our present day situation of common premarital sex, widespread use of the oral contraceptive, relatively easy divorce and the notion that any loving relationship must start with 'falling in love'. Some Indian couples whose marriages were arranged have told me that, far from being a disincentive to romantic love, their acceptance of their chosen partner laid a basis of commitment which grew, in time, into a deeply satisfying and loving relationship. Today, our western ideas of 'romantic love' may be in danger of blinding us to the fact that loving is hard work and often demands an act of will rather than warm feelings – though these may well follow.

Perhaps for many of the generation now in their 20s and 30s, the expected starting point for a relationship has moved from romantic love to sexual fulfilment. In the 60s Elvis Presley's hip wiggle was thought to be too sexy for TV viewing (and he was thereafter shown only from the waist up!). Today, only 30 years on, explicit sexual images are used to sell everything from cars to ice-cream.

We are bombarded with information and adverts with the message that sexual fulfilment is healthy and normal, and so it is, in one sense. This raises expectations that this should be our experience with almost any one at any time or there is something wrong with us. It is as though the genital aspects of sexuality can be readily divorced from the relational. The separation of sexual intercourse from fear of pregnancy by readily available contraception feeds this expectation, although the fear of AIDS has countered it to some extent.

An article in the *Guardian*, commenting on the Lovers' Guide video as 'Sex by numbers; a piece of plumbing sexology', says that 'romance and intimacy are far more no-go areas than sex'.[9] It is easier, it seems, to make a 'nuts-and-bolts' video for the mass-market than to tackle the intricacies of intimacy with all that involves.

How do we react as Christians? What effect has all this on our sexuality? If we are middle-aged do we throw up our hands in horror and bemoan the state of 'young people today' with their 'lax morals'? Do we throw out traditional Christian values as 'old hat' and happily join in with secular norms? Or do we struggle to find a Christian theology of sexuality which neither denies the biblical view nor condemns those who want to find a new freedom and joy in their sexuality? Without that ongoing struggle in our own lives, we will have little or nothing to say to those who seek sexual fulfilment as an end in itself. It seems to me that we need to find a way to make and express valid links between 'eros' at one end of the sexual spectrum and 'agape', the love that truly desires the best for the loved one, at the other. Eros can be a part of agape, but there is also a place for such biblical values as compassion, contentment, tenderness, non-sexual touch, creativity, nurturing and play – all of which are part of our sexuality because they are part of our humanity and our true humanity can only be experienced as a man or as a woman.

Christian teaching

'Headship'

Much theological debate has centred on this concept. For a considered look at the main strands of the argument I recommend Roy McCloughry's reference to it in *Men and Masculinity*.[10] We will come back to it in relation to gender roles in marriage. For the present I simply want to illustrate the kind of misery that rigid (and, in my opinion, unbiblical) interpretations can cause to both men and women.

Janet was brought up in a Christian home. Her parents were at pains to tell her that a woman's role was to be submissive. This they interpreted as meaning that she should subdue any tendency to assert herself or her own ideas (of which she had plenty), and meekly acquiesce to the 'headship' of her husband. Jack, her young husband, had been given similar teaching. He interpreted his 'headship' as the right to get his own way at all times! It was only as their marriage tottered towards disaster that they began, with the help of more enlightened Christian friends, to question their families' interpretation of Scripture.

Looking at St Paul's teaching in Ephesians 5, we begin to see that, far from reinforcing the existing cultural values of male domination and female inferiority and exploitation, it was revolutionary in its picture of the parallel of the man as 'head' of his wife and Christ as 'head' of his church. This was not bullying dominance but utter self-giving love – the servant king, not the dominating ruler. A wife's response to such love would be a joyous offering of herself to her husband. Mutual submission in love was the picture Paul presented to the early church. An ideal to work towards, maybe, but we distort it at our peril into something that feeds man's ego and need for power but is not consistent with the nature and image of God, or the relationships with women which Jesus demonstrated.

What we learn, as Christians, about sexuality is not only from formal teaching in sermons or lectures, but perhaps even more from the unwritten messages which make up our Christian culture. A further and highly significant element is the prevailing secular culture as it impinges on our understanding of Christian issues. It can be quite hard to tease out these influences on each of us and examine them, but I will illustrate a few here by way of example.

Sexuality is for marriage only

We can encounter a sort of working premise that 'sexuality is for marriage and marriage is for sexuality'. Sexual issues and teaching are related only to the married state, or to preparation for it, as if those who are single, divorced or widowed have no sexual feelings or longings. We know they do, if we think about it rationally, but it seems neither safe nor proper to discuss it in church circles.

Recently I was heartwarmed and encouraged to hear a courageous sermon by a single professional man. Courageous because he put into words some of the unvoiced thoughts of Christians about his single state. 'Poor Eric', he could almost hear them say, 'He seems such a nice man. You wouldn't think he would still be single at his age! Still, you never know, do you, he might be – well, you know . . .! At any rate there must be something wrong with him to stay celibate – that is we assume he *is* celibate!'

We tend to fear what we do not understand. I have learnt a great deal about sexuality from celibate and single friends, much of which has enriched me enormously. And we recognize that we can still make assumptions about our different states without really listening to each other – sometimes assuming that the 'grass is greener' on the other side. The celibate nun I mentioned at the beginning of this book read some chapters I had contributed to a book on psychosexual medicine. 'Well!' she said with a twinkle in her eye, 'now I know that it is not only the celibate who have problems!'

Our Christian teaching may have emphasized the married state as 'normal' and given very little indication of the possibility of a person being celibate and fully sexual, in spite of the example of Jesus. This can leave us, if we are single, thinking there is something amiss with our sexuality, and if we are married and perhaps struggling, unable to find a forum in which to explore our difficulties. We are led to believe that our married state, in itself, should be the answer!

Sexual failures

This brings us to another unwritten assumption, that failure or difficulty with our sexuality has no part in a 'victorious Christian life' and should therefore be tackled and put behind us as rapidly as possible. Many Christians have had to go outside the church structure – to wise friends, counsellors, marriage encounter weekends, etc. – to find understanding, forgiveness and healing of some of their sexual difficulties. Whilst I do not deny the usefulness of doing this kind of work with a person who is not part of our day-to-day life in the church, it is sad that in so many churches there can be little or no recognition that these issues even arise for people, and therefore no opportunity to discuss them there if that should be appropriate. In excluding sexual issues from the 'normal' life of the church, we are in danger of making those who struggle with them feel that they are unwanted failures, rather that the ones who are able to break new ground in understanding for us all, if only we would listen and learn. 'Failures, . . . more readily that successes, teach us to embrace the whole of our humanity and own ourselves without pretence, before God. Successes may lead us to believe that of course God must accept us now, look how he is blessing us!'[11]

Secular norms

Much traditional Christian teaching seems to say far more about the 'thou shalt nots' of sexuality than the 'thou shalts', in contrast to the secular climate of today which regards sexual intercourse as a natural and normal part of relationships at an early stage. The tension this can provoke, especially (but not only) in young people, is enormous. One young man in his 30s said to me, with real feeling, as he struggled to stay celibate and to follow God's will in the face of many opportunities for sex, 'You don't know what it's like to be single and 30 today!' The pressures are becoming greater as sexual 'freedom' is embraced more generally. What has the Christian community to say? In chapter 1, I tried to express something of the life-giving and creative nature of our sexuality, whether it finds genital expression or not. That doesn't remove the tensions or the powerful sexual drives of my young friend, or others like him, but it may help to put things into a wider perspective than simply the question of whether or not to have intercourse before marriage. 'Thou shalt not' teaching tends to breed either fear or rebellion. Neither pave the way for real intimacy. Henri Nouwen writes that, 'Fear is the great enemy of intimacy. Fear makes us run away from each other or cling to each other but does not create . . . the space where true intimacy can exist.'[12] To find such space for ourselves and for others is a real challenge in pastoral care.

Personal and professional expectations

Macrina Wiederkehr in *A Tree Full of Angels* recounts the translation of her Christian name as 'little great one' and explores something of the 'littleness' and 'greatness' in all of us. To embrace our sexuality means embracing the littleness *and* the greatness of our personal expectations and allowing them to meet. Gail and Alan, whom I mentioned earlier, had very different expectations. Gail's were great, Alan's were little. Somehow they had to meet and receive each other rather than try to make the other like themselves. Some of us may find these extremes in ourselves, co-existing in an uneasy truce rather than embracing. We may drive ourselves onwards in a need to fulfil our perceived capacity for sexual enjoyment 'if only I can find the right person', unaware that our very drive serves to blind us to our fear of true intimacy and commitment. Conversely, some of us live determinedly with low expectations in order not to have to face the disappointment of finding ourselves unable to live up to our 'great expectations' should we make the opportunity.

Eleanor was a successful young accountant. She came to see me because after six months of marriage she had not 'achieved orgasm' and she felt that something had to be done about it. Used to being able to control her professional life and be successful, she had tried books, sexual aids and all kinds of stimulation by her partner, to no avail. How hard it was to convince her that orgasms do not come by trying harder! I suggested that Eleanor might try to adjust her sights to a different level of enjoyment and satisfaction. She might allow herself to let go of her high expectations and take pleasure in what she did enjoy in lovemaking, as a prelude to being able to relax enough to let go of her need to control and allow herself to reach orgasm. Sadly she was unconvinced by this approach and went off to seek more 'active' help elsewhere.

For professionals, particularly in the 'caring professions', our own expectations and those of others can have an unhelpful effect on our growth in sexuality. Doctors, for example, by virtue of their medical training, can be expected to know all about sex, even when they may have had little or no personal experience. This can lead to a belief that we should be omnicompetent and, if we find ourselves floundering in our personal lives, can make it difficult to ask for help. It is as if a personal difficulty in this field is felt to be professional failure. Another professional who is able to model vulnerability in an appropriate way can open the door to sharing of ourselves and to growth and understanding.

At a time when I was troubled by our inability to conceive I went to see my GP who had a grown up family of his own. He carefully attended to the relevant facts, examined me and outlined further steps to be taken. As I left he said gently 'It took us seven years to conceive our first'. That tiny bit of sharing of himself made me feel human again and, curiously, considering what he had said, gave me hope.

We could look at many professional expectations which affect pastoral carers in similar ways but perhaps one more will do. Clergy, whether married or single, seem to be in particuar danger of being idealized as those who are extra holy; whose lives are lived in a bubble that is 'cloudless, untroubled, peaceful and blameless'.[13] This myth is explored helpfully by Wanda Nash in the Grove booklet *Living with God at the Vicarage*.

People on pedestals attract projections by virtue of their position. They may be objects of sexual fantasies just because they are set apart in this way. Clergy, particularly, may be seen as 'spiritual' rather than 'sexual' and therefore safe, in the sense that the fantasy is unlikely to turn into a reality. They may also be sexually attractive because someone unreachable and special is far more attractive than the man next door, with his darned socks and bristly chin!

To many of us, priests and religious represent people we would like to be but can't. We reach out in fantasy to unite ourselves with them and take some of their holiness into our earthiness. Others of us react by wanting to bring them down to our level, toppling them from their pedestal. Whatever the reason, projections and fantasies abound and fascinate, as a quick look at popular literature will illustrate. To take two very recent successes; Susan Howatch's *Glamorous Powers*, with its Anglican clergy and a monk as the main characters, and *The Thornbirds*, with its Catholic priest central to the story, are evidence in themselves.

Now the advertisers are jumping on the bandwaggon it seems. A recent issue of the *Prague Post* carried an article on 'Priest Kisses Nun'.[14] It referred to a current advert for a well-known clothes manufacturer.

> Not far from the towering spires of one of Prague's most beautiful churches, a billboard rises to depict a larger-than-life priest kissing a young nun in an elaborate white habit. Is it a forbidden fantasy, a tasteless mockery of the church's vows of celibacy, an aesthetic blunder, or an inspired message about love and religion? These are some of the ways folks on the streets describe the . . . billboards that . . . aim to sell clothes.

But there are dangers in all this for the professional. Either he may collude with the myth of super-holiness and deny his sexuality, spiritualizing sexual issues and ignoring his own sexual fulfilment, or he may take any sexual advances offered at their face value and respond with inappropriate sexual behaviour. The first response may, eventually, lead to such deprivation of love and physical touch that it could flip over into the second when the opportunity arises.[15] There is a real need for self awareness if we are to be responsible professionally as well as personally in this field. Richard Holloway puts it this way:

This is an extremely difficult area for clergy to deal with. Being close to the vulnerable as we often are, it is doubly important for us to know our own wounds. There are two contrasting sets of dangers we are exposed to. The first is to operate with weak or non-existent sexual boundaries and exploit the relationship of trust and affection we develop with others . . . to solace our own needs . . . The opposing danger is to be so afraid of our own sexual vulnerability that we enclose ourselves in emotional armour plating.[16]

As we conclude this chapter on embracing our sexuality, we return to the theme of being 'at home' with our sexual selves and take courage from some of Macrina Wiederkehr's definitions of 'home'.

It is (at home) that you are loved, cherished and accepted just as you are, with all your frailty, fears and flaws. It is there . . . that you discover that you don't have to be perfect to be loved . . . What is home but a place where forgiveness stands at the doors, peers out the window, and rushes down the steps to meet you?[17]

Perhaps such a place is beyond our wildest dreams, humanly speaking, but it is into such a home that God invites us by his loving gaze. As we dare to look further into his face, and see the love he has for us as we are, we may dare to offer our sexuality to his embrace, to embrace it ourselves and to open ourselves further to others. 'The call from God is to come home, to embrace both our littleness and our greatness and to come home. Come home to our families, our friends, our church, our selves, our God.'[18]

LISTENING TO SEXUALITY

To listen to a person sharing his or her sexual feelings is to enter holy ground in a very real sense. Holy, because of the place God has given to our sexuality in such intimacy, and because of the enormous potential for healing or for hurt in walking with another in this place, so deeply central to our humanity.

Sandra came to see me with her husband. She had been referred because she was uninterested in love-making. She looked prickly and pointed one sharp little foot at me from her tight ski-pants as if to say 'watch it'. The story at first was a bit rehearsed, ups and downs in libido, mainly downs, worse since the birth of their first child. Then Sandra made a reference to a 'difficult childhood' and I encouraged her to say more if she wanted to. Out poured resentment and anger about her parents' lack of affection towards her and her brother. 'A loveless childhood' she called it. There was a long pause and then she added 'I was sexually abused, too'.

I waited, gently, to see if she would go on. 'I only told one other person - someone at work. They said: "You must confront your brother, tell him how angry you are". But I *couldn't* do that!'

Again I waited, as if holding a wild bird in my hand which could fly off at any moment. Slowly, out came the words: 'It was like two people who loved each other, lying in bed together. I know it was wrong, but it felt so natural.' I acknowledged the goodness of that to her in her 'loveless childhood' and she relaxed visibly.

'What I felt angry about was that it stopped and I don't know why. I never knew. I felt so rejected.' Sandra had gone on to develop a pattern of greatly enjoying love-making and then switching off her enjoyment 'as though a switch had flipped'. Fearful of ever being hurt that way again, she would, as she later put it, 'prick her own bubble'. Unable to own her enjoyment of her brother's attentions because they were 'wrong', she was not in touch with the source of this pattern until she was carefully listened to. Then she could relax with her very supportive husband and begin to believe that he would not leave her as her brother had done. Enjoyment of motherhood, too, became more possible as she allowed her loving feelings to emerge.

Listening is both very simple and very difficult. Simple, because if only we will give a person space they may say what they have never been able to say before. Difficult, because we so quickly want to fill that space with our own ideas and advice. Preserving this space is like holding a wild bird in our hand – open too wide and it feels unsafe and unprotected, hold too tight and it struggles to be free.

For most of us it is a rare experience to be listened to well. At a workshop for clergy, on loss, I invited them to listen to each other about an experience of bereavement for ten minutes without interruption. One elderly clergyman, nearing the end of his ministry, described that ten minutes on his return to the group as 'sheer luxury'.

Jesus' listening

Just as we can look to Jesus as a person living fully in his sexuality, so we can look to him as someone who listened to people in depth and with real compassion.

In his book, *The Counselling of Jesus*, Duncan Buchanan makes several very helpful points about Jesus' listening, among them, the quality of discernment evident in all his encounters. Buchanan defines discernment as 'the ability to see beyond the obvious to the reality of the situation'.[1]

In Mark 5, we read of Jesus pressed in by a large crowd as he went to heal Jairus' daughter. A woman who had been bleeding for twelve years (presumably vaginally) touched his cloak. Amongst so much human contact, Jesus 'heard' the nature of this particular person's touch. He knew that power for healing had drained from him. Perhaps he understood something of the desperation of a person touching him in that way. Perhaps his love for individuals would not allow him to leave such a vital life-giving encounter at that and hurry on. At any rate, he stopped and looked around for the woman. How much greater her healing must have been at his words of recognition and blessing, especially since she had suffered so much under the 'care' of many doctors and others over the years. Such discernment requires openness to possibility - a breadth of vision which is not blinkered to the unexpected, nor set too firmly on the task at hand to notice it when it occurs.

Jesus listened to people as they *were*. He respected their differences in temperament and attitude and did not seek to force change, only to offer them new possibilities. In the story of Mary and Martha (Luke 10), Jesus hears and respects the different temperaments of the sisters - Mary's dreamy contemplative nature and Martha's compulsive activism. Whilst in no way condemning Martha, he offers her the suggestion that there are things more important to be concerned about at present than the details of preparing food; a way of release from her compulsion and from her resentment. Equally, he does not feel obliged to side with her and tell Mary what her duty is. Perhaps after Martha had relaxed and sat and listened for a while, she and Mary would have prepared a simple meal together and gone on discussing what they had heard - but that is just a flight of fancy!

Even if the heart of the matter was uncomfortable, Jesus did not avoid it for the sake of peaceful relationships. His love and concern for the rich young ruler (Mark 10) did not prevent him from putting his finger on what that young man needed to do in order to follow him freely. He had to give up his wealth, something on which he relied so strongly that he was unable to let go of it at that time. Such confrontations were not always in public, either. With

Zacchaeus, the tax collector (Luke 19), Jesus took him home to talk about his questionable business practices in private. Whatever was said in Zacchaeus' home, it had a dramatic effect afterwards in his putting things right and repaying money he had extorted – an effect that was evident to all.

One further point, from many which could be made about Jesus' listening, was that he was unafraid of showing his feelings. He wept at the grave of Lazarus, probably both at his own pain and that of Martha and Mary, before he raised his friend from the dead (John 11). In seeing the sorrow of the widow of Nain (Luke 7:13) his 'heart went out to her'. Jesus did not listen dispassionately. He listened with compassion, entering into the pain of others and responding appropriately in truth and love.

A 'climate' of listening

> If someone is in a climate of listening, he will say things
> he wouldn't have said before.
> (Dame Cicely Saunders – on a radio programme.)

Discernment, openness to possibility and to pain, respect and appropriate confrontation were all part of the 'climate' of Jesus' listening encounters. In her book *Listening* Anne Long writes about listening as a ministry. She goes on to identify a quality of hospitality in this kind of listening.

> Listening is the highest form of hospitality . . . hospitality is
> not to change people but to offer them space where change
> can take place. [2]
>
> HENRI NOUWEN

Later Anne goes on to say that this kind of listening requires us to put aside our own concerns for a while. Such 'hospitality' in listening is, 'costly, yet freely given, it can feel to the person needing a listening ear like coming in from a cold, dark street into a warm, welcoming home.'[3] This quality of listening can be healing in itself. It was part of the healing which Jesus offered to those who came to him in pain and which he offers to those who struggle with their sexuality. We need to draw deeply on him, because, as Duncan Buchanan puts it: 'We may have the finest counselling techniques, but if we have not the Spirit of Christ, we will lack the discernment, the love and the vision to see past ourselves and past the obvious, to the areas of failure, sin, inadequacy and self-rejection which are the cause of so many problems.'[4]

Enabling through listening

What are some of the qualities in the listener which are particularly relevant to listening to sexual difficulties? How might they be experienced in pastoral counselling?

Acceptance

What does it mean to be accepted by another? When I am unconditionally accepted, I feel free to be myself, exactly as I am now, with all my awkward and unlovable bits and with the jumble of past and present, thoughts and feelings, that go to make up 'me'. I am not only allowed to be me - I am loved as me. Held in that loving acceptance, I need not try to defend myself any more. I can slowly relax and even begin to consider change. This quality is a rare gift for most of us. We may experience it briefly 'on a good day' and give it, likewise. We are well aware of the terms and conditions of our acceptability to others. They vary from family, to friends, to colleagues - but are, none the less, conditions.

Part of the discipline of listening to another is to learn to 'screen out' those caveats we place on our acceptance of them, so that we come closer to incarnating the unconditional love of God referred to in chapter 1. We might, for example, only be prepared to accept a person if they have been faithful in marriage. To be trusted with a story of unfaithfulness can then put severe strain on our pastoral counselling relationship. Yet, if there has been infidelity, we have to start with acceptance of the reality of what has happened and how the person feels about it, or we cannot begin to help them evaluate the situation and decide where to go from there. Indeed, our very lack of acceptance, conveyed by a look, or by our tone of voice may mean that the speaker stops sharing with us in any depth. To accept is not to condone or to deny that we might view the situation very differently, but it does require the setting aside of those differences for a while in the service of the speaker. Having said that, we are all human and have our limitations. Even going on our own journey of growth will not prevent us from having some boundaries to our ability to accept others. Recognizing our own boundaries and taking appropriate action is vital, whether that is to seek some good listening or counselling ourselves, or to limit the listening we do in certain areas, as far as it is possible.

Catherine was an experienced single psychiatric social worker. She had managed to work with a variety of difficult clients in her professional life and although greatly challenged, had worked effectively. With the increasingly high profile of child sexual abuse, she was asked to take further training in that area. To her distress, this threw up vague but very powerful memories of her own abuse and she had to withdraw from the training in order to cope. She made a decision not to be available for child sexual abuse work and it was accepted by her senior colleagues. As pastors we need both understanding of ourselves and our own boundaries – and gentleness about our limitations.

Respect

Respect is part of acceptance. To respect another is to give them value, to treat them with consideration. In such intimate matters as sexuality this is especially important. Recently I visited a consultant gynaecologist with a friend, a single person in her sixties, who was fearful of examination. She was received gently and considerately with none of the false bonhomie that can be a way of countering a person's fears. When the examination came, it was uncomfortable, but that was acknowledged and the consultant apologized for any hurt caused. His sensitivity greatly reduced the pain. Afterwards I said to my friend 'that consultant really seemed to reverence women'. She agreed with me, saying 'He was a Christ figure to me'.

Integrity

Integrity is a quality difficult to define but one which we know when we see it. What does sexual integrity look like? We can have no better example than Jesus in his ease with his physical sexuality and his relationships with women and with men. We may be able to think of others who have about them that same sense of being in touch with both the physical and emotional in their sexual nature, the whole being ordered and available in a healthy and life-giving way. They are fully human and fully alive. Men or women whose capacity to love and be loved is fully available to those around them, neither repressed into a sterile asexual kind of loving, nor forced on others in a smothering way. Listening to others in this area is both a challenge and a gift to us as we work towards our own sexual integrity.

Empathy

Sometimes I have heard a person question the capacity for empathy in someone who has not had a similar experience. 'You can't really know what it is like until you have gone through it yourself.' Whilst experience can, once integrated, allow for rapid empathy, it can also lead to a tendency to say 'I know exactly how you feel'. We do not need to have experienced child abuse, miscarriage or impotence to be able to empathize with feelings of violation, loss or helplessness. We require an ability to be in touch with these feelings in ourselves and to recognize them in others. Our own life experience is a rich resource, rightly used. We cannot wait to offer pastoral care and compassion until we have experience of rape, or of sexual abuse, but by careful listening I have learnt much from my patients about the wide range of feelings and effects they can cause.

Humour

Another very different aspect of respect in listening to sexual matters is dealing with the humorous – intentional or otherwise – with care. An Irishman who was in real distress at his impotence following his wife's desertion said dolefully 'Ach, doctor, I am about as much use as a chocolate tea-pot'. To him, it was just a figure of speech. I had never heard it before and had to struggle hard to contain myself as I let the mental picture develop in my mind. Laughter at that point would have been a distraction, if not an insult. But I have often laughed at it since because it was so apt. At other times, shared laughter can be immensely healing. An elderly lady I visited in a nursing home was shaken and embarrassed by having had an uncomfortable catheter change performed with a male nurse holding her legs apart. She is a cockney with a lively sense of humour and after hearing her story and understanding her shame, I said, as I left, 'Well, Mollie, keep your legs crossed for a while now!' She roared with laughter at the bit of suggestiveness in that, as she can be quite a flirt at times.

'Unshockability'

As human beings we may well be shocked by some of what we hear. Respectful attention to the other requires that we do not show that inappropriately. A couple on a very low income were trying to overcome the wife's vaginismus – spasm of the vaginal muscles on penetration making consummation impossible. They decided that something like a vaginal dilator would be useful but couldn't afford to buy a set. They told me that instead they had used a scrubbed carrot! I was torn between admiration at their ingenuity and concern for the delicate vaginal skin. Without wishing to discourage, I asked gently whether they had covered it with a condom and was highly relieved to be told that they had!

Confidentiality

Confidentiality is always a necessary aspect of listening, even more so when sensitive things are shared in a pastoral care setting. Assurance of complete privacy builds trust, never more so than when a person is talking of child sexual abuse or of homosexual involvement. Frequently these feelings have not been shared with anyone before and to have such a confidence betrayed would be devastating. Church settings can fall down here when it comes to sharing 'for prayer' more details than are necessary, or anything which raises curiosity and sets people guessing.

Sometimes it can be hard to keep pain to ourselves and this is where good supervision is vital, providing a setting in which the counsellor can air his or her own reactions and learn from them. However experienced we are, to be listening to others without some element of supervision is irresponsible. It is with a person who has supervisory skills that we can look at the denied and hidden aspects of ourselves as they affect our pastoral counselling. It goes without saying that the supervision relationship, too, must be absolutely confidential. I will say more about this at the end of the chapter.

Hard work

I need hardly mention the hard work involved in staying with a person's pain, particularly the pain of abuse. I will say more about the cost to the listener in that area in chapter 10, but any pain is costly and hard to go on listening to. We require the self discipline to put our own concerns and reactions aside for a while (though we may well need to come back to them in supervision). We need to be wary of the avoidances mentioned below, and to find ways of enabling the person to go on sharing, saying in effect, 'your pain is your reality and I am with you in it'. Sometimes, if a person begins to weep, the simple comment that 'it is all right to cry' will be enough to convey the sense of a 'safe place' for the expression of pain.

Prayer

Above all, we need to be people of prayer, resourced in our own lives by our relationship with God and able and willing to lift into his love those for whom we care in his name. Sometimes, between sessions, I just name in prayer those with whom I am working. God does not need a comprehensive case history, fortunately! Whilst I am with them I sometimes cry to him for his perspective on this person - longing to be able to see them through his eyes rather than with my very hazy spectacles, and to see their potential for change. If the person is a Christian, so much the better as they can do their own work of prayer too. At times, God seems to honour that particularly.

Part of the cost of the unconditional acceptance I mentioned above is that we will hear things we wish we did not have to hear. Recently I heard a young prison chaplain say 'Can you imagine what it does to us to have spent a day hearing about incest, rape and buggery?' Most of us, fortunately, will not be exposed to those issues to the same extent, but what we do hear can be very heavy at times, none the less. We need to develop a discipline of handing over what we hear to God, giving what we cannot bear to the one who can and does bear it for us. For some of us, it is helpful to picture ourselves leaving such burdens at the foot of the cross. This is not because we can, in some way, forget them, but because we need to shed the weight of them and share our responsibility with our Lord, so that we may have strength and space in us to go on listening.

Hannah was a rather frail woman emotionally. She would often be lost for words when she came in to see me, even though she knew beforehand what she wanted to say. Her low self-esteem and long history of mishandling by doctors (as she saw it) had caused withdrawal from her husband, from her friends in the church, and from her children. I encouraged her to pray between our sessions, just to bring her pain to God and open herself to him, without using lots of words. 'Let him hear the cry of your heart' I would say. One day, to her amazement, she heard a voice inside saying 'You are precious to me'. To an outside observer this may seem like a cliché.

To Hannah it was like a door opening on the possibility that she could be lovable and loving. From then on she improved rapidly and became a much happier person. God knew what was needed and how to tell her in a way that she could hear.

This is not meant to be a comprehensive list of all the desirable qualities in a person listening to sexual issues. Even if I could make such a list I doubt if any of us would match up to such an ideal profile! The best we can do is to be aware of any qualities in which we feel we need to grow and change, and to find ways of doing so, under God.

Some ways in

Probably most people reading this book will have learnt by experience and many by training how to enable a person to share more of their story and feelings. There are lots of different listening and counselling approaches which can be used and I do not believe that any such skill can be learnt from a book, but only by teaching and supervised practice. However, there are some basic 'ways in' which I have found to be invaluable and it might be useful to indicate a few here.

Mirroring

Reflecting back the person's own feeling words is part of a process called 'mirroring' which we teach in Christian Listener groups[5] and which is outlined more fully in Anne Long's book *Listening*. The factual details are summarized, but the feelings reflected back in full. This enables a person to go deeper and to begin to hear themselves more clearly. It requires practice and careful attention to the actual words a person uses as well as the general and non-verbal communication, but even the occasional feeling word reflected back can give insight and impetus to go further.

Gemma was inarticulate with fear in her first visit to me. She sat, screwed up, her legs twisted around each other like a corkscrew.

Direct comment on the palpable terror in the room would have been too much at this early stage. She said, slowly, 'I feel I can't tell anyone in the church what happened, it's too awful'. She deflected quickly to issues of confidentiality and where the notes were kept and who might read them. The words came more easily on this topic. I reflected her concern back to her, told her about arrangements for the records (they are kept in a locked cabinet) and then said 'But you feel you can't tell anyone because it's too awful, is that right?' 'Yes,' she replied, 'I'm so ashamed'. Gently, after a pause, I reflected again 'ashamed . . .' 'Yes, and so guilty'. She began to cry, corkscrewing up even tighter and hiding her face from me. I waited a while and then said 'Gemma, it's hard to be feeling ashamed and guilty and not able to tell anyone'. Still simply reflecting although by then I had a pretty good idea of what might be coming. With deep sobs and a sense of a dam bursting at last the story flooded out – an early marriage to a 'suitable' Christian man without much idea of how to hear his wife's sexual feelings, let alone make love to her. 'In and out and turn over' was how she described it. A caring older boss in the office, 'misunderstood by his wife' and skilled as a lover, had swept her off her feet into an affair. Only weeks later did she discover that he had done the same with several others. Hurt, angry, humiliated, she had sought help from her GP who had suggested some counselling. There was much work to do with Gemma and her husband, but reflecting back Gemma's feeling words had allowed her to find a way in to telling her story.

Other 'ways in' could be the kind of response to a person's initial silence which says 'it is hard to start, isn't it?' Given permission like this I have never known anyone to fail to begin somehow, although they may have needed help to progress to the nub of the matter! Again, reflecting back their own feeling words, and occasionally offering a short summary of what has been said can help a person on.

Open-ended questions

Open-ended questions are part of the 'stock-in-trade' of good pastoral counselling. Questions such as 'Would you like to say more about that?' 'Would you like to say how you are feeling/thinking at the moment?' Used appropriately they can take a person deeper. In a later chapter I will look briefly at couples work, but for the moment will just say that it is so easy for sexual partners to react to the other's words in a personal way and so hard to take the time to listen to the feelings behind those words. The response to an open-ended question by a counsellor, in the partner's presence, can be life-changing.

Sam drew up the shutters in a response to his wife's anger. The more she demanded physical and sexual touch, the more he withdrew. He could only hear his father's voice nagging him to 'get it right, or else'. My question to Flora, his wife, 'Would you like to say more about how you are feeling?' revealed her deep hurt and sense of rejection. Sam looked at her, wide eyed. He had never imagined she felt like that. His process of withdrawal did not change overnight, but he had the motivation to change as he received his wife's hurt feelings and responded to them.

Another part of the process of mirroring is what we call the 'essence' question. After a person has been speaking for a while, when much of the story may have been told, at least for this occasion, it can be helpful to ask something like 'What do you think is the most important thing in all that you have said?' We may well be surprised at the answer as it is often not what we thought most important. This question allows a person to focus down for the present and, perhaps, to find a way of identifying how to move forward in one area rather than being overwhelmed by everything. It can help counsellor and client to see more clearly where they will go next. I use this question on its own at times, particularly if someone tends to go round in circles!

Towards the end of the process of mirroring comes the 'action' question. Again, this can be used usefully on its own as it helps someone, at the end of a session, to identify any further action they would want to take, however tiny a step it might seem. To ask 'Is

there anything you might want to do about what we have shared?'
is to invite the person speaking to take responsibility for moving
on in their own way. I remember once asking this question of an
experienced parish priest. His answer, after much thought was
'Well, I pray about many things, but I haven't really opened my
sexual relationship to God in prayer - I think I need to do that'.
God greatly honoured his 'action'.

Barriers to Listening

Lack of experience

In our training seminars we would sometimes hear a doctor say
that a man had come into his surgery, sat down, and said 'Doctor,
I'm impotent'. 'Help', the doctor would say (to the seminar) 'What
do I do now?' If the man had said, 'I've got a painful ear', there
would have been no difficulty in examining it. But impotence -
well, that was another thing altogether. One barrier to listening to
sexual difficulties can be either real or presumed lack of knowledge
or experience on the part of the listener. Obviously we may find
ourselves out of our depth and need to say so, and help the person
to find further help; but because the topic is a sexual one, we
sometimes freeze too soon. Encouraging a doctor to ask his patient
to 'tell me about it' was often sufficient for him to see what the
difficulty might be about and to advise accordingly.

Embarrassment

Even a seasoned professional in other areas can find himself
embarrassed when faced with a sexual difficulty. Perhaps as a child
he was taught that these things shouldn't be talked about, or if they
were, it was with giggles behind the bike shed. Talk of masturbation
or sexual fantasies, for example, can make for such embarrassment
that it is hard to go on listening, let alone enable the speaker to
share more. One very experienced counsellor found himself
blushing when masturbation was mentioned, although it was not

a problem for him in the present. One day he discussed his embarrassment with a fellow counsellor and discovered, to his relief, that the cause was related to an incident in his early life which he had completely forgotten. Now he no longer blushes and can listen with relative ease when this topic comes up.

Excitement and touch

It would be a rare person who does not respond to certain sexual topics with excitement - even arousal at times. This might well be coming from the speaker, either directly, or in an unconscious communication. It can, none the less, cause such dis-ease that the listener stops attending to the other carefully. In itself it is something to note, to wonder about, and to try to understand; not something to be ashamed of. Clearly it must not be acted upon inappropriately, either by gratifying the need for physical contact or by asking to hear more titillating details for the listener's sake. But it should not be ignored either, as it can be a finding that tells us something about the person (why do some people cause us to feel sexually excited, and others not at all?). If it recurs a great deal it may be saying something about our own sexual needs which may not be being adequately met.

Gary was trying to help Philip, a new Christian with deep needs for friendship and difficulties in making and keeping relationships. Neither had any homosexual experience but gradually the pastoral care relationship developed into one with a lot of hugging and holding and eventually into sexual contact. When I asked Gary what he thought had gone wrong, he said at once, 'We got into far too much touching and holding, it just took over'. Whilst a gentle hand on the arm can give comfort when a person is distressed, I feel strongly that in discussing sexual and relationship matters, the use of touch should be kept to a minimum, as it can so easily be misunderstood. It can lead to boundaries being crossed that are hard, if not impossible, to put back. We can give a great deal of love by our tone of voice, eye contact and availability, and even acknowledge the felt need for touch, but we need to know ourselves very well as pastoral carers, our own needs and boundaries, if we are to discern when to offer more than brief touch in a sexual context. Exceptions to this would be when working either with another pastoral counsellor present or in a group. Then I have seen the real value of 'holding' touch whilst a person moves through an area of fear, usually in a regressed state. The little child may need adult holding in an actual as well as psychotherapeutic sense, but I would not personally try to do this myself whilst working alone. Having said that, a person can feel very vulnerable and exposed after sharing sexually and needs all the warmth and affirmation we can give in other ways, such as a smile as they go and careful attention to arrangements as to when to meet again. Someone in difficulties with their sexuality can have very 'thin' boundaries, between tenderness and passion, friendship and sexual love, for example; and we as carers need to be very clear about *our* boundaries or we could be in danger of wounding them by our attempts to care. A good 'rule of thumb' about touch in sexual counselling is 'if in doubt, don't'.

Some Avoidances

Asking for more information

I recently heard of a person who was talking about a fearful experience of child abuse and saying she had been strapped to a chair. Her counsellor asked her 'What kind of chair was it?' Whilst open-ended questions can help a person be more specific and to explore the event in more detail, this question was not only irrelevant but indicated to the speaker that her fear was not being heard. She quickly lost all trust in the counsellor and failed to return for further help. When we get stuck or embarrassed as we listen, one way to ease our own discomfort is to ask questions, to elicit more information and detail which is known to the speaker anyway. All of us do this at times, but we need to notice it if it is an avoidance of discomfort and, if possible, return to the area of dis-ease to give the speaker a chance to say more. Open ended questions such as 'Would you like to say how you feel about that?' or, 'Would you want to say any more about that?' are very helpful and not intrusive, if used sensitively.

Advice giving

'If I were you I would . . .'. Advice-giving before we have had time to hear and weigh a person's story and to give them time to consider what to do can be another way of avoiding the discomfort of apparent inactivity. Sandra was given advice by someone at work which was entirely inappropriate and prevented her from sharing her story for a long time – with serious consequences for her sexual and family relationships. If a relationship is good, we can tell how useful our advice is by how it is used. If a basic trust is not there we may never know whether it was acted upon or not!

Siding for or against

It is hard not to feel critical or judgemental about some of the people we listen to. Work with couples is a particular challenge here – siding with one or the other is likely to prevent any useful work on their relationship. The counsellor who is known and trusted can occasionally confront one partner about an unhelpful attitude without losing the respect of the couple. However, getting the balance right is not easy!

Recently, Bill and Helen came to see me in crisis. Bill had left home after 20 years of marriage. He said Helen never made any sexual advances (though she responded to his) and that was so unreasonable as to be unbearable. When Helen tried to express her side of the story he just said 'Rubbish' again and again in different ways. To me this was like a red rag to a bull! Feeling as deeply as I do about the value of listening and acceptance (though I often fail to practise it!) I bent over backwards to be neutral and to enable them to hear each other. Obviously I somewhat over-did it because as they left Bill shook my hand warmly and made a further appointment. Helen was not so sure!

Jesus' model and teaching allow no place for judgemental or critical attitudes. In Luke 6 he is unequivocal.

Do not judge, and you will not be judged. Do not condemn, and you will not be condemned. Forgive, and you will be forgiven. Give, and it will be given to you . . . For with the measure you use, it will be measured to you . . . Why do you look at the speck of sawdust in your brother's eye and pay no attention to the plank in your own eye? How can you say to your brother, 'Brother, let me take the speck out of your eye', when you yourself fail to see the plank in your own eye? You hypocrite, first take the plank out of your eye, and then you will see clearly to remove the speck from your brother's eye. (Luke 6:37-38, 40-41)

There is only one judge – God. In his ministry the only people Jesus ever publicly condemned were the Pharisees. Otherwise, in confronting, he simply gave loving opportunity for repentance, forgiveness, and new life. The model that Jesus offers for pastoral care is frequently one in which he gives space for a person who is open to change to explore their situation and find out what they want from him. His question to the man at the pool of Bethesda was 'Do you want to get well?' (John 5:6). To blind Bartimaeus it was 'What do you want me to do for you?' (Mark 10:51). He had no need to point the finger, except to those whose hearts were closed and whose spiritual and moral ears were deaf – the Pharisees.

For a person who is searching, just to come close to holiness is enough to increase sensitivity to sin. To experience light is to be aware of darkness. Pastorally, if a person is wanting change (and if they do not, nothing we can do will change them!) we need to enable them to explore freely and to centre the encounter on Christ. His holiness will do the rest. Such pastoral care requires real discipline and personal prayer but is very much in line with Christ's pattern. When we condemn others, we crush them. When we condemn ourselves we put on our shoulders a burden that is not from God at all and live under it, bowed down and unforgiven. This is not God's way. Indeed, Jesus offers to take our burdens from us so that we may live free and forgiven lives.

Some resources

As Christians our great resource for growth in our sexuality and for helping others on the journey is God himself and our relationship with him. But there are other resources too, which bear looking at at this stage.

Supervision

Here I am using the word supervision in a specific sense. A person who has supervisory skills is one who can enable us to spread out our working relationships and methods and examine them carefully, learning from our mistakes and understanding some of our blind spots. Some social workers, psychologists, counsellors and psychotherapists have this training, as well as a few clergy and doctors.

In our Psychosexual Institute training we meet in seminar groups of about twelve doctors with a leader, whose job it is to enable us to share our work honestly, and to find out about our blind spots and avoidances so that we can do better with our patients. Deeply trusting relationships develop in a good seminar – it is not possible to be seen falling on our face regularly by colleagues without learning to 'bear each other's burdens'. This is one model of supervision, similar to peer groups whose members meet regularly to share their work and offer comment and criticism in a supportive atmosphere. Other training may require one-to-one supervision or written work to be submitted for comment.

All these models have in common accountability to others and opportunity for learning through our difficulties and mistakes. I find such supervision an invaluable resource and whilst I may groan at the preparation necessary, I rarely regret going. In listening to sexual difficulties there is an added safeguard in a good supervisory relationship. From time to time there can be a strong sexual attraction between the two people involved in a pastoral counselling relationship. If this is discussed early on with a supervisor, a decision can be made as to whether it is safe to work with or not, and if not, what action might be needed.

Finding a good supervisor is not necessarily easy, but it is worth the effort. Where courses in pastoral care and counselling offer supervision as part of the training they will be in contact with people with suitable skills and might be able to suggest someone. The Association of Christian Counsellors[6] is in the process of accrediting those who can offer supervision as well as counselling skills and could also be a helpful contact point. Obviously other local counsellors, too, might be able to help.

Personal resourcing

This leads us to another resource: those people who meet our own needs for friendship, love, touch (whether genital or general), listening, play and creativity. In short, those who share and enhance our capacity for loving relationships. From time to time it can be helpful to take stock of who our resource people are and whether we need to make more time to be with them. We may never get enough of what resources us, but if we have a reasonable amount we will not be in danger of meeting our relationship needs through those we try to help - a real danger for busy carers.

The challenge of listening

We have looked at some of the qualities in the pastoral counsellor which enable another to share. Skills of listening and counselling; growth through encountering some of our own barriers and avoidances; our resources in God and in others - all are things which contribute to the 'climate of listening' which we are able to offer in pastoral care, or in more formal counselling settings. The challenge of listening to a person struggling with his or her sexuality is summed up in the words of Jean Vanier, the founder of l'Arche: 'In effect, love is not primarily to do something for someone, but it is to reveal to that person his or her value, not only through listening and tenderness, through love and kindness, but also through a certain competence and faithful commitment.'[7]

FURTHER DIMENSIONS

So far, we have spent time looking at a biblical perspective on sexuality, at our own journey towards sexual integrity and at some of the ways in which we can listen to others so as to build trust and enable disclosure of intimate and sometimes 'shameful' sexual thoughts and feelings. Often our listening will take us deeper into the hidden and denied aspects of another's inner world. We need to be aware of non-verbal clues to feelings or attitudes which are not being voiced. And we need to be sensitive to the many and varied defence mechanisms which can be used to protect a person from discomfort and pain - not to rip them down, but to respect them and to examine them together at the right time.

A model of the different layers, or levels making up our inner world derives from psychodynamic theory and may be helpful here.

TABLE 1. DUAL LEVELS OF AWARENESS BETWEEN SELF AND OTHERS. [1]

	known to self	unknown to self
known to others	A public self	B blind self
unknown to others	C secret self	D unconscious self

Counselling can be said to include information coming from C to A (self disclosure), from B to A (contributions from others, including the counsellor) and sometimes from D to A when material which has been completely repressed comes to light. The latter group is particularly the province of more intensive psychotherapy, but can crop up in pastoral counselling with a sensitive listener.

Obviously this diagram applies to the carer as well. In the area of defences, particularly, we can be utterly blind to our own defence mechanisms, but others can spot them easily. Here, good supervision can help us to grow in insight so as to be able to separate out our personal and individual reactions from those which are provoked by our working relationship with a client.

For example, if I have had a row with my daughter before leaving for work and arrive hassled and late, it will not be surprising if I am irritated when the first person comes in to see me, looks pointedly at his watch and says he has been waiting ten minutes! My anger with my daughter could easily get displaced onto him with a rather tart and defensive reply. Only by being well aware of my own anger and its source and my guilt at being late, would I be able to observe his anger as a separate event and wonder what had provoked him to complain. Such discrimination takes time and practice but without it we run the risk of acting out our personal feelings and missing the interactions with others which may give important clues as to how they function in relationship and what they are feeling.

Non-verbal communication

One piece of research has suggested that as little as seven per cent of what we communicate is conveyed by our words alone.[2] Whilst I find it hard to see how such figures can be the same for everybody on every occasion, it is still an indication that we communicate far more than we are aware of in a non-verbal way. Much of the communication between the sexes is non-verbal – ways of dressing which are attractive to the opposite sex, perfume or after-shave, an inviting smile or a toss of the head. We see it in the young (and not so young) every day. So what clues might present themselves in pastoral care settings?

The eyes – the 'windows of the soul' – can give away a great deal. We may see guilt or embarrassment in a person's avoidance of eye contact. We may see a teasing look, or the brimming of tears as feelings come to the fore. Like any non-verbal communication, though, we should never assume that we know its meaning, but always try to find a way to enable the other to tell us, if and when they wish to. We can be very wrong in our assumptions, especially cross-culturally. In some cultures direct eye contact would be avoided as a matter of courtesy, not of guilt!

Theresa was a pretty woman. A real carer herself within her family and through her work. She hated feeling in need, or feeling unhappy. She was the one others turned to in distress. After a very heavy two years with much to bear, including her own illness, she was lacking in any sexual desire for her husband. The story came out brightly and apologetically until I said that it was all right to feel tired and in need of care herself after all she had been through. Then her eyes brimmed with tears as she allowed herself to feel some of the damned up feelings of the past two years – anger, self-pity, fear of losing her looks and her ability to 'cope'. She had enjoyed her identity as the pretty, happy person in her family and was having to face real changes in the present which threatened that identity.

A person's choice of dress may tell us something important if we note it in the context of the whole. An older man or woman dressed either sportily or in a younger style may signal fears of loss of fitness and attractiveness or of ageing. When dress is incongruous we need to take note – what might it be covering up? Again, finding the right opportunity to allow the person to express their feelings rather than using any direct personal comment which could be both hurtful and wrong in its inference.

Very drab or non-sexual dress can indicate a person's ambivalence about their sexuality. Vera, for example, wore dark green and brown clothes, thick black stockings and flat lace-up shoes. She had a short hair cut and no make up. She hated her husband's requests to look at her naked and had, to her acute embarrassment, found lately that she was sexually attracted to her women friends. Her dress was an attempt to hide her uncomfortable sexuality.

Sometimes unusual mannerisms can give us clues to unvoiced feelings. Rose, a pleasant 68 year old, came asking for Hormone Replacement Therapy (HRT). A reasonable request in a younger woman but unusual at 68. She made it sound so logical: her husband was sexually active and she was not able to respond as he desired. She opened her handbag and took out a sharply folded lace hanky. Instead of blowing her nose she sat folding it further into very precise points and pressing them down with her fingers. After a while I said she seemed very determined to get that hanky to behave as she wanted it – was that indicative of anything to do with her sexual difficulty? Out came a torrent of anger about her husband's affairs in the past, and now he wanted her again she felt she had no choice but to force herself to try to respond or risk losing him. Exploring this together allowed her to choose how to respond, and HRT was not mentioned again.

A person's manner as they enter our room may speak volumes: confident, sure I'll get what I'm after, accusing, too tired to care, slapdash, flirtatious – all telling us something important if we listen carefully. A colleague described a man who came to her as 'enormous, he filled the room'. Intuitively she had picked up the enormity of his need although he was only an average sized man in fact. A deep need for mothering and a history of abuse became apparent. No wonder he 'filled the room'.

Silences, too, can be listened to. In the past week, I have 'heard' all these silences in everyday life – rebellious, sad, angry, fearful, embarrassed, despairing, surprised, and prayerful. Quite often someone who is about to go deeper or to share an intimate fantasy or fear, will be silent first. It is as if they are waiting, weighing our trustworthiness before taking the next step. At such sensitive moments just holding them to God in the quiet may be the most loving thing to do. It may be a revelation to us when we first appreciate that silences can be listened to. Taking time to 'weigh' them rather than jumping in to avoid discomfort (ours, usually) is a vital skill in listening.

Other clues in the 'here and now'

People present themselves with sexual difficulties in many informal ways in a pastoral care setting. They may come for healing prayer and be offered a more leisurely counselling time, for example, or raise a difficulty in the course of a pastoral visit. If they specifically ask for help with their sexuality or are referred by another person, the mode of referral may tell us a little about how they behave in sexual relationships. A person who has to be 'seen at once' may be in a real crisis, or may be someone who demands attention whether it is convenient or not. In relationships this can be very wearing! If they are given an appointment quickly, often at inconvenience to the carer, they may well cancel or change it later.

A referral letter to a doctor seemed to indicate urgency: a handicapped wife, married only six months and having sexual difficulties such that the relationship was in jeopardy. When the receptionist rang to offer an early appointment she was amazed 'it was like drawing teeth' she said. Nothing was convenient - it clashed with evening classes or social activities - 'couldn't it be another day instead?' They were put back on the waiting list!

Some people come with a message of 'treat me gently, I'm so fragile'. Referrers who would not normally fuss ring us up to 'pave the way' as though this person is delicate and requires special treatment. We may well find that in relationships and sexually they are hard to please and have everyone running around them.

Beginnings and endings

If we are flexible enough to notice, we may see that we begin and end consultations (or meetings) differently with different people.

Sometimes this can be very revealing. Although time is short we may find ourselves using a lot of small talk to 'put the person at ease'. One of my colleagues reported to a seminar that she had spent the first 10 to 15 minutes of a 45 minute consultation discussing the latest episode of a TV serial with her patient. Such was the power of this lady to avoid consummation that the doctor saw nothing unreasonable until the seminar asked if she often discussed TV at length with her patients. Of course, she did not!

A person's opening gambit and our response may be very relevant. Caution about trusting anyone can be expressed as 'the last person I went to didn't understand, so I don't expect you to'. Vulnerability may be hidden under a rather confrontational 'I'd like to know what training you've had, and exactly how you will work with me'. Another person has us feeling like God's gift to all in need within minutes: 'I *know* you are going to be able to help me, I trusted you as soon as I saw you'. Hard to confront and very seductive! Listened to carefully these say a lot about the person as a sexual partner.

Currently on the TV soap 'Neighbours' a scheming lady called Fay is making a blatant pass at a widower, Jim. Everyone else sees her ability to deceive but to Jim she is all sweetness and light and somehow manages to present to him a face of tender vulnerability which puts others in the wrong, not her. Jim finds it hard to refuse her anything, even going against his own wishes to please her. Some people try to put a counsellor in a similar position!

The way a session ends can be equally interesting. Most of us at some stage will encounter the person who seems to prolong the time way beyond what we had offered. We go on and on, feeling increasingly resentful and getting nowhere. Although this can be due to inexperience, it can also indicate a person who 'gets no satisfaction' in spite of their partner's best attempts in bed or otherwise. Confronting them with their own responsibility for satisfaction and limiting the time to what we can reasonably give, can help them to find out what they need and how to achieve it.

Abrupt endings can signify different things: for instance anger with the client or with the carer can lead to an abrupt withdrawal. The client may be passed on - to a GP for a medical check up, for example - as a way of getting free of a difficult working relationship as well as for better reasons. Some people 'get better' very fast, without clear evidence of why they have improved, rather than saying that they are not finding the counselling helpful. Beginnings and endings can represent elements of the person's sexuality, if they are allowed to 'speak'.

When writing about defences in a previous book I quoted the example of the young civil servant who came to me about his impotence. He always began cautiously giving me a 'progress report': there was slow progress each time. He made use of the consultations to find out the next point at which he was stuck and to explore possible ways to move on. He was always in charge, making the next appointment three or four months ahead. He always ended the interview himself, a little before the time was up.

Gradually this man achieved intercourse with a measure of satisfaction. In all, the process took about three years. Finally he said goodbye and later wrote a very nice letter thanking me for my help, and enclosing a cheque to use as a donation to a charity of my choice. All along I kept pace with this man's progress, not pushing him in any way. His need to control his sexual feelings and go slow were put to him gently at times, and perhaps that helped him along. He needed to begin the consultation in his way with his progress report and to end it in such a way that he was in control. A rather nice postscript happened in this particular case. About two years later I had a little card from this man and his wife saying they had given birth to their first child. He may have been slower than the average person to develop sexually but he got there in the end!

Defences

We all need and use defences, or 'defence mechanisms' as Melanie Klein called them in her original work, to protect us from too much emotional pain or discomfort. At times we can tolerate a lot of anxiety, before a performance or an exam, for example. It raises our adrenaline and gives us the extra energy we need. At other times our defences help us to ward off feelings which are felt to be intolerable.

In the area of sexuality both the body and the emotions can feel very exposed and vulnerable. The 'private parts' are not so called for nothing! The interplay in this area between the sexual organs and the feelings associated with sexual expression gives rise to a rich and varied range of defences. In response, as I have already indicated, the listener may use his own defences to ward off the discomfort felt. If we can learn to spot our own use of defences at critical points we may be able to face the underlying painful or embarrassing feelings in the client which caused us to adopt them. This may only happen as we reflect later on what occurred, but it may not be too late to pick up on those feelings the next time they arise.

There are examples in the early chapters of Genesis of man's use of defences to protect himself from reality. Dr Marion Ashton, an experienced doctor and counsellor, has said that there are two basic defences, illustrated in the Bible by Adam and Cain. When Adam was found by God in the Garden of Eden after eating the fruit of the tree of knowledge of good and evil, he said: 'I was afraid because I was naked: so I hid' (Genesis 3:10). Cain's words, after killing his brother and being confronted by God in what he had done, and condemned to restless wandering, were: 'Whoever finds me will kill me' (Genesis 4:14). Underlying most, if not all, human defences are these two basic fears, of being found 'naked' and of being hurt by others.

As our sexuality draws us into relationships of closeness and intimacy, whether emotional or physical, we need to be able to tolerate loss of control and helplessness. Each partner is open to the other's touch, words, reactions. Having an orgasm in the presence of another requires us to 'let go' at every level. Intimacy always increases the risk of conflict. We bring to our loving relationships not only our 'good' feelings but also our less acceptable ones: anger, jealousy, and fear. Not only our attractive parts but those we are less proud of. With such exposure and the risks involved, no wonder we need defences!

Defences will be encountered as a person tries to control the degree of vulnerability that he feels he can tolerate sexually. This will vary greatly from person to person. Martin Seligman noted that a person's ability to tolerate helplessness depends on his previous experience of situations of uncontrollability, his ability to tolerate loss of control in some areas while retaining it in others, and the personal significance of the situation felt to be uncontrollable.[3] To some extent this will affect the defence mechanisms used and the degree to which they are employed. Such defences against exposure may protect a person from growing up and from facing disappointment at unmet expectations. They may prevent the facing of negative feelings such as anger at infidelity (real or imagined) and losses such as youth, health and physical attractiveness.

Caring professionals are not noted for their ability to tolerate helplessness either! Indeed one of the less praise-worthy reasons for entering a 'caring profession' may be a need to be in control in some way and to be seen to be powerful. To stand alongside others does require a 'letting go' of this power, an ability to tolerate the helplessness of *not* understanding, of *not* knowing; to remain ignorant and questioning in the face of uncertainty. No wonder we, too, use our defences to protect ourselves at times!

> Defences are not only universal, they are at times life preserving. They should be recognized and treated with respect, not battered down willy-nilly as if they had no right to be there, but examined with the person in order to understand the reason for them. The person will then have the choice of deciding whether to keep the defence in place or remove it and work with what is behind it.[4]

Myra Chave-Jones puts it this way:

> We need defences. However, when they become too thick and heavily fortified they can work against us. A tortoise needs its shell ... but if the shell were too thick and heavy the

tortoise would not be able to move about at all . . . defences
serve us best when they are appropriate and flexible.[5]

Some of the common defence mechanisms encountered in people
presenting with difficulties with their sexuality are illustrated
below. Those familiar with psycho-dynamic theory as described, for
instance, in Brown and Pedder[6] will recognize familiar patterns,
such as denial and projection, but because of the inter-relationship
in sexuality between body and mind, physical problems may form
major defences in themselves.

Denial – 'this far and no further'

Andrea, a pretty girl of 24, looking about 18 and rather giggly, came
on her first visit accompanied by her aunt. She had been unable
to allow penetration since her marriage. She said she was afraid
of pain but when examined vaginally she was reasonably relaxed
and only said 'it stings'. Suddenly, after being examined, she
volunteered 'I think I am keeping this part of me private, as if I
don't want to grow up'. Later, after a gap of two years, she came
again with her husband. No change. She admitted that she just
wanted it 'put right' as if by magic and got angry and impatient
at having to work at her feelings. If things did not go her way she
behaved like a sulky child, rather than the adult woman she was
and denied her own responsibility in the relationship with her
husband and with me. It was easier for Andrea to remain a child
than to face the anguish of her actual childhood (with beatings and
rows) and grow into an adult. It was as if she was still hoping for
a good childhood and good parents to love her. The pain of facing
how it had actually been for her was too great to bear. Eventually
she did decide to 'grow up'. When I last saw this couple they were
having regular intercourse and planning a family of their own.

Denial allows us to put a brick wall between ourselves and what
is unacceptable or even unconscious in our external or internal
worlds. Only when that brick wall prevents us from doing what
we want to do will we have the motivation to look behind it. (In

this case, Andrea wanted a baby as well as a 'normal' sexual life.)

Regression - 'Don't leave me'

In the last example, Andrea had remained a 'child' to deny the pain of her 'lost childhood' as she put it. It is normal and healthy for all of us to have times when we relax and are playful and childlike, as on holiday. But reverting to a dependent childlike state can, also, be an avoidance of conflict in an adult relationship. Brian and Wendy married young. Both lacking confidence they gave each other a certain security and status, but it was fragile. Twenty years on, after having a family, Wendy decided to do a law degree, something she had planned before marriage but had abandoned. Her new-found confidence and independence threw Brian into a frenzy of anxiety at his lost 'security'. He became sulky and angry by turns at being asked to help with shopping and take his turn at cooking. Worse, he became impotent, and it was only when he began to understand that his feelings related to his view of Wendy as his 'mother' who he felt was abandoning him that he was able to readjust somewhat.

Reaction formation - 'smoke screen'

We may go to one extreme in our behaviour to hide the opposite - excessive cleanliness to cover a feeling of being dirty, for example, or excessive tidiness to hide a wish to be messy. Sally had been abused as a young girl. She had been looked at, naked, and then touched sexually. She felt as though she was still being looked at by everyone and was quite unable to go out without being beautifully dressed, her hair and nails immaculate, in case anyone should see the dirty and used little girl she felt herself to be underneath.

Projection - 'It's not me, it's him!'

Commonly we 'throw out' our unacceptable feelings, attributing them to others and then reacting critically to them. Christ was very familiar with this: 'How can you say to your brother "Let me take the speck out of your eye," when all the time there is a plank in your own eye' (Matthew 7:4). We blame 'them' for our own shortcomings. Who has not heard the poor old tax man castigated because he wants our money, whilst to want to hold on to it ourselves is only reasonable, after all!

Disowning our own homosexual feelings and then over-reacting to the slightest hint of them in others, even in what may be entirely innocent same sex friendships is, sadly, not uncommon in the church. It is this kind of homophobia based on unconscious projection of homosexual feelings that can preclude any loving and understanding dialogue with those who are orientated towards the same sex. It can even push them into genital relationships where they might have chosen to remain celibate had they felt sufficiently accepted and loved to make such a choice.

In work with couples, projection and mutual projection can be a bit of a minefield. We need to take care, when seeing one partner, not to collude with their description of the other, whom we may not have met. A wife who felt that she should not feel sexual now that she was a mother, described her husband as 'lacking control' because he got an erection so easily! Another lady insisted that she had to be 'strong' because her parents' marriage had nearly broken up when she was six. She had felt as though it was up to her to keep them together (not an uncommon feeling) and despised her own feelings of 'weakness', loudly contemptuous of her husband's tendency to indecision. She could only relate sexually on her terms, never when *he* felt the need of *her*.

Conversion – of emotional pain into physical symptoms

It is not uncommon for gynaecologists to see women with abdominal pain or pain on intercourse for which no physical cause can be found. Sometimes this can be a conversion into physical pain of an emotional hurt (such as unfaithfulness) which cannot be expressed, or is felt too risky to acknowledge. Men, too, can convert emotional pain into physical symptoms.

Anthony was 21, thin, pale and anxious. He was sure his penis was only half-grown and far too small to give satisfaction. In fact, he had quite a sexual appetite but wasn't sure it was at all acceptable, especially since he had used fantasy and pornography from a young age. He now longed for exciting and loving sex, but felt inadequate in relationships. All this he had converted into his 'small' penis. When I examined him, he was quite normal in size and, as he had a slight erection, I said his penis looked good to me - how did it look to him? 'Oh, it's okay *now*' he said, smiling at me shyly, 'but it gets *very* small when I'm scared.'

In most pastoral care relationships, it would not be appropriate or possible to examine a person physically. That is an extra dimension only open to the medically trained, I realize. If we are asking for an examination of this kind, it is as well to brief the doctor or nurse beforehand that it may have a psychological element and, if possible, to use someone trained in psycho-sexual work.

Displacement

We are all familiar with the scenario of a man given a hard time by his boss, taking it out on his wife, who has a go at the children who take it out on the cat! Feelings not directed appropriately to the person who aroused them may be displaced elsewhere.

Bill brought Brenda to me because of non-consummation of their marriage. They were an older couple and likeable in their eagerness to reach sexual fulfilment. Although the problem was presented as Brenda's, I noticed that Bill, who had a bad back, always limped slowly along the corridor, so that we had to wait for him. He would never 'force' his wife to allow penetration and quickly drew back if he hurt her. His own mother, he said, had been raped. In any case, his back was so painful that intercourse was, quite simply, not on the agenda. Bill managed to displace his sexual inadequacy on to Brenda and onto his back. Only when I stopped looking at those and invited him directly to address his sexual fears did we begin to make progress.

Splitting – black and white

This is a version of projection in which we separate good and bad feelings, retaining the good and getting rid of the bad. Among some Christians, the 'animal' bodily sexual functions have, in the past, been regarded as bad and rejected, whilst sexuality on a purely 'spiritual' plane was to be enjoyed in all its purity. Some Levitical taboos rendered certain bodily fluids unclean – menstrual and seminal fluids amongst them. Richard Holloway comments on the 'momentous consequences that still reverberate' from the carrying over of these taboos into Christianity. In the early church a menstruating woman was not allowed to take the sacrament.

> Long after this particular taboo has been removed its influence is still felt. There are many Christians who are uncomfortable with women in the sanctuary or choir, and find themselves incapable of receiving the sacrament from female administrators of the eucharistic bread and wine. For people of this particular tenderness . . . ordaining women to the priesthood is shudderingly unthinkable.[7]

Similar taboos about seminal fluid have been carried over, in some cases, as the reason for priests remaining celibate. As Richard Holloway comments, however, it is possible for a man to control his ejaculations (apart, perhaps, from wet dreams) but not for a woman to stop her periods!

Rationalization

The substitution of a *good* reason for the *real* reason is such a common defence that it deserves a mention here. Perhaps a useful example among the many that we hear and use with regard to our sexual feelings is related to the high profile of sexual abuse at present. Sexual abuse is a deeply traumatic event and many women have been badly wounded in this way. Having said that, there are a few who rationalize their present difficulties in sexual relating by saying it is all because of an incident of abuse which, in the end, proves to be almost irrelevant. Someone may have been 'flashed' at by a stranger and use that as a reason for hating all men, totally avoiding the real roots of such hatred.

The Sexualized Interview

Sexual attraction in pastoral care work is bound to occur from time to time, especially when sexual issues are being talked about. We have already looked at the need for self-awareness, care with touch and attention to our own resources. Sometimes, though, a person may sexualize the interview as a way of deflecting attention away from their sexual fears and inadequacies. For example, it is much harder for a clergyman, even one experienced in pastoral care and counselling, to help a woman to examine such fears if she is sexily dressed and fluttering her eyelashes at him. Most men would cut and run in this situation and might be wise to do so, offering to refer her to a woman counsellor or to see her with a chaperone! I am referring here to flirtatious behaviour. Not all attractively dressed women are flirts, by any means.

To de-professionalize the carer by treating him or her as a sexual partner is an effective defence and yet can be worked with if we can keep our cool and find a way of offering understanding. I have been offered 'dinner for two' or 'a walk in the park' on occasions as a way of avoiding the discomfort of working at a man's sexual difficulties. Even harder to deal with is the statement that the caring person has featured in the client's fantasies. Even if not *said*, this can often occur as closeness develops. It is not every time we can say calmly 'How interesting, what does that tell us about what is going on in our working relationship'? However, acceptance, refusal to be shocked or seduced and time spent examining what *is* going on may be the turning point in understanding for that individual.

What does the sexualizing of the interview achieve? If it seems safer to make it sexual than therapeutic, what is so *unsafe*? Presumably to be a person with needs and feelings. Such a person may have learnt to cut off such feelings early on in life and relate more as a sexual object than someone whose sexuality is part of his whole personality. If he can be offered the chance to see his process in action (rather than having it studiously ignored) he may be able to change. Saying something like 'You seem to find it easier to flirt with me than to relate to me as a counsellor' is one way of opening up the agenda.

With experience this kind of defensive sexualization can be distinguished from the person who comes for titillation (perhaps not so common in church settings but it can easily occur in Christian Counselling Centres, for example, where someone could more easily self-refer). Again it has a different 'feel' from the recognition of the other as a sexually attractive person which is simply a part of mutual respect and liking in a pastoral care relationship and which doesn't in any way prevent growth and understanding. Again, as carers we do need to know our own boundaries. If we are feeling sexually attracted to a client, it is best not to open up this particular area, but to discuss it with our supervisor.

This is not a comprehensive list of defences, but may serve to indicate some of the avoidances that we, and those we counsel, use to deal with our sexual pain and ambivalences. Any insights we offer should be given gently and at a time when we sense a person is ready to receive them. When noticed and explored with honesty and respect a person is given a choice of looking at what was thought to be unacceptable, uncontrollable and unimaginable and finding, in the process, that the 'buffalo' of Macrina Widderkehr's dream can be seen for what it is and become manageable – even tame.

Transference

This occurs in a general sense in every-day life and may occur in a special sense in a therapeutic working relationship. In a general sense we transfer feeling patterns from the past onto new relationships, especially when there are no clear clues as to how we should relate. I was told by colleagues that an analyst, whose seminar I was going to join, was capable of being very harsh at times – even reducing doctors to tears. I quaked in my shoes at this, but when I saw him, my instant reaction was one of warmth and liking. This was inexplicable to me until I realized how much he reminded me physically of my father (something I had not expected from his description). I had transferred some of my love for my father onto him and was responding accordingly. My reaction to him never quite gave way to terror and probably helped me to confront him when necessary during my training. His ability to be direct and critical was, in fact, tempered by a deep concern for the truth and his way of caring was to offer that truth to us, however uncomfortable.

Transference is intensified when we are ill or anxious. Patients in hospital can become dependent on the 'parent' figures of the nurses and doctors, reverting to adult perspectives on them when feeling better. In a therapeutic relationship intense feelings can develop towards the counsellor or carer as if they were a parent figure, or less commonly, another person from the past. In long-term counselling and psychotherapy this can be worked with as a useful tool to investigate forgotten or repressed feelings. In other areas of pastoral care it may be noted, but not used specifically, although it can be a helpful clue to a person's relationships with others. When transference includes sexual feelings it can be a bit difficult to deal with and we need good supervision to sort out what is going on. If we find this hard to handle we are in good company! Brown and Pedder quote Breuer, a colleague of Freud, as reacting with alarm to erotic feelings in a patient. He was treating Anna O, a patient with numerous hysterical symptoms, by putting her in a light hypnotic trance and inviting her to talk of her thoughts and feelings at the time of nursing her dying father.

Towards the end of treatment, erotic feelings emerged towards Breuer which alarmed him as he took it for an adult-

adult (or frankly adulterous) reaction. He is said to have taken his wife for a second honeymoon to reassure them both, and thereafter he withdrew from further explorations in this field. [8]

Counter Transference

This has two distinct meanings within the field of counselling and psychotherapy. The first is the response of the counsellor to the patient which comes from his own conflicts and problems, past or present, i.e., his own transference onto the client. Hopefully, as we grow in our own self-awareness, we may be able to screen out this kind of personal response to the other and see it for what it is; not to condemn ourselves for it - it is part of life - but to set it aside to hear the other more clearly.

The second meaning is the response of the therapist or counsellor to the person's unconscious communications (i.e., to *their* transference) uncontaminated by the counsellor's own agenda, as he listens to the person and to himself. This can be a useful tool in understanding a client's reactions when they do not seem to make sense on a rational level.

Bryn was a charming single man of 27. He always made me feel that I was helping him and although I was aware of his desire to please me, I looked forward to seeing him. One day he told me that even with his closest group of friends he felt an outsider, on the edge and never as welcome as the others. The group consisted of a couple, a single girl and another single man. Bryn's feelings were out of proportion to what was going on in the present and we began to wonder about echoes from the past. Sure enough, Bryn had never felt good enough for his parents (especially his father) and compared himself unfavourably with his younger brother and sister. He had transferred his feelings of not being good enough to this group of friends and, in measure, to me too, trying so hard to please but never believing he had succeeded. I did not need to comment on his transference with me (or my counter-transference which had alerted me to it) to help him see what was causing him so much pain in his relationship with his friends.

Our response as carers to this myriad of conscious and semi-conscious communications will depend on our level of training and experience and the role in which we find ourselves. Our own defences against anxiety may be to retreat to our known professional role (i.e., for a clergyman, for example, to offer prayer, communion or the fellowship of a housegroup), not because these are the best way ahead for the other person just at that moment, but because we are feeling anxious or inadequate. For others of us, there can be a retreat to the role of the 'person who knows', in advice-giving or teaching. These responses are not wrong in themselves – they may be highly appropriate at other times. Used defensively, however, in response to a fear of 'not knowing', they may prevent us, and the person we are working with, from gaining new and vital understanding.

How do we spot such defensive behaviour in ourselves? It is hard, because for a defence to be effective there also has to be a subtle reasonableness about it. Two things are particularly helpful here: good supervision, essential to everyone involved in counselling, when our blind spots may be only too apparent to another, and an intuitive feel for changes in the working relationship. If we think of the latter as a kind of 'dance' – the emotional energy between two people allowing movement – changes in which the speaker's emotions become either very intense, or absent, will clearly affect the 'movement'. Sometimes it is as if the 'dancers' stop and sit on the sidelines commenting on the 'absent partner' or the 'state of the world' and no progress is made. Noting these changes and our reactions to them can be helpful in addressing the avoidances – ours and those of our clients.

Another way of putting this is to use the concept of 'hospitality' and 'hostility' borrowed from the writing of Henri Nouwen. The movement into flight from discomfort has about it the feel of moving from an attitude of 'hospitality', with space available for the person and his feelings, to one of 'hostility', when they must be held at a distance. Recognizing this . . . allows for movement back again to the attitude of 'hospitality', with openness to hear and understand . . . what is happening.[9]

This area of further dimensions in sexuality, as in life in general, is a challenging one. It demands much of us in personal growth and thinking and reflecting on what is happening in a disciplined way, often within the kinds of supervisory relationships mentioned in chapter 3. Although at first it may seem rather overwhelming, I believe it can be hugely rewarding. Indeed not to attend to it in measure can be to deprive another of comfort and help. To avoid these areas by offering bland reassurance or ready advice is rather like 'singing songs to a heavy heart'.

Like one who takes away a garment on a cold day . . .
is one who sings songs to a heavy heart. (Proverbs 25:20)

SEXUALITY AND MARRIAGE

This chapter covers a huge subject. Many good and helpful books have been written about it and I can only touch briefly on some facets of sexuality and marriage which I hope will be useful in pastoral care.

Marriage is rather like Christmas! Looked at from a distance they may both hold very special hopes and expectations – warmth, good gifts given and received, celebration, family intimacy, tradition, and Christ at the centre, giving it life and meaning. They can be idealized or dismissed as disappointing rubbish, according to our temperament and past experience. The reality is rather different. Surrounded by busyness and commercialism, at least in our Western culture, the central values can become eroded and almost choked out by the pressures of materialism. The 'gifts', when they are opened, are a mixed blessing. Some are just right for us and we treasure them. Others are hard to like, they don't fit or are simply not our taste at all! Just when all could be sweetness and light, something goes horribly wrong and feelings explode destructively. And perhaps, when we least expect it, there is a moment of life-giving encounter with each other (and perhaps with Christ through each other), in which we receive acceptance and understanding. In both situations there are, too, those who are not included, who stand outside alone.

Despite the ups and downs of reality most of us never quite let go of our hopes for marriage or for Christmas. And that is right, for we are looking back to God's created order for us, and forward to its completion when Christ brings in his kingdom. Meanwhile we have to live with the mixture of hope, reality and glimpses of redemption that colours all our relationships, but which, because of its great potential for intimacy, marriage, like Christmas, brings into particularly sharp relief!

Two years ago we celebrated the first Christmas in our new home. I had imagined it from the time we moved in August - the family gathered, the fire lit, the tree glowing and all the preparations joyfully made. A real celebration of hard work done, on the house itself and in ourselves in making the move. The home-maker and the mother in me were finding fulfilment and focus. On Christmas Eve my brother and his wife joined us for mulled wine and mince pies. The turkey was thawing and the vegetables were prepared for the next day (I had tipped all the peelings with joyful abandon into the new waste disposal unit - a novelty for me). As I settled down to the warm glow of it all (helped by the mulled wine) my husband's anxious voice came from the kitchen, 'Moy, come and help, the dishwasher is flooding!' Within minutes my beautifully ordered kitchen was pulled apart and cupboards had to be emptied and fascias removed to get at the blocked drain caused by all the vegetable peelings. It was 'all hands to the mops', apart from the two grannies, who, mercifully, stayed in the sitting room. My husband said we would not be able to use the sink over the holiday and at the thought of Christmas dinner for 11 with no sink, I blew my top and stated emphatically that he had to do something! Finally we got our heads together and used the Yellow Pages. A delightful plumber turned up at 10.45 pm and (also warmed by the mulled wine) wrestled with our drain until midnight. Never had there been a more unusual or more welcome Father Christmas! Our celebrations turned out pretty well in the end, but not without effort. In marriage, as at Christmas, realizing some of our ideals can be very hard work!

A love relationship is like a dance in which the partners keep in step, together and responsively, through the various changes in tempo. That sounds enjoyable and straightforward. It actually demands a marked degree of concentration, intelligence, awareness and sensitivity.[1]

It seems to me that the place in which ideals, hopes and reality meet in marriage is in the place of intimacy. The word intimacy comes from two Latin words, *intimus* meaning 'innermost' and *intimare* meaning 'to make known'. So intimacy is the making known of that which is innermost. I want to look at intimacy in marriage as the sharing of truth – emotional, physical and spiritual truth. That sharing demands a great deal of both partners. In some marriages it barely begins; in others it reaches real depth. Most of us, if we are honest, are still struggling with the barriers to intimacy that we encounter inside and outside ourselves. But a moment of shared intimacy in a love relationship, whether marriage or friendship, is so precious that it is well worth the struggle.

Emotional intimacy

Pat Collins, in his book *Intimacy and the Hungers of the Heart*, draws a very useful distinction between closeness and intimacy. He points out that intimacy and self-disclosure are not always the same thing. It is possible for a person to talk at length about himself without any real self-knowledge, and the effect on the listener is draining. The pouring out has been a sort of catharsis rather than a communication with another human being. In fact, the same story may be poured out again and again without any significant change. Couples can spend many hours together each day, sharing their thoughts and feelings about everyday life, and make no progress at all in hearing more of the truth of each other. Such closeness is important. Without it they could lose touch altogether, but, as Pat Collins puts it:

A good relationship, marital or otherwise, includes a mixture of closeness and intimacy. But if the oxygen of true intimacy is lacking, the sense of closeness will, in time, become stale and boring. Perhaps that is one of the reasons why so many apparently 'good marriages' eventually break down and finally split up. [2]

In contrast, intimacy in the sense of sharing of the truth, whilst it can be painful and hard, is also energizing. It does not necessarily take long, or many words. However, the process of getting to the point of sharing can be a lengthy one, as we face the truth in ourselves, first, and then risk sharing it with our partner. The fear is that we will not be liked or accepted. 'I'm afraid to tell you who I am, because, if I tell you who I am, you may not like who I am and it's all that I have.' [3] Such sharing of 'who I am' must, inevitably, include 'who I am' sexually, with all the attendant problems that brings! But intimacy is the life blood of marriage and loving relationships. It is the place of life, growth and change and, for all the hard work involved, it is the place of freedom in loving. 'You shall know the truth, and the truth shall make you free' (John 8:32).

My husband and I have been on two marriage enrichment weekends during our marriage and found them, in prospect, daunting to say the least. However, just carving out the time and space to be with each other, with the opportunity to look at important issues and to hear dissatisfactions as well as good things, has been life-giving. The first time, many years ago, I felt so ill I nearly didn't go. The second faced us with an area we found so hard that we nearly didn't go back on the second day. So I don't write lightly about the sharing of truth. But, when it does come, such intimacy is like the sun breaking through grey clouds and lighting up what, until then, has seemed a rather dull landscape.

On Easter Sunday I heard Archdeacon Yong Chen Fah from Sabah in Malaysia preaching about the way in which busyness erodes our intimacy in relationships. He said 'When you first get married, it is all wonderful, isn't it? You feel so close. But after five or six years you may have children and jobs and so much to think about and it is not the same at all!' We were just about to go away for a three-day break – the first time we had spent alone in ten months.

I wondered what I would discover about our marriage in that time, under the grey 'silt' of busyness. Sitting on the bed next day, I asked Mike how he was feeling about his work just now. Hearing at leisure, not only his plans but his thoughts and feelings about them, immediately drew me to him as a person who seemed more real than before, and I felt in some way enlarged also. We decided that we needed such breaks in the future, not as a luxury but as a necessity, to 'feed' our relationship.

Physical Intimacy

For Christians, marriage is the relationship for which full sexual union is designed. The Bible is unequivocal on that. However hard we may find it to stay within those boundaries, and however often we may need to seek the forgiveness of God and others for crossing them, we do need to keep in sight, at least, what God designed and created and why he did so.

To return, for a moment, to my analogy of marriage and Christmas. I seem to see more people for counselling after Christmas each year than at other times. They are disillusioned and fed up. They had hoped that, somehow, Christmas would 'put things right' but it only made it worse! We cannot have, in Christmas, what is not there the rest of the year, in relationships at least. If we try to do that, it becomes a travesty. Meeting together and spending time with each other highlights what is good and not good, true and untrue in our family and friends, as if it were under a magnifying glass. Sexual union, also, cannot create what is not there in relationships, although we often treat it as though it can. It can be a profound reflection of a couple's intimacy, deeply satisfying as well as fun; or it can highlight, by its very physical closeness, the lack of intimacy between them. It needs the relationship to give it true meaning, just as the marriage needs physical expression in this way to make it fully alive and whole. For this reason, I believe the genital expression of sexuality has been set, by God, within the boundary of a committed and permanent relationship; not to restrict it, but rather to let it take its full place in our growth into love.

As a child needs loving boundaries in order to develop, so our physical sexuality needs them too. I have often ached for those people who seek help with their sexual difficulties when they have assumed that sexual ease should come naturally and at once. They get so bruised and bumped by their shortcomings in casual relationships that they are afraid to risk anything more permanent until they know they can 'get it right'. In this chicken and egg situation you can't start with the chicken *or* the egg - they need each other!

Whilst the sexual union has profound implications and meaning, it also needs a sense of humour. The sharing of our physical truth with each other can be, at times, a clumsy and even embarrassing affair. C. S. Lewis has written of this: 'Nothing is more needed here than a roar of old fashioned laughter.'[4] I was talking to a young woman recently who had lost interest in love-making after five years of marriage. At first it had been 'earth-moving', now she was always thinking of other things she preferred to do. She sounded so serious as she talked about it, yet seemed capable of much playfulness in the rest of her life. She said of sex 'I feel so *silly*'. I answered her with a smile, 'well, sex *is* silly, isn't it?' We both laughed at the truth of this and I think it helped.

Sexual union needs tenderness and shared laughter if it is to survive the ups and downs of marriage. In the early days there may be premature ejaculation and fear of penetration. Later on the man's erections may fail and for both partners, as they age, there can be changes in their libido and in their capacity for love-making. Set in a relationship where truth can be shared, such changes can be integrated, though they may not be welcome. Without that, the physical difficulties may become obstacles on which the marriage may founder completely without help. In counselling a person our own experience can colour our approach. We need to be aware of our own perceptions but prepared to stand back from them to hear what is true for this particular person.

Spiritual intimacy

What does it mean, as men and women, to share our 'spiritual truth' with each other? Spiritual intimacy is far more than a couple attending church or Christian functions together, or praying and reading the Bible – all of which, though valuable and necessary, can be a form of 'going through the motions'. It is a sharing of part of who I am, with God, at any given time. Like any other facet of intimacy, it demands that I know myself well enough to have something to share. In each of us there is a central quiet place, an 'inner temple' where we can be alone with God, speaking, listening and just being. So often we fail to get there, distracted on the way by preoccupations, busyness and feelings. But in that place alone, we can find our spirit in harmony with God's Spirit and it is from there that we can share some (not all) of our spiritual truth. Sometimes that truth comes as we let God's word speak to our spirit directly from the Bible. At other times we meet him through our other senses or in silence.

In that same break with Mike that I referred to earlier, I was reading the lectionary passages for the day, alone, before he was awake. Restless, for a variety of reasons, including a recent bereavement, I heard God's Word that day as a word of peace and direction into my fragmented spirit. First from the Psalms:

> My help comes from the Lord,
> the Maker of heaven and earth.
> He will not let your foot slip . . .
>
> The Lord will watch over your
> coming and going
> both now and evermore. (Psalm 121:2,3,8)

Then from the Epistles:

> Clothe yourselves with compassion, kindness, humility,
> gentleness and patience. Bear with each other and

forgive whatever grievances you may have against one another . . . Let the Peace of Christ rule in your hearts, . . . And be thankful. (Colossians 3:12,13,15).

I don't always share these things with my husband, but in this case I did, at a later point in the day. From his response, I think it spoke to him too and to our time together.

Headship

There is an even deeper dimension to spiritual intimacy in Christian marriage in the parallel drawn by Paul with the relationship between Christ and his Church. In an amazing and mysterious way, the relationship between a man and his wife can reflect that of Christ with all Christians, individually and corporately. From that point of spiritual truth the values and resources of the whole relationship flow. So it is vital to look at what Paul is saying in his teaching and at that point I quail in my shoes because even the most respected theologians fail to agree, it seems, on the issues which are debated under the term 'headship'! However, I have read and thought about this a great deal, both from a personal and professional point of view and I share some of my conclusions, drawing on the experience of others where I can.

Our starting point on any discussion on gender roles within marriage has to be the created as opposed to the fallen state. As I said in chapter 1, the creation story in Genesis 1 and 2 indicates no superiority of man over woman but an equality between different and complementary human beings. The New Testament follows this theme in Paul's teaching in Galatians 3:26-28. 'You are all sons of God through faith in Jesus Christ, for all of you who were baptized into Christ have been clothed with Christ. There is neither Jew nor Greek, slave nor free, male nor female, for you are all one in Christ Jesus'. So, whatever Paul means by the use of the word 'head' in relation to men and women in marriage, he cannot mean it in its English usage of 'the boss' in a way that speaks of superiority and power over others. As Roy McCloughry says: 'If there is no hierarchy in Eden, and there is not, will God introduce it in redemption? The answer must be 'no'. Equality, freedom and mutuality remain the goal and the characteristics of all relationships in the kingdom of God.'[5]

For the moment I want to focus on Paul's use, in Ephesians and Colossians in particular, of the word *kephale*, generally translated 'head' (but with the sense in the Greek of 'origin' also or 'source').[6] There are two reasons for this particular focus. One is that many writers have managed to be convincing about what 'head' does *not* mean, in the sense of a 'boss' or someone in authority, but have not said a great deal, in a practical sense, about what it *does* mean in a marriage of equality. I have never been fully satisfied with conclusions about mutual submission in love and equality of man and wife in God's sight – although I entirely agree with them and defend them further on. What still has to be explored, I think, is what is meant by the particular place a man is given in marriage, if it is not one of superiority. We cannot entirely argue ourselves away from the different emphasis in Paul's teaching for a husband in relation to his wife. The second reason is that where headship has been an issue for couples I have met, it has been mainly one of a power struggle, due I think to a wrong understanding of the word. I wanted to explore the positive side of Paul's teaching.

It was without much enthusiasm that I set about this task. My wise and knowing friends and husband indicated the wealth of study which had gone before! But slowly, as I looked at Ephesians and Colossians with the help of various commentators' detailed studies of these and other passages relating to the role of women, I began to see something exciting and potentially life-giving in the parallels Paul draws with Christ as the head of the Church.

In chapter 2 I referred briefly to the servanthood of Christ as a model for self-giving love of a husband to his wife (Ephesians 5:23). Christ is the head of the Church – not as a ruler, but as a saviour, giving himself up for her. Similarly, a man is to love his wife 'as his own body'. This is a hugely important parallel and must have turned upside down the standards of the day, when men could divorce women at will and commit adultery with single or unattached women without any penalty at all. The wife's response of loving submission would make for a relationship of mutual submission in the character of that of Christ and the Church. 'Submit to one another out of reverence for Christ' (Ephesians 5:21). As Richard Foster says in *Celebration of Discipline*:

> Submission is an ethical theme that runs the gamut of the New Testament. It is . . . obligatory upon *all* Christians: men as well as women, fathers as well as children, masters as well as slaves. We are commanded to live a life of submission because Jesus lived a life of submission, not because we are in a particular place or station in life.[7]

Submission is *not* being a doormat, one partner dominating the other or constantly giving into the other against their real feelings. It is *not* about stunted development. Submission *is* offering all we are and have to others freely as gift and not as duty, yet without denying our unique personhood. It is about *freedom* - it brings the freedom to lay down the burden of always needing to get our own way.

Richard Foster goes on to say that submission has limits to it. 'The limits of submission are the points at which it becomes destructive. It then becomes a denial of the law of love as taught by Jesus and is an affront to genuine biblical submission' (Matthew 5-7 and especially 22: 37-39).[8] There are no hard or fast rules about this. Sometimes the limits are relatively easy to see. Perhaps parents disagree on the best way of disciplining a child. A wife should not submit to using a harsh approach (such as beating) which she feels to be harmful. A boss might require an employee to do something unlawful. A conflict of law and conscience would not require submission to the boss, but a polite and firm refusal.

Sometimes the limits are much harder to define. Perhaps the professional career of her spouse causes a wife to feel stifled in her personal fulfilment. Should she deny her own needs or would that be too destructive? What if a student is given a reference from a tutor which he thinks is inaccurate – should he challenge it or just accept it?

Barbara eventually divorced her husband because she thought his sexual demands were unreasonable. He wanted intercourse several times a day and demanded oral sex (which she disliked) and sado-masochistic practices. Her dilemma came when her daughter reached 14 and was going alone on access visits, staying overnight. Barbara had no evidence that her husband meant her any harm, but knowing what she did about his behaviour created a very difficult conflict for her over her wish to protect her daughter's sexual integrity and her husband's legal rights.

Discernment of what the limits of submission may be throws us into deep dependence on the Holy Spirit to lead us into all truth. If our attitude is one of willingness to serve rather than to be served, we can ask him to show us the right limits to submission.[9]

The alternative translation of *kephale* as 'source', 'origin', or 'fountain-head'[10] has about it the sense of a life-giving dynamic process. How might this be worked out in marriage? Obviously, the relationship of mutual submission just described is life-giving in itself. But I wonder whether the man's particular responsibility for initiating and sustaining that kind of loving might extend a little more widely in Paul's use of *kephale*. In Ephesians 4:15 and 16, for example, there is the picture of Christ as head of the Church providing life, cohesion and growth for his body. Again in Colossians 2:19 'the Head from whom the whole body, nourished and knit together through its joints and ligaments, grows with a growth that is from God'. Perhaps in God's loving provision for marriage, he has given the man primary responsibility for initiating the provision of a climate of life and growth, of mutual submission and respect, within which the relationship with his wife and children can develop, drawing directly on the resources of Christ to do so.

What I am suggesting is about differing responsibilities in marriage, not about the ways these are worked out in gender roles. We might say, for example, that a husband has a God-given responsibility to watch over the basic values in his marriage – of equality before God, mutual submission and respect - and to engage his wife's help and her gifting in working these out appropriately. This is a part of God's creative and life-sustaining initiative through Christ to his Church, drawing us into greater wholeness.

This has nothing to do with a man having power over his wife. Rather, as in the principle of mutual submission, it turns traditional values on their heads and demands of a man qualities which are often denied and may be seen as 'womanish' - a capacity to nurture and protect his closest relationships. If this kind of nurturing is to bear fruit he will need to allow himself to risk vulnerability and show compassion. In chapter 2, I explored some of the reasons why this can be harder for men than for women. When a man is able to offer to his wife and family even a little of this part of himself he enriches the marriage and all his relationships in a very special way. He becomes for them, I believe, a more 'whole' man, a more sexual man in the fullest sense of the word. Perhaps it was to bring out the full potential of a man that Paul drew the particular parallel he did and emphasized his special role in relation to women. But to fulfil this role, the requirement of him is that he relinquish any sense of power or superiority, just as Christ himself did. As Roger Hurding puts it:

> If men will cling to power over women, even if they use biblical terms to describe it, they can openly do so only at the expense of wearing a mask which hides their vulnerability. Until a man is willing to lay down power, with its connotations of superiority, he cannot be whole.[11]

Being human, none of us will get this absolutely right! I believe, though, that there are many examples of this kind of Christian marriage around, just as there are many in which a man may have opted out of responsibility almost entirely and his wife's cry is 'he leaves it *all* to me - he never takes any initiative for our home and family. All his energy goes into his work.'

Philip has a very responsible executive job. Many men in his position are so tied up with work that they exude a kind of 'don't bother me, I'm already over burdened' message. Not so with Philip. He is disciplined with his time in such a way that he guards weekends for home, church and family. He and his wife both work towards this. I have been greatly impressed by the effect of Philip's disciplined approach. They have space for others, an unhurried sense about them and, above all, they have a lot of fun.

Gilbert Bilezkian sums up this whole issue very aptly:

> The meaning of head-body duality is not authority but reciprocity. *Because* Christ is the wellspring of the Church's life and provides it with existence and sustenance. [in return,] the Church serves him in loving dependency . . . the head-body metaphor applied to the husband and wife relationship serves to emphasize their essential unity, deriving from creation. Because man as the fountainhead of the woman's existence was originally used to supply her very life . . . he continues to love her sacrificially as his own body in marriage. In return, a Christian wife binds herself to her husband in a similar relationship of servant submission that expresses their oneness. The imposition of an authority structure on this . . . balance of reciprocity would paganize the marriage relationship and make the Christ/Church paradigm irrelevant to it.[12]

Basics and variables

In working out biblically creative roles in marriage there are certain values which could be seen as basic, and others which are variable, according to the gifts and personality needs of an individual couple. The basics might be the principles of equality before God, mutual submission in love, complementarity, interdependence and respect. Variable 'styles' of marriage can then be chosen; perhaps more traditional role models are followed - the husband as provider and decision maker, the wife caring primarily for the home and children; or a very different balance of shared responsibilities, even to the deliberate reversal of these roles. Where the basics are at least acknowledged and accepted (if not always held to) these various styles seem to me to be perfectly acceptable. Where there is any kind of manipulation or domination, in other words where there is not freedom of choice for one or other partner, marital stress can be severe and breakdown may occur.

I have focused so far in this chapter on how marriage has been designed by God (as I see it) and its possible strengths. I have approached it this way because many books have been written about marriage counselling and there is much expertise to be learned from in helping couples in trouble. No such skills can be learnt from a book. Like any counselling they can only be learned by 'doing' under good supervision. However, as we seek to help couples pastorally I hope that this background will serve to give us a sense of direction, if not an actual goal. I now want to go on and take a necessarily very sketchy look at some difficulties in marriage.

Emotional needs and marital stress

In chapter 2 we looked at some of the factors which affect our developing sexuality. If our emotional needs are not adequately met in childhood and adolescence then a spouse might be chosen in the hope that he or she will meet those needs. As the couple grow and mature this can lead to a lot of stress along the way! A few examples may illustrate more clearly what I mean.

Dependency

Gill had a very over-anxious mother. She worried over every little detail. When Gill started school, she felt as though she was being torn apart from her mother. She had picked up her mother's need to hold on to her and that, in turn, led to a deep fear of separation in Gill. Finally managing to leave home, she met and married Ron, a cheerful extrovert. Six years and two children later, she can still feel abandoned if Ron is away from home on a training course, but she is not so incapacitated by the feeling that she prevents him from going at all.

Submission/rebellion

Stan felt that he could never get it right with his father. He grew up with a great need to please but when he met a girl he loved and marriage began to loom as a possibility he suddenly rebelled. His friends were amazed, they had seemed such an ideal couple. Stan said he could just feel the trap closing in on him in which he would have to please his wife at all costs, but he would never be good enough. He was not yet ready to commit himself to marriage.

In his very readable book on counselling, *Restoring the Image*[13] Roger Hurding describes three kinds of marriages which may be an attempt to answer emotional needs.

(i) Lean-to marriages. Two people with a great need for care and protection may gravitate to each other. Because we often give out what we most need, each may seem to the other just the strong, confident man or the warm, mothering woman she or he desires. As the underlying needs emerge, the pattern changes and each meets another deeply needy partner, with few resources to give out. Sadly, the temptation can often be to have a baby to cement the failing relationship.

(ii) Marriage of rebels. Both partners are fleeing from authoritarian parents, but as soon as there is conflict (and there will be in any close relationship) they react as they did to their parents and the pattern of rebellion and fighting continues!

(iii) Domination/submission marriages. Here opposites are attracted. A rebel, not intending to be dominated again becomes the dominant partner. Such a man might meet a woman longing for security. For a while things work well until she matures and begins to react against his 'rule'. Equally, the woman might be the dominant partner in an 'Andy Capp' style marriage with a husband treated like a doormat. However, even doormats eventually get worn out with being trodden on, and again, the marriage is under threat unless the dominant partner is willing to change.

Lack of self-confidence

I have met many people in whom there is a deep script of 'I'm no good' or 'I'm not good enough'. In some measure we may all feel like this, but in some people it runs so deep that no amount of loving by spouse, friends or family seems to touch it. Often it is a childhood theme where the child has felt rejected by one or both parents. They may have been unwanted, disliked for some particular characteristic, or the parents may have wanted a child of the opposite sex. Love and approval has been withheld and a small child is quite unable to do anything about this or even understand it. They are helpless in the grip of the feeling of being unloved. Such helplessness, in the face of any amount of reassurance in adulthood, can prompt us to help a person look for a childhood source for such feelings. To change the script is no easy task and it is often more a matter of God's grace than human understanding in the end. The depth of this feeling of unworthiness may prevent any relationships growing with the opposite sex, in extreme cases. It may be a persistent and stressful theme in a marriage where the spouse eventually gives up trying to offer loving reassurance because their love seems to go unheard.

Sexual needs and expectations

The greatest recurring theme I hear in my clinic with couples goes something like this: 'He always wants sex, he would have it every night if he could. I feel like an object. I long for just a cuddle sometimes, but I know it will lead on to more'. And: 'she is just not interested in me and my needs. She always brushes me off if I try to kiss her or touch her bottom – even at the sink!' What has gone wrong here? Differences have become huge barriers with the couple entrenched behind them firing their respective shots at each other and getting nowhere. It may be that the relationship is sick and sex has simply become the focus for their discontent. But even in marriages where the partners are relating well, there can be considerable inbalances in demand and desire.

Most of us, if we are honest, think that others should be like us in some ways and, if not, they are rather odd. 'All the world is queer save thee and me, and even thou art a little queer.[14] (This was written before the word 'queer' was used as an insult to a homosexual person.) So it can come as a real shock, in early relationships with the opposite sex, to realize what different needs we can have sexually, and how the sexual act can have such very different meanings for each person.

Some years ago I took part in preparing couples for marriage using a Church Pastoral Aid Society course 'Side by Side'. Some of the sheets on sexual matters were an eye-opener to the partners as they studied them separately and then discussed them together. I wonder how many older couples have had the opportunity to look at similar questions. The preliminary sentence on one sheet is a good one: 'You will need to approach these questions with sympathy for each other and imagination. This is no bad thing because the same approach is right for sex itself!'

Here is a selection of questions adapted from the material:

1. How frequently might I want to make love?
2. Will the sort of day I have had affect my desire for sex?
3. How will I know if you are in the mood for making love?
4. How will I know if you fancy closeness without sex?
5. How can I tell you I'm not in the mood for sex without you feeling rejected?

It seems to me that to listen with sympathy and imagination to a partner's sexual needs requires an openness to the truth of that person and the mutual commitment to share that truth in a way which is neither demanding nor manipulative. In a hurting marriage this is a tall order! In a healthy one it is not easy, but creativity and imagination come into play. For sex *is* play and I have to be free in myself to be willing to play with another. If we understand that neither of us can have our needs fully met, but each can have some of what we need, then we may have room for flexibility and understanding. In a later chapter I shall refer to the more specialist help required if one partner has needs which seem to be so compulsive or bizarre that the other cannot respond to them without doing violence to his or her own sexual integrity.

Loss of interest

There are many physical and emotional causes of loss of libido; bereavement, menopause, ageing and resentment, to name just a few. But here I want to focus on an area which is not just loss of libido but a more general loss of interest in the marriage partner. I suspect that many marriages (Christian and otherwise) have become boring and are increasingly vulnerable to adultery because of that. It is not easy for partners to admit to it, for fear of hurting the other and for fear that it would make things worse, not better. I have already referred to the erosion of intimacy that busyness causes and hinted at how that can be countered, in measure, though it is no easy business. Perhaps the motivation to work at it can only come as the couple face into the loss of interest they are feeling and look at what might be contributing to that.

Chris and Sam were finding that they 'niggled' each other more and more. Secretly they both dreaded coming home to the other – their spirits fell with each encounter and they became tired and de-energised in the other's company. Chris found some solace in her work and relationships with friends but Sam became more tired and depressed and did not go outside the home much except to work. One day they faced into their dread that their marriage might have died. They both reviewed what resources they needed to continue and have something to give to each other. Much to Chris' surprise Sam decided to take a week alone and walk the South Downs Way. The simple act of talking through their feelings had energized him enough to take responsibility for his own resourcing and not to look to Chris to supply it all – a task she was finding heavier and heavier.

Marriage needs emotional energy. If we are using up all our energy outside marriage, in work or in other relationships, we cannot expect our marriage to make it up for us. Yet sometimes we behave as if it should. Adding resources or plugging unnecessary emotional drains can be a vital step to take before one or other partner finds someone else who *can* resource them and the marriage breaks up.

Pastoral care

What is a realistic aim in care for couples? Roger Hurding says that our aims must be modest: 'We must not expect to revolutionize a marriage into the union of the century!'[15] He quotes Jack Dominian as saying that: 'Marital reconciliation ultimately depends on the ability of the spouses to change sufficiently to meet the other's minimal needs.'[16] Some forms of prayer counselling nowadays seem to have quite unrealistic expectations, both of the couple and of the Holy Spirit. They seem to assume they can circumvent the difficulties and in some ways 'zap' the marriage into a changed state. Whilst God's Holy Spirit does work miracles of grace, he works with the pain of change and its demands, enabling and gracing the change, not circumventing it.

Listening to a couple

Marriage counselling of couples in distress, especially where there are personality difficulties causing complex projections and transferences to arise (see chapter 4) is the province of the trained marital counsellor or therapist. Many pastoral carers, though, will find themselves listening to, praying with and helping couples to grow in their relationships. I want to offer a few guidelines and 'danger warnings' here which might be helpful.

Listening to one partner

This may be the only option we have if the other will not come for help. Sometimes one partner may wish to work on a sexual or emotional difficulty which has arisen from childhood experiences and they need the space to explore that alone before sharing it with their spouse. In the latter case, we are in true one-to-one counselling. In the former we are trying to look at a relationship with only half of it present! Here we need to be careful.

It is all too easy to take sides – either for or against the absent partner. 'No wonder he backs off if she goes on and on like this!' Or, 'she sounds a real cold fish'. Remember, we only have that person's perception of the partner. Stay with their feelings and keep an open mind about the absent one. It can be tempting to try to be a 'better partner' to a misunderstood or hurting spouse. To be lovingly *for* them is right, but any sense of an internal urge to make up for the partner needs recognizing because it could take emotional energy from the marriage and, worse, on occasions it has led to a sexual relationship forming with the counsellor or priest who is trying to help.[17] Gentle but firm confrontation may be needed to bring a person back from a tendency to blame all the marital difficulties on the partner and to help them to look at their part in it. 'There is nothing wrong with me, I've just got the wrong spouse' is a stuck place from which no change, other than divorce is likely!

Listening to both partners

This really is a minefield! It can be highly rewarding as they begin to hear and meet each other in new ways, but it is hard work for all concerned and requires both discipline and skill on the part of the listener. For all that, I have sometimes felt like a referee at a fight, blowing the whistle at intervals but having little effect as the couple go on fighting down the corridor as they leave!

Though many couples will require the services of a skilled marital counsellor, some may be helped by some careful pastoral listening if the following principles can be followed:

i.   This kind of listening requires a formal structure – a time and place. It is not something to be done casually over coffee.

ii.   Listen to the *relationship*. What is going on between them? For instance, is one being a 'fractious child' and the other a 'consoling parent'? Is one criticizing the other by underhand remarks rather than being straightforward? (Enable them to hear themselves rather than pointing these processes out too quickly. They will accept your comments only when some understanding is dawning and when trust is present.)

iii. Lay the ground rules for clear communication and help the couple to stick to them. These are:

   a)   Each person should own his/her own feelings and express them without criticism or blame.

   b)   Each person should give time for the other to speak and wait until he has finished, not interrupting except for clarification. He should then repeat back in summary what has been heard to make sure he has got it right – 'So what I heard you say was . . .'
   This may take time and repeated attempts before the partner is satisfied. Then it is the turn of the other.

iv.   Know your limits. This is *listening,* not marriage guidance.

v.   Listening in this way is very demanding. It may spark off painful feelings in you as you listen. Supervision is both necessary and responsible in this kind of work.[18]

Conclusion

Sexuality finds a particular focus in marriage and genital sexuality has both its protection and (hopefully) its fulfilment there. Such a focus has the potential for deep intimacy *and* for considerable conflict. Relationship without conflict is relationship without growth. We can idealize marriage and find the reality very different; but in our reality, individually and together, is the seed of truth. In finding and sharing that truth we find intimacy. All of us need some help along the way from partners, friends (single and married) and perhaps from professionals. That is not a sign of failure but of a willingness to work at a relationship which, for all its difficulties, is a very special gift from God – one which is life-giving and life-sustaining, and deserves to be protected, fed and cared for.

CELIBACY AND SINGLENESS

'As a Christian person my primary identity is as a child of God. My secondary identity is as a married, single, celibate, or widowed person.' This comment was made in a sermon at our local church. It sets celibacy and singleness in their true context. A person who is celibate is a person who is sexual in the full sense of the word. For the purposes of this chapter, I would define celibacy as a state in which a person does not give full genital expression to his or her sexuality, for whatever reason. This might be from choice or circumstance, within marriage or without. Singleness is an unmarried state, including widowed and divorced people. Singles are not necessarily celibate, just as celibates are not necessarily single, though often, particularly in Christian circles, the two do coincide.

What a celibate person does with his or her sexuality is crucial. Sexuality, owned and integrated, including genital feelings, can be harnessed in a wide range of loving relationships, from brief contacts to deep intimacy. Repressed sexuality takes with it into a person's unconscious (and out of their use) a great deal of their capacity to love. Such a person relates in a dry, sterile way and can be agonizingly lonely. Sexuality which is not integrated can become split off into a secret life of real or imagined sexual encounters. By definition, these can only be partial and superficial because they are unrelated to the person as a whole and to loving relationships.

Like marriage, in celibacy there is an ideal to strive for and a reality to live with. The ideal of celibacy in a Christian sense is well defined by Donald Goergen in *The Sexual Celibate*:

> Celibacy in this sense is not a negative thing; it is not sexual abstinence. It is choosing to forego the genital within inter-personal relationships in order to be free ... to do the work of God. The celibate person, to the degree that he or she is mature in his or her choice, sees celibacy as a positive non-involvement in genital relations in order to be free to love God and to work for his kingdom.[1]

In a sense, singleness and celibacy are issues for us all. Each of us is single for part of our lives and if we marry, we are still part of a family which includes single people. There is a sense, too, in which we all 'walk alone'. As Margaret Evening puts it in her book *Who Walk Alone*:

> Whether we are married or single, male or female, old or young, there is a sense in which each of us 'walks alone' ... It may be in relationship to others that we begin to find ourselves, but there is that about our selfhood which is alone and individual, sacred and inviolate. It is alone that we enter the world and alone that we leave it. And ultimately it is alone that we must stand before God, our Judge and Father. . .
>
> Indeed, if we are able to accept and enjoy our 'aloneness', then the particular circumstances in which we find ourselves (single or married) become for us not strait-jackets but a framework for positive living.[2]

Over the years I have learnt so much from my patients and friends who have shared something of their struggles with singleness and sexuality with me. There are those who have never married, those who have been widowed or divorced, those who never want to marry and those who long to do so. Some, as single people, have opted for sexual relationships outside marriage. Others have remained celibate for a whole variety of reasons. Some have chosen celibacy after previous sexual experience, so celibacy is not necessarily the same as virginity. These different perspectives each have their own pain and their own cost. I have learnt the most from those single Christians who, whilst owning their sexuality, have chosen celibacy, at least for the time being.

At present, many of my colleagues and dearest friends are single and celibate. They have shown me something of the breadth of sexuality. They have had to find ways of expressing themselves as sexual people when they have chosen to forgo genital expression. The richness of their creativity, ways of giving and receiving nurture, gentleness and tenderness and of being genuinely fulfilled and whole as persons is staggering. It is also a great gift. Far from being 'second class' people, many of them are amongst the most interesting, gifted, creative and genuinely loving people I know. And I know that any degree of fulfilment and integrity in lifestyle is very costly and doesn't just happen overnight.

Such expressions of sexuality are not necessarily different in kind from those open to married people, but there is a freedom that comes from singleness and celibacy which can bring a difference in quality and even in time available. I think of Elizabeth, in her sixties, a gifted teacher and deacon. She has time for so many friendships in her busy life. To talk to her is always to be encouraged – not in a trivial way, but through a depth of meeting, even on the telephone. Elizabeth prizes family relationships highly and, despite her busyness, tries to give quality time to her sisters and her nephews and nieces. I think, too, of Gerard, a single man in his forties, who has a busy 'peopled' job but also spends many hours counselling church members. I have not been to his home as he is someone I have recently met, but I know he loves to give hospitality, not only to single people but to families and children. Or I think of Madge, a doctor in her fifties, who was widowed ten years ago. As well as her full-time job, she lives with an adult step-daughter and an elderly and frail aunt. Her household is every bit as much of a family as that of a married couple.

A biblical perspective

A biblical understanding of singleness and celibacy cannot be based on anything to do with elitism, either spiritual or relational. Yet Christian teaching has often erred that way. On the one hand there was the splitting of the spirit from the 'impure' body in the Greek thinking of Plato and Aristotle which elevated celibacy to a higher and more holy plane than marriage. On the other hand, the adoption of current cultural norms in a couples-orientated society, has elevated marriage as the more desirable state. Singleness is seen as a second class option (if it is an option at all). Protestantism, in particular, has tended to err that way in contrast to Roman Catholicism with its requirement that its priests remain celibate. We have looked at the creation perspective on sexuality in Genesis 1 and 2 in chapter 1. This must be the biblical starting point. 'In fact, the biblical starting point for both marriage and celibacy is identical: man is a sexual being who accepts the goodness of his own sexuality and values deeply the richness of human relationships.'[3] Clearly this perspective has been altered by the fall. Neither marriage nor celibacy reaches God's ideals for humanity. Some single people behave as if their problems would be solved by marriage – they would not, they would only become different ones! David Gillett, speaking of celibacy says: 'the problems encountered in that calling should not be seen primarily as the natural results of not being married, but the inevitable consequences of being part of fallen humanity.'[4]

The Old Testament deals almost exclusively with the married state – singleness being virtually unknown apart from the nomadic holy men. In the New Testament, in the person of Jesus and in the teachings of the celibate Paul, we have a revolutionary new dimension. The call to singleness becomes a normal possibility for those who are Christ's disciples and part of his Kingdom. 'As in Adam, the first man of creation, we discover the perfection of marriage, so in Christ, the second Adam and the first man of the Kingdom we are confronted with the perfection of singleness.'[5]

We have already explored something of the sexuality of Jesus in chapter 1. He was fully human – in touch with his sexuality in all its dimensions. A celibate man without a woman as a sexual partner, none the less able to give and receive love freely and unashamedly. He was tender, gentle and able to weep. He could be strongly confrontational in his protection of the weak and oppressed (the woman taken in adultery, for example) or of his Father's honour (overturning the tables in the Temple). He could touch others in love, sometimes reaching out to touch and heal people who were deemed untouchable. He received with joy the hugs and cuddles of little children and the sensual touch of the weeping prostitute in Simon the Pharisee's house. Jesus' life and example give the lie to the assumption that the person without genital fulfilment remains stunted and incomplete in his or her sexuality.

Whatever our state, married or single, celibate or sexually active, we can know that we are equal and precious in God's sight. He watches over us to the very end of our lives, sustaining us in our struggles and sometimes rescuing us from our pits of despair as we go on our journey of sexual integration.

> Listen to me, O house of Jacob,
> all you who remain of the house of Israel,
> you whom I have upheld since you were conceived,
> and have carried since your birth.
> Even to your old age and grey hairs
> I am he, I am he who will sustain you.
> I have made you and I will carry you;
> I will sustain you and I will rescue you. (Isaiah 46:3,4.)

Singleness and emotional stress

Before going on to the more positive aspects of celibacy, I want to identify some of the difficulties experienced by single people. These are not necessarily confined to the single state but may be accentuated by it.

Loneliness

Carol was surrounded by people in her management job. She was often tired out by her tendency to be a workaholic. Carol recognized that some of this was avoidance of her empty flat. She said that sitting alone at weekends was awful – it tended to produce self-pity and weepiness in her and she spiralled down into apathy and depression. In this condition it was impossible to reach out to friends to meet them for a walk or a drink. She rarely took holidays because she had no one to go with. Carol had to force herself to make arrangements for company in her leisure time which married people generally take for granted.

Sue was reasonably content with her own company at home, having a good network of friends who called or phoned, and plenty of work to get on with. She found herself feeling most lonely at weddings when she was not part of a couple and there was so much expectation in the air. At these times her longing for a marriage partner surfaced in an almost unmanageable way and she wanted to escape as soon as possible. Christmas, too, with all its emphasis on family affected her similarly.

To own our sexuality is to own our need for satisfying relationships at all levels and with both sexes. It seems to me that one of the hard things about being single is that such relationships often have to be initiated and looked for – an effort that a married person surrounded by a family does not necessarily have to make. With an adequate sense of self-acceptance this is not so difficult. When a sense of self esteem is low or lacking it can feel nearly impossible. Here good pastoral care within the church family can be a great help. As pastors or carers we can be watchful for those people who need to be asked to join in activities or family gatherings and who would not necessarily ask for that inclusion for themselves.

Lack of identity

Sylvia was deserted by her husband for another woman. Before he left he criticized her for her lack of understanding. He said she spent too much time at her work and too little on their home. She lacked imagination in bed. Much of this criticism was an attempt to rationalize his guilt at leaving her. She was left with a profound sense of rejection and her identity as a wife was in fragments. She even doubted her capacities in areas such as mothering (at which she was gifted), as a result of her husband's criticism.

For those who have not experienced this kind of rejection there can still be real questions of identity and self acceptance. Am I so unattractive to women that no one wants me? Who am I and where is my life going if I am not to marry? These questions are particularly hard for single people who wait passively for a hoped-for marriage to give life a purpose. For those who have had such a marriage and then are widowed, especially if that happened early or suddenly, there can be a profound loss of identity. Anger and shock may persist for years.

Barbara was widowed in her late thirties with two young children. She loved her husband deeply and fully expected to be married into old age. Even fifteen years later when I met her, she introduced herself as 'living alone but not wanting to'. She still felt only half a person in spite of her many outgoing activities in which she gave herself generously to others.

Family pressures

Doreen was the only single child in the family. As she was living at home she was expected to look after her elderly father when her mother died. She gave up her job and sacrificially cared for him. He was a dear old man in many ways, but used to his wife's constant companionship. He got ill and irritable if Doreen wanted to go out with friends and a holiday was a major crisis. It would have taken a more determined woman than Doreen to fight with him. Her fear was that, if she left home for a holiday, he might die and she would be responsible. When he did eventually die, she had no close friendships at all and no one with whom to share her feelings. Fortunately she was able to relate well to a bereavement visitor who listened to her distress and gradually introduced her to new friends and a different lifestyle.

Many single people find themselves under pressure to care for elderly parents when their married brothers or sisters are assumed to be too busy. Some do it gladly and by preference but others find it a heavy load to bear alone. Again a caring church family can be watchful of these pressures and provide support and help when needed.

Bringing up children as a single parent is a particularly stressful situation. Taking decisions without a partner can feel very frightening. It is bad enough doing it with two! Teenage rebellion can hit out at the single parent, often with blame for their singleness. It needs good supportive friends and a resilient sense of self to weather that. However, there can be bonuses too. A friend who brought up two small boys after her husband was killed in an accident, told of a special treat they would have on Sunday mornings. She allowed them into her bed and they ate apples together.

Sexual needs

A poem by Michel Quoist is often quoted by writers on the sexual needs of the single. It is from 'To love – The Prayer of the adolescent' and because it is so vivid, and applies to all ages, I will quote it here:

I want to love, Lord,
I need to love.
All my being is desire;
My heart,
My body,
       yearn in the night to an unknown one to love.
My arms thrash about and I can seize on no object for my love.
I am alone and want to be two.
I speak, and no one is there to listen.
I live, and no one is there to share my life.
Why be so rich and have no one to enrich?

Where does this love come from?
Where is it going?
I want to love, Lord,
I need to love.
Here this evening, Lord, is all my love, unused.[6]

Margaret Evening says that the problem of how to cope with sexual gifts and energies comes second only to the problem of inner loneliness. She also says, rightly, that no one knows all the answers to this! Certainly in some single people - especially, but not only, the young - the biological and physical drives for genital intimacy are very strong.

Some single Christians today reject the biblical view that sex is for marriage only and opt for genital relationships outside of it. They search for fun, acceptance and bonding without waiting for life-long commitment. The Western secular world sees this as the norm, regarding celibate people as deprived or repressed in their sexuality. But what does it do to a Christian? In a very helpful book, *Sex and the Single Christian* Audrey Beslow writes about the effects of sex in singles. She describes three effects. Firstly, there can be a *bonding* effect - a sexual bonding that might then trap a couple into marriage against their better judgement. Secondly there can be a *splitting* effect - a tendency to split off sexual fulfilment for 'kicks' from feelings of love and tenderness. Even when these feelings are later felt they cannot easily be expressed. Thirdly there can be a *fragmenting* effect which comes from the different sexual bonds formed with several partners. All of these interfere in some measure with the full expression of sexuality as God intended it to be.

Celibacy

So what of celibacy as an option? How can someone who is celibate express his or her sexuality in a way that satisfies and fulfils them? Donald Goergen draws a helpful distinction between *affective* and *genital* sexuality. Whilst a celibate person chooses not to use genital expression, they do not forgo the affective aspects of their sexuality - indeed these become even more important in the absence of genitality. Anne Long writes:

> The affective dimension concerns the affectionate, compassionate, tender aspects of our sexuality, which need not be genital but can be socialised - though only as we confront and become comfortable with our own biological drives ... This will lead us into many different expressions of caring, loving, praying, creative activity.[7]

There is a whole variety of ways of expressing sexuality through creative activity. The physically active may become involved in sport - coaching or team building. Others put much energy into music-making. One lively American friend plays the saxophone in her church band with great panache! For some people their pets provide outlets for nurturing, exercise and fun. Hobbies such as painting or wood-carving can be highly expressive of a person's sexuality. Times of celebration, too, can be very special, as single and married friends and family meet together to give expression to their love and mutual commitment. However, these expressions, if they are not to become a resentful 'second best', do need that degree of comfort with our biological drives which Anne Long emphasizes. They require, also, a sense of freedom of choice about celibacy which is not always felt to be the case.

Some reasons for celibacy

Celibacy from fear

Dave longed for a sexual relationship. Once, as an adolescent, he had got close to a girl and ejaculated prematurely. Her derision had been the beginning of the end for him. In fear of being scorned for sexual ineptitude ever again, he avoided any closeness which might lead to sex. Dave was celibate because of his fear of rejection.

Ginnie was also celibate through fear. She had been through a very difficult birth when she felt she was at the mercy of the doctors who used forceps to deliver her baby. She was out of control of her own body and vowed never to let it happen again. Her marriage broke up as a result of her inability to allow intercourse from then on.

Some people never get as far as Dave or Ginnie. Their fantasies about what will happen if they allow themselves to have sexual feelings are so strong that they repress them. There are all sorts of reasons for this. Many people have taken on board dire parental warnings such as 'men only want one thing', or 'nice girls keep themselves pure'. They key into deeper, more primitive fears. These might be fears of sexual attraction to parents of the same or opposite sex, for example. It is interesting that not all members of the family react in the same way to such warnings. Some are more prone to these deeper fears than others.

Celibacy as a spiritual ideal

Paul and Diana came to see me about the non-consummation of their marriage. They looked a bit like Hansel and Gretel as they shyly held hands and told me how close they were in their relationship. I found myself thinking, rather oddly, 'If I blow too hard they will fly away'. They seemed to be all spirit and no body. Before their marriage they had spent a lot of time in prayer together, sharing spiritual thoughts and priding themselves on their lack of sexual temptation. No fumbling in the dark for these two! Now they were married, the physical aspects seemed far less attractive than the spiritual 'oneness' they had shared – though there were times when Paul felt aroused; and Diana did want a baby. Letting go of the idea that genital sexuality was somehow 'unspiritual' took some time. I am not sure that they ever really did so, though they did consummate their marriage eventually.

Other single people hold to celibacy as an ideal on the basis that they can be more single-minded in their work for the Lord that way. That is fine, so long as they do not become smug and out of touch with their own sexuality, otherwise it can erupt unexpectedly with disastrous results. Some of the heart-rending things that have come to light recently in the lives of celibate priests (Anglican and Roman Catholic) who have fathered children, and abused young men speak of the tensions of this state and the dangers of repressed sexuality.

Celibacy as calling and gift

In Matthew 19:10-12, Jesus gives his disciples teaching on the possibility of celibacy as an option for some of his followers. He gives three reasons for celibacy. Some have an incapacity from birth. Some have been made that way by men (this would include physical and emotional castration, and possibly homosexual orientation). Others are called to be celibate for the sake of the Kingdom of heaven. David Gillett writes: 'Jesus clearly regards both marriage and celibacy as difficult and demanding – both are to be seen as part of the radical call to forsake the ways of the world, to follow him and to live as heirs of his kingdom.'[8]

Paul's teaching in 1 Corinthians 7 on celibacy and marriage emphasises the *gift* of celibacy. There is freedom from the anxieties and ties of married life and the potential for undivided concern about pleasing the Lord, rather than a husband or wife. Though Paul would wish others to be as he is (celibate according to most theologians) he does not decry marriage. Rather, he gives it a very high place in his teaching.

Creative celibacy

In some of my single friends, I see real fulfilment and creativity in their celibate state. I (and they) have sometimes struggled with the 'grass is greener' syndrome as I envy their freedom and they envy my family life. It has been through honest discussion about these feelings of envy, rather than looking through idealistic rose coloured spectacles, that I have learned about some of the practicalities of how to be creative and celibate. In other words, such creativity is born of struggle and a positive acceptance of the present, together with a disciplined approach to the temptations to envy the married! We have found that the 'grass is greener' perspective denies reality and puts us in a place of discontent which is far from creative.

The celibate mind

This is a phrase which Audrey Beslow uses effectively and which I want to explore here. Our sexual responses do not originate in our genitals, but in our mind and heart. Certainly, once our bodily responses are aroused they can sweep away our thinking. Consider the different effect of a woman's breasts being touched by her lover when she is feeling tender and when she is feeling angry with him; or by a child or someone fondling her in an uninvited way. Sometimes, too, our bodily arousal can be inhibited by a thought or feeling. Couples have sometimes said to me, 'We were getting on fine until the phone rang and that was the end'. What did the phone call mean? Distraction? A diversion? A threat? Whatever it was, it switched off sexual arousal.

> Do not conform any longer to the pattern of this world, but
> be transformed by the renewing of your mind. (Romans 12:2)

Whether we are celibate or married we need to train our minds and hearts to focus on what is good and healthy in our sexual expression and not get caught up in fantasy which leads to unhelpful sexual arousal. Audrey Beslow writes:

> The more occupied our minds are with true caring for
> people, with achieving our goals, with beauty, truth, projects,
> and communing with God, the less our bodies will become
> aroused sexually. However, training the mind to shift its focus
> . . . can be a slow process . . . One does not necessarily
> achieve the desire to control one's mind in a month or even
> in a year. [9]

Chastity is rather an old-fashioned word now. This disciplined approach to sexual thoughts and feelings, striving to direct them into an integrated sexual and spiritual wholeness which is honouring to God, is chastity in its true sense. Chastity is not confined to those who are celibate. Married people who, as Christians, integrate their sexuality into the whole of their Christian life and reserve its genital expression for their marital relationship are also practising chastity in their own context. There is real freedom to be found in this discipline, but it cannot be achieved by ourselves – we need God's transforming and enabling grace as we stumble and fall along the way. In *Celebration of Discipline* Richard Foster says:'The Disciplines of the spiritual life allow us to place ourselves before God so that he can transform us.'[10]

The freedom of celibacy

For celibacy to be a creative choice it has to be focused more on what *is* possible than what is not. A celibate person may be free *from* certain responsibilities – such as care of a spouse and children – sometimes from possessions (in the case of a religious community), AIDS, VD, pregnancy and the disapproval of the church family for a single person who chooses not to have sexual relationships. But far more importantly, he or she is free *for* a life which is a joyful expression of relationship with God and service in his Kingdom. This freedom does not come all at once. As Donald Goergen puts it, 'At the end of a celibate formation process, a person should be more free. I speak here of interior freedom, the freedom of the sons and daughters of God, which comes from prayer as well as from a well integrated personality.' And when it comes, it brings joy. There are three spiritual joys which are the heart and soul of celibacy.

The core of celibacy is not living an austere life nor abstinence from sexual life. Celibacy means friendship, ministry, and prayer. Intense joy comes from each of these three: prayer so intense that it bursts forth in dance, ministry so rewarding that it leads to a loss of self-consciousness and the feeling of simply being, friendship so beautiful that it shines forth in laughter, kisses, and tears.[11]

Friendship

My mother at 75, is a single widow. She is a person who is happy with her own company, but who also likes a good chat. Around her are neighbours of different kinds. One pops in regularly and they gossip away over a cup of tea about anything and everything. This neighbour also takes Mum shopping, introducing her to bargains and to delightful new areas of the city where she has not been before. If Mum goes away, it is this friend who often meets her at the station. She has a husband and family and is much younger than my mother, but fulfils a vital function as a person who gives almost daily contact and companionship.

Jesus' close relationships were based on friendship. He had the home at Bethany of Mary, Martha and Lazarus to go to, a place where he could be fully at home. He had women who loved him and men too. He was closer to some than others and I am sure children were among his friends and gave him great delight.

Friends of differing ages can be a special gift. When I was suffering from a bout of depression, two elderly single nurses, retired by then, were always willing to receive me with a cup of tea by their fire. They were not counsellors, nor did they try to be, but they mothered me when I needed them, even tucking me up in their guest room for a sleep. They did so without in any way being possessive or smothering in their love. I am so grateful for what they gave in friendship at that time.

A single friend in her fifties has a very close relationship with her godson in his teens. They exchange letters in which he shares some of his discoveries, excitements and concerns and she is able to respond with some of hers. They are very special to each other.

Touch

It is within friendships of all kinds that a single person can give and receive touch. Some will need more touch than others for their well-being and they will need it at some times more than others. But for a person with no married partner, touch can be life-giving. Celibate friendships can be both intimate and tactile.

Marion, a friend of mine, was in hospital after a hysterectomy. She had a further operation for a haemorrhage and then received the news that her father had died suddenly. I visited her and waited to greet her whilst a nurse fiddled with the tubes draining her stomach and feeding her blood. Then I reached out and kissed the part of her face that was not taped to a tube. 'Oh', she said with feeling, 'I thought I was untouchable'.

Massage, especially back massage, can be wonderfully soothing and can communicate love in a very different way from words. It can have a sexually arousing effect, especially with the opposite sex, but used with care it is a wonderful way of giving and receiving bodily affirmation.

I think we can offer far more than we do in pastoral care for single people, especially those who are elderly and live alone, in the use of sensitive touch. A hand on the arm as we speak or an arm round the shoulders can be the only physical touch that a person receives that day or even that week. Studies have shown the beneficial effect of touch when a person is sick, especially in women. Some men would seem to be slower to respond, perhaps because of their conditioning against weakness and dependency. 'In pastoral care, appropriate use of touch can be more important than words. It can say things that words cannot easily say – such as 'I'm here, today, in *your* present situation and I care about you.'[12]

Intimacy

Intimacy is a need for us all, single or married. At best, marriage will provide intimate friendship as well as genital union. Not all friendships are intimate, but intimacy is always found within friendship, not apart from it. Jesus saw intimate friendship as the closest of all relationships. He called his disciples 'friends' because he had opened himself fully to them – sharing his intimacy with his Father and drawing them into that amazing 'oneness'. We too are called his friends if we love him.

> I shall not call you servants any more, because a servant does not know his master's business; I call you friends, because I have made known to you everything I have learnt from my Father. (John 15:15)

For Jesus, such intimacy and friendship includes, 'genuine choice, complete giving, self-disclosure, unpossessiveness, sharing joy and sorrow, motherly or fatherly concern, a sharing of the Father, and real life together or intimate union.'[13]

> A man can have no greater love than to lay down his life for his friends. (John 15:13)

There is a sense in which intimate friends are 'in each other', part of each other. If one hurts, the other feels it deeply. Physical separation does not change this. They are also, in the deepest sense of the word, 'at home' with each other. Just as Jesus and the Father are 'at home' together.

> Believe me when I say that I am in the Father and the Father is in me. (John 14:11)

Again Jesus draws us, too, into this loving hospitality.

> If anyone loves me, he will obey my teaching. My Father will love him, and we will come to him and make our home with him. (John 14:23)

Intimacy at its best is a life-giving creative and fruitful kind of friendship. But we need to learn how to be intimate and to do so involves making mistakes and taking risks. I like the way Gerald Vann puts this: 'Our Lord did not say "I am come that you may have safety and have it more abundantly".'[14]

Some issues to be faced in intimate friendships

Expectations

Often, expectations in friendship are unvoiced, at least initially. As the friendship deepens, conflicts arise, which, if faced, allow expectations to be shared and explored. Will we always spend our free time together? Will we take holidays together? Will you consult me about significant changes in your work or leisure plans? Will you always tell me where you are going and what you have been doing? Will we share our family gatherings? We always bring to a friendship expectations which antedate the relationship.

Early on in one close friendship I had arranged for a third person to join the two of us for coffee at my friend's flat. She knew about the arrangement and I took it to be a relatively informal one. Later on, it became clear that a snack lunch would fit better into our day, and I changed the plan. When I told my friend she was very cool. Since I would share in the preparation I couldn't understand why. Later, I realized that, for her, lunch, however informal, felt much more of a chore than coffee. Being more used to entertaining, I had expected her to be as flexible as I was. I had been insensitive to her needs and expectations as to the use of her home. Part of facing conflict is to face anger, in ourselves and in others. Avoidance of the anger in friendship means avoidance of growth.

Exclusiveness

As Margaret Evening points out, 'Possessiveness is a very ugly ingredient in any relationship.'[15] There are, of course, times when two friends wish to be alone. That is healthy and right, because there is some sharing which cannot take place with a third person present. It is when other people become a threat and are excluded from friendships by one or both friends that the relationship becomes unhealthy. Jealousy so often springs from a wish to be the preferred person, the 'special one'. Its roots are frequently found in the sibling rivalries of childhood. The lie is that we cannot be special *and* share our friend with others. We are special not because we are *preferred* to others, but, simply, because we are *not* others. In other words, each of us is unique and no one can take our place. But the place of friendship is a gift and not a right. We cannot grasp it and the tighter we cling to it, the more likely we are to lose it. Friendship is a basis for freedom and growth and yet so often we bind it up tightly with our anxieties and need for security. A deepening friendship will allow honest discussion of these feelings (and they will occur!) and the finding of a way forward which neither denies them nor bows to them.

Dependency

The biblical goal of maturity as a Christian person is not independence nor dependence, but interdependence. People with strong dependency needs may form friendships with each other or with their opposites. Unless such a person is growing into interdependence, there will be little basis for true intimacy. Dependency says 'I want you to be always there for me – available, loving, caring'. And the unvoiced part is, 'like an ideal parent'. Whilst stable relationships and marriages can be built on this basis of meeting needs, intimacy will not flourish. There is a place for occasional parenting in friendship, provided it is acknowledged and can be mutual, and provided it is not the *basis* for the friendship.

Space

'The greatest danger of an exclusive and absorbing relationship (with a person of the same sex) is not the risk of homosexual practice, but the temptation to throw away all occasions and opportunities for solitude.[16] Learning how to give distance as well as closeness in friendship is vital. Space for solitude is a need for all of us, though some avoid it at all costs. Space for other relationships has to be given too. A friendship between a couple and a single person can be enriching, but there are times when both the couple and the single person need to be alone, or their identities get blurred and they have less to give to each other. Dryness and boredom in friendship can often respond rapidly to some 'time out'. The mutual sharing afterwards is much the richer.

Sexual feelings

Donald Goergen draws a useful distinction between intimacy, tactility and genitality. Intimate relationships usually involve touch. Being sexual people we will sometimes feel genitally aroused also. Where there is a commitment to celibacy such genital feelings can be recognized but not followed. Special care is needed here, when pastoral care involves touch. A person who has other outlets for intimacy and especially for genitality has to be particularly careful not to arouse genital longings in a single person which may be very hard to control. Having said that, where celibacy is the underlying commitment, genital feelings do not need to cause panic, whether in heterosexual or homosexual friendships. They are simply part of our sexuality. Intimate loving involves the holding and cherishing of each other's sexual boundaries. To follow genital feelings by touching or kissing would be to do violence to celibacy and to the relationship.

Shalom

A friend drew my attention to a weekend study group entitled 'The marriage within'. Although I could not go to it, I went on reflecting on the title. It seems to me that part of growth in wholeness is that movement towards inner harmony, the integration of maleness and femaleness present in all of us, and an inner completeness or *shalom*, the Hebrew word for peace and well-being. In every person there is a different balance of 'male' and 'female' characteristics. A woman may need to integrate her strength into her softness, or it can appear as over-bossiness. A man may need to integrate his tenderness and need to nurture. If these needs are not owned they may be expressed unhelpfully, such as a man making his work project his 'baby'. In this respect I think singles may have a ministry to the married, as they have to learn to convert loneliness into solitude in a way that can more easily be avoided in marriage. As Anne Long puts it: ' "Shalom", harmony at every level, can become a growing reality as spirit, mind, attitudes, emotions, behaviour, body, past and present become integrated into personal identity . . . There is a self-nurture that is not selfish but part of maturing.[17]

The place of pastoral care

Space is limited here so I recommend Ruth Fowke's section in *A Place in the Family* on 'The Church and Single People' for further reading. A good church can be a family for everyone, single and married, young and old. But a fundamental condition is that each person is accepted as of right, and there are no second-class family members. Single and celibate people have real gifts to offer and they should be welcomed and respected.

Perhaps the more specific place of pastoral care is in helping single people make their own choices before God about when to stop looking for a marriage partner, whether celibacy is right for them, and how to structure their time and relationships in a positive way. To do this, we have to be able to share some of the pain of loneliness, the agony of sexual needs which are to be unmet this side of heaven and the deep doubts about identity that may be around. Standing with a single person in these places of hurt can be very hard. It demands of us that we, too, feel some of these unmet needs. We will all experience helplessness and hopelessness at times in such caring. What we are doing is nothing more or less than offering friendship. Roger Hurding writes, 'Jesus restored friendship to its rightful place as an expression of God-centred living. One of the main outcomes of pastoral care and counselling should be that such friendships, across the barriers of sex, class and race, are repaired, renewed or discovered for the first time.' Later on he says, 'And so, as we encounter one another to forgive and be forgiven, to befriend and receive friendship, and to journey from loneliness to solitude, let us ever be open to the God who delights to offer companionship on the way.' As James Nelson has written:

> Surely, it is the friendship of God to which the Christian affirmation of grace points. If we say that God loves us, what we are saying is that God confirms us, God confronts us, God celebrates us. And when we have experienced that kind of friendship . . . even momentarily, we know that everything is transformed and we can never be quite the same again.'[18]

As clergy and as carers, as we stand alongside those who seek to live as single, celibate people, we, and they, are striving towards an ideal.

> The moral ideal is neither celibacy, marriage, genitality nor virginity. The moral ideal is life with Christ and through him, union with God. The important question for all of us is not whether to marry or to be celibate; the important question is: where am I going and to what am I called?[19]

SEXUALITY AND OUR INNER WORLD

In this chapter we will explore some of the ways in which our sexuality expresses itself through our imagination in fantasy and in dreams. Listening carefully to these dimensions of our inner world can give insight into some of the hopes, fears, conflicts and concerns relating to sexual experience which are unvoiced - either because they have yet to be realized or because they are felt to be problematic. Attending to this inner world of the imagination taps into one of our most potentially creative functions. Because many of the problems experienced by Christians with masturbation relate to its links with sexual fantasies, I will include that here also.

Fantasy

There is a sense in which all our imagination is fantasy in that it differs from objective reality. The difference may be very slight or widely at variance with the reality, depending on the subject and situation. If I phone my elderly mother and she sounds unwell, I begin to picture her in my imagination. The reality, though it may be close to my picture, will not be identical. If, later in the day, I get no reply to the phone, my imagination could take flight. I might picture her unconscious at the foot of the stairs - or worse. I begin to fantasize about telling the rest of the family. I plan her funeral . . . The reality is that she has felt better and gone into the garden for a while. Fantasy and reality have flown apart!

Differing expressions

Our imagination is a God-given gift. It is part of what distinguishes us from the animals. We all have some kind of inner world in which we reflect upon the past, experience the present and project into the future. There are wide variations in the use we make of imagination and in our ability to visualize. Some of us have very vivid mind pictures at the drop of a hat. Others are 'word' people and tend to think in words and concepts rather than pictures. Yet others experience and respond to life more through their senses. They imagine by 'feeling'.

We can, if we are interested, listen to the language that a person uses to convey something of this inner world. A 'visual' person might say things like 'Ah, that sheds light on the problem. I really see what you mean'. A 'word' person might respond with 'I hear what you are getting at now, I can really tune into that – I am on your wavelength'. A 'sensing' person might put it this way: 'I can grasp what you mean now, I am getting the feel of it'.

There are some marvellous images used in the Bible to describe aspects of God. These can be looked at in similar ways. It might be useful to see which ones we are drawn to, as this can serve as a clue to our preferred inner language. Christ is described as 'the Light of the world' (John 8:12) – *visual*; the 'Bread of Life' (John 6:35) – *senses*; 'the Word' (John 1:1), 'The Truth' (John 14:6) – *auditory*. The Holy Spirit comes as a dove (Matthew 5:16) – *visual*; the sound of a violent wind (Acts 2:2); as a Counsellor (John 15:26) – *auditory*. God the Father is often described as a rock or a fortress in the Psalms (95 and 59) – *senses*. He reveals himself to Moses in Exodus 3 first by the visual image of the burning bush, then by the words of his name I AM. Our amazingly creative God uses his word, the Bible, to speak to our imagination as well as to our reason!

These different ways of processing information and making sense out of life are called visual, auditory and kinesthetic orientations. We generally have a capacity to use all three, but one may be preferred and used much of the time. The development of a counselling and communication approach based on these functions is known as neuro-linguistic programming. For our purposes I simply want to emphasize the way such preferences influence both our inner lives and the communication which flows from them. Asking a person about their fantasies may yield pictures, words, senses, or a mixture of all three, depending on their orientation. Some who say they 'never fantasize' may respond to questions such as 'What do you think about?' or 'What do you sense, as you imagine that situation?'

Creative or destructive fantasy?

Clearly, our imagination can be used creatively or destructively. The creative use of fantasy relates the inner world to the outer world in an integrative way. This might include imagining or planning a course of action, or developing an idea or image - exploring and examining different possibilities and deciding on the best one. In time this could be translated into reality. The worlds of art, science, literature and music have many examples of such 'imaginings', often formed in a half-waking state of reverie. The psychoanalyst Jung was interested in this creative use of the imagination. In his technique of 'active imagination' he encouraged his patients to draw, write, paint or sculpt their inner world. Given conscious access to their fantasies they could explore their meaning and relevance.

Destructive fantasy is disintegrative in its effect. It would include planning to destroy, damage, or manipulate another person. It would also include those fantasies which simply deepen negative patterns and 'scripts', making for self-fulfilling prophecies. It would certainly include fantasy that becomes a substitute for warm relationships or leads to an obsession with genital sexuality.

If we are to listen to our own inner world more carefully and to the inner worlds of others, we need both care and discernment. Care - that we don't trample on or intrude wrongly into what is, after all, a very private area. Discernment - to know the difference between creative and God-directed use of the imagination and its destructive side. We all make mistakes as we learn. Some of the ways in which secular therapies have been used by Christians to help people take control of their lives have perhaps erred too far towards 'self-actualization'. Gestalt, for example, has huge creative and integrative potential. But it needs discrimination in its use if it is not to lose the fine balance between the paradoxical biblical concepts of unconditional acceptance and self-denial. Ultimately for a Christian the centre is Christ, not self.

The Bible has much to say about the influence of our thought life on our character and relationships. We can find biblical encouragement as well as the promise of help as we focus our minds on God:

> You will keep in perfect peace
> him whose mind is steadfast,
> because he trusts in you. (Isaiah 26:3)

> Finally, brothers, whatever is true, whatever is noble,
> whatever is right, whatever is pure, whatever is lovely,
> whatever is admirable – if anything is excellent or
> praiseworthy – think about such things. (Philippians 4:8)

The influence of feelings

It is not as easy as all that to control our imagination! Our thoughts are greatly influenced by our feelings – conscious or unconscious, and won't always 'come to heel' as we might choose. Jealousy, anger and fear can be powerful influences on our ways of thinking and imagining.

Beryl had been living with Steve for three years. One day she found a rather scanty pair of woman's knickers in his drawer. Immediately, in her mind, her greatest fear was realized – he was having an affair. When she confronted him with the situation he said that the office secretaries had played a joke on him and the knickers were just a bit of fun. Quite unable to trust him because of her underlying fear that she was not good enough for him sexually, Beryl lost all interest in their love-making. She needed to unravel her jealousy, anger and fear in order to make some sense of what was going on for her. Part of good pastoral care is listening with a person to the feelings and perceptions which underlie such destructive thought processes. Only then will such processes be amenable or accessible to change. It does not help, in the initial stages, to quote biblical verses about the 'renewing of the mind'. Often if a person *could* renew it, they would! Prayer, openness to God's Holy Spirit and careful listening are necessary. Later, Scripture can reinforce and confirm God's grace and holding love in the process of renewal and healing.

Sexuality and fantasy

There are many ways in which our fantasy lives express something of our maleness and femaleness other than in the explicit sexual (genital) fantasies usually associated with arousal and masturbation. I will come to those later. For the moment I want to look a little more widely at the ways in which fantasies can be expressive of aspects of sexuality such as unrealized hopes or unresolved conflict.

Unrealized hopes

A young man who is fond of a girl may imagine ways of approaching her until he finds one he is comfortable with. He may use his imagination to work out how to give her pleasure. Eventually, if all goes well, this will lead to actual contact and the relationship will grow. The details of the reality will be different, in part, from his imaginings – but the one will have paved the way for the other. Sadly, such planning may fall foul of some negative thought processes.

Bill often fell for girls from a distance. He would fantasize about asking them out, but in his fantasy they would always reject him.

He never translated his wishes into reality and the repeated fantasies of rejection reinforced this destructive pattern. Bill had been rejected by his step-mother when he was six and was convinced that no woman would like him, though he longed to find one who would. His hopes remained unrealized.

Unresolved conflicts

Conflicts, especially between uncomfortable aspects of our maleness and femaleness, can be heard more clearly by listening to fantasy, however odd or embarrassing it may seem. Rescue fantasies, for example, are fairly common. A man may daydream about saving the life of the woman he fancies. He is her hero and she loves him forever. What might this be saying? Interpretation of fantasies must never be automatic, but related to what they mean for the individual and to the feeling content of the story. However, such a need to rescue may indicate a feeling of powerlessness as a man in real life. A wish to make a woman helpless and in need of his care, can mean that he wishes she did not seem so powerful and independent. The fantasy allows an uncomfortable and unacceptable dynamic (real or perceived) to be changed to a more manageable one. If this is examined, the man may be able to explore other ways of relating comfortably to a woman. I would stress here, though, that we must never assume that we understand the meaning of the fantasy, but find out what it means to the person who shares it. It is only in finding the specific and unique meaning for *that* person that light will be shed on the nature of the conflict to be worked on.

If we look at the rescue fantasy from the other side, a person might imagine themselves as the victim. Suzy was an intelligent and decisive business woman in a world in which men predominated. She was well able to hold her own in her field. She felt embarrassed and ashamed of her fantasies of being weak and vulnerable and needing a big strong man to carry her off. In contrast to her working life and rational beliefs, this was, as she put it, a 'me Tarzan, you Jane' situation. Suzy found as she explored this contrast that she had pushed into her subconscious much of her softness and vulnerability as a person in order to succeed in her career. She had 'toughened herself up'. Recognizing the conflict this created in her, she was able to find ways of expressing some of her vulnerability and femininity without losing any of her business acumen. With the help of a male friend she found more confidence in dressing attractively and softly, something she had not dared to tackle before.

The child who has not grown up

Some fantasies give clues to aspects of personhood which are not yet fully integrated. Someone who is at a subconscious level still a child or adolescent may demonstrate this. Parental values may colour the imagination. Wishes to please or rebel may be acted out in day-dreaming.

> To pass sexually from childhood to maturity requires sufficient internal freedom from parental values, be they actual or perceived, and sufficient freedom from the wish to please or to rebel against such values, as to feel sure that one's instincts and desires are one's own. Any unconscious difficulty with this ... process can lead to sexual problems, as well as to other emotional or psychosomatic problems. Without such freedom, both men and women can be sexually 'children' to a greater or lesser degree all their lives. [1]

Sally, although 42, was still an adolescent at heart. She had never really left her parents emotionally and felt a compulsion to please them. She would take them presents, ring and visit frequently, even though she knew, rationally, that they did not demand all this of her. One day she shared with me a fantasy of driving down a one way street the wrong way – hooting as she went. She was in touch with a wish to rebel, not against her parents' demands, but against her own need to please. The fantasy signalled the beginning of growing up for Sally!

Jeremy was also 42. As a very young man of 17 he had a girl

friend with whom he was deeply in love. They had a quarrel and she sent a message asking him to ring her to make it up. He left it for two weeks, feeling very angry. Finally he realized he loved her but couldn't bring himself to ring. His 'perfect' love was ended. He felt no emotions even when his mother died. He had blocked them off completely. Eventually he met and married Christine. He was unable to verbalize his love for her and, although he functioned sexually, he could not allow himself to enjoy making love. He slowly recognized that he was still expecting the perfect love of the 17-year-old adolescent. Jeremy was not a 'visual' person but his words were graphic: 'If I blow my own trumpet, something is sure to go wrong!' His adolescent experience had been turned into a self-fulfilling prophecy in his imagination. I have found that when listening to a person who has blocked off feelings for some reason, access to fantasies in the usual way is not possible. They are not consciously in touch with much of their inner world. That is when a phrase like Jeremy's can give a valuable clue as to what is going on in his thought life and to what has become distorted there.

Fantasies and genital sexuality

Depending on a person's sexual maturity and on whether they have a sexual partner, the inner world of the imagination may influence genital relating. Jeremy could not allow himself to 'blow his own trumpet' genitally or emotionally. Suzy, the business woman, had no sexual partner at the time, but we could imagine that she might have difficulty in letting herself be vulnerable and 'out of control' to the point of orgasm with a man.

'Thin Walls'

Parental values, internalized, can have a loud voice in the bedroom! Many couples who enjoy pre-marital lovemaking, with or without intercourse, find that their enjoyment dims with marriage. Suddenly they are on the 'other side' – 'in the club'. What was their own private world of love becomes, in a sense, common property and less enjoyable. In her case anthology, Prue Tunnadine quotes a good example of this.

> She (Lily) remembered turning from the signing of the register, and setting off radiantly down the aisle on George's arm, all the family and friends smiling, and 'I suddenly thought', she recalled, 'they know' - and she had found herself blushing.[2]

I have often been told about the difficulties of 'thin walls' though which neighbours can hear. In the CPAS course on preparation for marriage - 'Side by Side' - to which I referred in chapter 5, there is an amusing video scene. A rather inhibited couple are listening to grunts and groans from the neighbours' bedroom in the next door semi and drawing the obvious conclusions. 'They are *really* enjoying themselves!' Suddenly the door bell rings. It is the wife from next door asking if they could give them a lift to the hospital as her husband is having severe stomach pains!

If we take the comments about thin walls at their face value, clearly the only remedy would be sound-proofing or a move! What is needed is to find out what it means to be 'heard' in an internal sense and how to establish the inner privacy to be free to be sexual. Often what is needed is permission from the internalized (perceived rather than actual) parent to grow up and leave home with its 'thin walls'.

Another woman

Terry had lost all sexual interest with his wife. He could no longer get a full erection. Sheepishly, and rather guiltily, he told me that 'there is someone else'. His difficulties dated from that time. He had felt pushed away by his wife who only welcomed intercourse to get pregnant. Though he longed to make love to his girlfriend he was unable to get a full erection with her either. Gradually, in talking, he said that he feared the implications of full lovemaking with his girlfriend. 'What might those be?' I asked. 'Well, I might want to be with her all the time because I would enjoy it so much.' In his subconscious imaginings, Terry foresaw himself torn unbearably between the two women in his life. He could not bring himself to face leaving his wife and he did not want to give up his girlfriend. He resolved the conflict (irrationally but subconsciously) by failing genitally. At the end of our session he asked me 'Do you think I'm doing wrong?' I simply put the question back to him. 'Well,' he said, 'I suppose I must think so, or I wouldn't have asked.' Then he added that he had expected me to give him a lecture about going back to his wife (more fantasy). I pointed out that he could do that for himself if he chose to. 'How would you have felt if I had given you a lecture?' I asked him. 'Oh, I would just have written it off as the text book answer', he said with a wry grin.

Terry needed to hear his own inner thoughts and the conflict they were creating in him, not have my text book answers put upon him. Sometimes in pastoral care, we may quickly pick up a person's guilt, but if we respond by giving a lecture or telling them (however gently) what to do, we may block the process of change. If their guilt is so near the surface they can best be helped by being enabled to own it and respond to it with our encouragement – and advice *if and when it is asked for.*

Masturbation

I do not think that death is the greatest taboo in this country – certainly not within the Christian Church – but masturbation. Priests who hear confession say that when this has been mentioned they *know* they have heard all there is to hear. I once sat over coffee with two friends in a busy shopping centre. We were deep in conversation about issues relating to sexuality and the subject of masturbation came up. The more extrovert of the three of us talked on regardless. The other two gradually became aware of a lull in the conversation at the surrounding tables. A waitress had been wiping a nearby counter top for several minutes, over and over again! Masturbation is something which arouses much guilt and shame, particularly among Christians, but by no means exclusively. It also provokes, I suspect, a great deal of curiosity.

It requires a very trusting and intimate relationship indeed for most of us to share our personal thoughts and feelings about this subject. Many Christians are deeply troubled about habits of masturbation and sexual fantasy which they feel are destructive to their spiritual and emotional life. Where they have been able to share this with other Christians for support and prayer, the results have sometimes been quite dramatically helpful. Richard Foster makes a case for sharing sexual fantasies with a 'soul friend' in this way:

> One of the most healing ministries we can render to each other is to pray for one another about our sexual fantasies. In this realm I have a friend who prays for me and I for him . . . We pray that Christ will enter our sexual fantasies and fill them with his light. We pray that our sexuality will be full and pure. It is a gracious, wholesome, happy ministry and I would commend it to you.[3]

Biblical guidelines

Since the Bible is silent on the subject of masturbation we must find our biblical guidelines indirectly rather than directly. As we have already seen there are biblical principles to guide us in the use and abuse of our imagination and thinking. We must not lay on people impossible moral burdens which are unjustified by biblical teaching. Neither must we perpetuate myths that are untrue - that masturbation is physically harmful. It is not. It has been blamed, in the past, for many things from blindness to insanity. There is absolutely no connection, in a physical sense. 'Many honest folk, told of the evils of masturbation, have prayed desperately to be set free, and in reality have been expecting God to take away their sexual desires . . . if God were to oblige, he would be doing violence to his own creation.'[4]

Positive Value

Masturbation is a common experience for most people at some time in their lives. It is not inherently sinful and can have positive value. Adolescents, for example, develop sexual desires and awareness far earlier than their capacity for committed relationships and emotional intimacy. Without the relief of masturbation they might be driven into disastrously early genital relating. Many do go this way, in spite of masturbatory relief, and their maturation process can be seriously interfered with. At this stage of life masturbation provides a way of exploring a young person's sexuality and sexual identity. The danger is that it may become obsessive and distorted.

Within marriage mutual masturbation can be greatly enjoyable. If one partner is absent, the other may masturbate whilst fantasizing about them and there is nothing inherently wrong in that.

For a single person without a sexual partner this issue causes the greatest concern. Some are able to use the occasional physical relief of pent up sexual energy to good effect, whilst not becoming reliant on masturbation and channelling their sexual energies into other directions also. For others it becomes a guilt-ridden and shameful cycle of masturbation, repentance, determination never to do it again, failure and self-condemnation. It is here that, if trust is sufficient, listening to what accompanies the habit – the situations which lead to it and the fantasies which accompany it – can be helpful. What is *not* helpful is to collude with the attempt to 'stamp it out' without examining the feelings and needs which are being expressed in this way.

Areas of concern

So what are the legitimate areas of concern for Christians about masturbation? The first is its link with sexual fantasies, which may be a form of 'adultery of the heart' (Matthew 5:28). The second is its obsessive quality which can grip a person in a way that becomes uncontrollable. The third is a focus on self rather than relationships. As the agony aunt Marge Proops once said 'You don't meet interesting people that way'. In this third sense, masturbation can cause difficulties in that a person relies on a pattern of arousal which is ideal for them, one which is unlikely to be carried out as satisfactorily by a partner. It may then become their preferred form of genital stimulation.

In practical terms, how can we as pastoral carers help with these concerns? I have found that a gently accepting approach to sexual fantasies is necessary as a first step. After all, we all have them and the question is how do we deal with them in the wider context of intimate relationships? To understand that such fantasies may have something to say to us can be a new insight. To share these imaginings with a trusted pastor or counsellor may be a first step in seeing them more objectively. A word of caution here though. If we ourselves are struggling with habits of masturbation and fantasy over which we do not have control, we should seek help ourselves before attempting to listen to others. It could make our own difficulty worse by titillating us. If, on the other hand, this whole area is one in which we feel highly critical and judgemental, we are not likely to be of much help either. It may be that, in that case, we should confine our pastoral cares to other issues about which we can be more relaxed and help a person to find someone else to work with.

Barry was greatly troubled by a habit of masturbation accompanied by a fantasy of two men wrestling with each other. He feared an unrecognized homosexual orientation although he had always been sexually attracted to girls. We explored together the situations which led to the compulsion to masturbate. They were usually times of loneliness and boredom. Then we examined Barry's feelings about the two men. One always overcame the other. He identified with the weaker one. Relating this to his present circumstances, Barry was a person who was easily bored. He had lots of ideas about what he would like to do but rarely took initiatives for fear of being rejected. There was a constant battle in him between his gentle, pleasing side and his more forceful, initiating wishes. When trapped by this conflict, bored and lonely, he felt a compulsion to masturbate. Barry had much to offer as a young Christian man and this habit greatly distressed him. It was also getting in the way of a relationship with a girl he loved.

While Barry's fantasy may have had a number of meanings, the one which made most sense to him and which related to his present circumstances was the one for him to follow. He found that he could explore his conflicting needs (to take initiatives in order not to be bored, and to please others by doing what *they* wanted) in more depth in our sessions and find ways of resolving them. We prayed together about his masturbation and agreed it was not the end of the world if he had a 'bad patch', though acknowledging his desire to be free of his compulsion. A measure of healing came gradually with the help of other Christian friends with whom he developed real trust.

Adultery of the heart

Sexual fantasies which come into the 'adultery of the heart' category need to be recognized as such, but not by condemnation, as I have already indicated. Sometimes as they are explored in a counselling situation new insights may come as to what is going on. Is a married person, for example, escaping into fantasy from an unresolved conflict? Does the marriage need attention? Is there an indication of unmet needs in a single person? Is that person in need of more intimacy and more physical touch? Having a good look at these kind of issues together, in the context of trustful pastoral care, could be a very important aspect of 'preventative medicine'.

No change

Not all problems of masturbation yield to counselling in this way. They may have their roots in early deprivation and deep lack of self-esteem. Here I think that loving understanding and acceptance of the person *with* the difficulties presented is what is most needed. Whilst not condoning or colluding with an obsessive habit, a light touch and prayerful approach to making new relationships will often be far more helpful than concentrating on what is already receiving too much attention! Sometimes God is more concerned with other areas of life and growth and we must certainly not load people with burdens of guilt which are not of him.

Dreams

Dreams in the Bible

Your young men will see visions and your old men will dream dreams. (Acts 2:17)

The study of visions and dreams in the Bible is richly rewarding and exciting. Russ Parker's book, *Healing Dreams*, is a well informed and readable introduction to the subject. The following is a comment from his chapter on the Bible and dreams:

Herman Riffel says that if we added together all the direct references to dreams and visions, all the stories surrounding them and all the prophecies that issued out of them, we would find that about one third of the entire Bible is related to our subject. So we can easily conclude that the subject of dreams plays an important role in the whole biblical narrative. [5]

Visions and dreams have much in common. Both may have a personal message for the individual. The unconscious may put into dream form a truth which a person has consciously denied. God may use such dreams to show the sleeper something he wants him to see and attend to. Many of the dreams and visions in the Bible are of this kind - in which God challenges, guides, encourages and warns a person and through him, others, even nations. Although the word 'vision' has a range of meanings today, it is generally used biblically in the sense of a 'waking dream', the content of which is given and directed by God. [6] Space does not permit many examples here, but a few will illustrate the point about God's use of dreams.

In Genesis 15 Abram has a vision in which God speaks to encourage him:

> Do not be afraid, Abram.
> I am your shield,
> Your very great reward.

Abram could not conceive of reward from God as he was childless. Later in the vision God gives him, with poetic beauty, this picture of his future offspring:

> Look up at the heavens and count the stars – if indeed you can count them. So shall your offspring be. (Genesis 15:5)

Later in the same chapter God speaks to Abram in a deep sleep. He warns him of his people's future exile, promises him old age and a peaceful death and makes a covenant with Israel, giving them a specific land to live in (verses 12-21).

The baby Jesus was protected from King Herod's desire to kill him by God's warning to Joseph in a dream. Joseph was told to go to Egypt with Jesus and Mary and he obeyed, staying there until Herod was dead (Matthew 2:13). Like other uses of our imagination, dreams can be beneficial and integrative or harmful and destructive. I do not go along with some writers who see them as 'out of bounds' because they can open us to occult influences.[7] My own view is that, as God used such means in the Bible to speak to his people, so with prayerful preparation we can expect him to do so today. This does not mean that we can dispense with discernment! We need to be very alert in our understanding and interpretation of dreams, but we can ask for and receive the Holy Spirit's help with the process.

Dreams and sexuality

It would be surprising if the varied aspects of our sexuality did not, at times, appear in our dreams and, of course, they do. Some dreams are clearly sexual, involving arousal, ejaculation and orgasm. 'Wet dreams' during puberty can be embarrassing, but are a normal part of a young adolescent boy's life. Girls, too, may experience orgasm whilst dreaming, but it is less common than the more romantic sexual dream. Specifically genital dreams, unless they are unhelpfully persistent, are not usually a problem. Occasionally they can face a person with desires they would rather forget!

Dream disguises

Quite often if we listen to dreams, we encounter aspects of our sexuality 'in disguise'. A friend dreamt of a powerful white horse on which she was riding bareback. By attending to the associations for *her* of the dream she discovered that the horse represented sexual energy. I dreamt of a woman in a wheelchair: I had to push her around and look after her. She did not speak – only 'bleeped' at me. Exploring that dream in a Gestalt group I found that this represented an aspect of my femininity which appeared weak but was, in fact, very powerful. Later in the dream the woman got up out of her chair and walked. I realized that she was only 'playing weak'. I learnt some important new truths about the powerful side of myself through that dream!

Exploring dreams

This is not the place to discuss in detail how to interpret dreams, but a few principles might be useful. Freud related all dream symbols to the genitals and to sexual drives. I do not think this is justified. Jung took a different approach: 'He tried to read dreams as one might approach an unknown foreign tongue. In interpreting a dream, Jung asked for his patient's associations to each image which appeared in it.'[8]

I find Russ Parker's approach very helpful. He encourages us to play close attention to the feelings contained within a dream, to check out everyday events and circumstances, and to make links, where relevant, with childhood experiences and feelings. He says: 'Here then are a number of routes by which we can gauge the direction or basic thrust of the dream message. They may not explain the meaning of every symbol and element in the dream, but they help to pinpoint the 'punchline' for which we are looking.[9]

Warning dreams

In pastoral care, we may need to know how to deal with dream material, particularly if it seems to be arising as a result of our counselling. Sometimes we can look at it in the ways outlined, at other times it may serve as a warning that we should not delve further into sexual material for the present. In my experience, this kind of warning dream comes, for example, in relation to memories of childhood sexual abuse. A person may be able only to look at a little of the memory and its implications at a time. Nightmares or repeated distressing dreams may indicate a need for supportive rather than exploratory care for the time being. Prayer of a 'covering' nature is helpful until the person is less distressed and ready to proceed. Incidentally, I would suggest that someone who has memories of abuse with distressing dreams is counselled only by an experienced person with training in this field, otherwise they could be made worse.

Hayley had been sexually assaulted as a young girl. She had many difficulties relating to this and other emotional problems which were unrelated. She was not a strong person emotionally. After hearing Hayley's account of her ordeal several times, I noticed that, far from helping her in going over the feelings involved, it seemed to deepen her anxiety. She recounted a dream in which she was in her bedroom and frightened. Snakes began to appear from under the bed and approach her. They had heads like penises. She always woke before they reached her.

For several reasons I decided not to work with the content of

the dream at that point. Instead I invited Hayley to imagine herself
in the dream and look around to sense the presence of Jesus there
in the room with her. She was immediately drawn to her cross on
the wall. For Hayley, that was a point of contact with Jesus. I asked
her to find out what she wanted him to do for her. She wanted
him to get rid of the snakes. In her imagination she saw Jesus open
the door of the room and all the snakes fled. When the dream came
again, Helen was able to visualize that ending and see the cross
on the wall as protection.

It was significant, I think, that Hayley's request to Jesus was to
'get rid of the snakes'. I had rightly judged, I think, that she was
not ready to face them and find out more about them at that
stage.

A prophetic dream

I would like to end this chapter with a dream recounted in an essay
by my father towards the end of his life. He may not have seen it
as a sexual dream as such, but its symbolism of the tower with its
life-giving core can be seen as an expression of his sexuality as well
as his humanity. For that reason, (and because he was 72 at the
time and our sexuality does not diminish with age, though it may
change shape) I shall include it here. This dream, though personal,
also has a prophetic message, I believe, if we care to hear it.

I had a wonderful dream last night and 'Brother Pain' was
responsible for me remembering it. I dreamt I owned a piece
of land and on it had been built a tower. The tower was old
but there was reason to believe that an older tower had been in
existence on this site. As I passed, there was a loud crack and
when I went to look, the tower had split from top to
bottom . . . exposing the older tower within. This old tower
was quite remarkable. It was built of glass . . . transparent and
shining white . . . and was in two layers as it were. The outer
part consisted of this shiny, white space, occupied by creatures,

men and angels, who were continually and gladly offering praise to God. Within was God, his hands raised in blessing and constant giving of Life and Goodness to these creatures.

LOSS, CHANGE AND BEREAVEMENT

Give sorrow words. The grief that does not speak
Whispers the o'erfraught heart, and bids it break.[1]

As I write this chapter I am looking out onto our small terrace – bright with orange and gold nasturtiums and monbretia, flanked by pots of gaudy petunias, fuchsias and busy-lizzies. It is a part of our garden that draws me like a magnet to gaze, titivate and enjoy; a deep resource in all its changing patterns of colour and texture. Yet this terrace, and the rest of our small steep garden has grown out of loss. Loss of a lovely larger garden, gently sloping upwards to woodland and full of birds and insects. We grew together – the garden and the family – over 18 years. I knew all its quirks, what would and wouldn't thrive in it. I knew its changing seasons with their reassuring sameness and subtle differences each year. The loss of that garden, when we moved two years ago, was so painful that I can still feel a yearning ache when I think of it. Once or twice it has featured in my dreams – changed now but still recognizable. Slowly, out of the loss and with the encouragement of family and friends, I worked at making a new garden beautiful. It can never replace the old one, but it is finding its own place in my heart and in my life.

Bereavement and loss can affect not only our relationships with people we love, but also with nature, places and parts of ourselves. A part of my sexuality – my ability to love and relate creatively to the natural world (and thereby to God its Creator) was cut off for a while, with the loss of a loved garden. I needed to mourn it, express my distress and the gulf inside, and my anger at having to leave it, before I could begin to work constructively on a new and very different garden.

Loss, whatever its nature, HURTS. We are familiar with the pain of loss through death and expect the bereaved to hurt and mourn – though very often the extent and depth of mourning is not fully appreciated except by those who stay alongside and are prepared to listen again and again. But other losses may go almost unnoticed and unsuspected, leaving the mourner feeling silly or stupid to be experiencing such pain. The pain may then be put smartly away and, like anything else that is 'buried alive', will make itself felt in other ways such as depression, physical symptoms and changes in sexual responsiveness.

The grieving process has been described as 'work to be done'. It is part of loving to mourn what we have loved and lost, be it a garden, womb, child or spouse. Our sexuality, our capacity to love and be loved, is inextricably bound up in the grieving process. It would be amazing if it were *not* so. We mourn physically with our bodies as well as our emotions and spirits. A newly bereaved person will experience deep tiredness – as if a plug is pulled on their energy. Yet, they may not be able to relax, their bodies restlessly moving about and finding something to do. The body is reflecting the mind's distraction.

In his section on death in *Anger, Sex, Doubt, and Death*, Richard Holloway says that 'human beings are rememberers'.[2] We remember with mixtures of sorrow and joy what we have lost. That memory affects our present and our perceptions of the future. Most memories, especially of people, are not untinged with regret and guilt. Regret about things unsaid or undone, guilt about hurts given or imagined. Part of the work of mourning involves facing these uncomfortable feelings and owning them for what they are – accepting ourselves *with* them even if we feel unacceptable. But our 'remembering' may become distorted. We may be unable to own such feelings and need to idealize or vilify the deceased in order to cope with them. It could be that this loss is distorted by echoes of a previous one which may be only partly imagined because it occurred in our early years. Such distortions in remembering are some of the ways in which the work of grieving gets 'stuck' and is unable to progress without help. As pastoral carers we have a role in enabling the 'normal' work of grieving, helping people to understand the bewildering and confusing range of feelings experienced. We also have a role in identifying grief which is 'stuck' and finding ways, when the person is ready, to enable him or her to move on. This may sometimes require professional help beyond our own skills.

'Death is the Church's business'[3]

Self-evidently the Church has a ministry to many who are bereaved, whether believers or non-believers. A ministry which at its best, can bring the incarnate Christ to those who grieve as the one who blesses 'those who mourn' (Matthew 5:4). Anyone who has experienced the sensitive and loving handling of funeral details and post-bereavement care by a pastorally hearted minister knows how vitally important this ministry is, and how deep the wound if it is mishandled. But there is, of course, a far wider sense in which death is the Church's business. Where the secular world views death as failure or 'the end' – as something to be avoided at all costs and for as long as possible – for Christians it has a very different meaning. Death, far from being failure, is the gateway, through Christ, to eternal life.

> Lo! I tell you a mystery. We shall not all sleep, but we shall all be changed, in a moment, in the twinkling of an eye, at the last trumpet. The trumpet will sound, and the dead will be raised imperishable, and we shall be changed. For this perishable nature must put on the imperishable, and this mortal nature must put on immortality. When the perishable puts on the imperishable, and the mortal puts on immortality, then shall come to pass the saying that is written: 'Death is swallowed up in victory'. (1 Corinthians 15:51-4.)

For Christians there is always the tension and paradox between the agony of loss and the appropriateness of mourning, and the hope that looks beyond. Hope in the utter dependency and faithfulness of a God in whom our relationship is eternal and unchanging. In a Christian sense, therefore, loss of any kind, whilst not something we would seek (or we become masochists) can be something which, more than anything else, shows us our full dependency on God. That is gift indeed. And such dependency takes great courage.

Jenny Francis, an experienced social worker and wife of a vicar, speaks of this in her deeply moving book *Belief Beyond Pain*. She writes from the perspective of 12 years of severe pain from chronic pancreatitis:

> It takes great courage to allow oneself to remain in such weakness, to be exposed, stripped naked in all senses before God himself. Bereft of clothes, layer upon layer of self stripped away to reveal a puny body and a more puny spirit, we find our feet placed on rock and know in our innermost being that this is God: he it is who wraps us in his love, but does not necessarily exempt us from the world's evil.[4]

She goes on to say that this is a process she has to keep working at: 'It is not a one off experience, rather a process through which we often struggle, aware that in it God draws as close as we will permit.'[5]

We might ask: 'Where is our sexuality in all this?' In the genital sense the answer could vary from promiscuity to a sense of real deadness. Or, as one man with chronic back pain following injury put it, 'The battery is completely flat, doctor!' In a wider, relational sense, the answer seems to be 'at the very heart of it'. For if our sexuality, freely expressed, draws us into increasingly loving relationship with God and with others; then loss, by its very vulnerability, can be a doorway to deeper encounters with love. And, if we are honest, we come to this point (if we ever do) agonizingly - kicking and screaming all the way in our protest. The comfort is that the Son of Man, too, screamed in protest in the face of death - but then submitted to it.

> My Father, if it is possible, may this cup be taken from me.
> Yet not as I will, but as you will. (Matthew 26:39.)

As we stand alongside others in loss and bereavement, we stand in the tension between suffering and hope. If we try to avoid the tension by moving too far to the one or to the other then we fail to love with integrity. As Jürgen Moltmann writes, 'Genuine hope is not blind optimism. It is hope with open eyes, which sees the suffering and yet believes in the future.'[6]

Pastoral care of the bereaved
There is so much helpful literature on the pastoral care of the bereaved that I have not set out to make that the focus of this chapter. Rather I hope to show how loss and bereavement relate to sexuality in a range of different ways. Issues of sexuality can be overlooked in bereavement, as can the significance of losses in difficulties with sexuality. For those who would like more specific guidance on the care of the bereaved, I list some further reading at the end of the chapter.

Some specific losses and their effects

Before we look at the effects on our sexuality of loss through death, I want to illustrate the effects of the 'little deaths' (some far from little in their impact) which are part of everyday life.

Loss of relationship
Separation, divorce and adultery are increasingly common features of people's stories inside the Church as well as outside it. The losses they may bring are compound: loss of 'status' (being one of a couple rather than alone), companionship, sexual relating, trust, self-esteem, confidence, support - to mention only a few. The effects on an individual man or woman can be very different and can be

long-term. Much help and support is needed by anyone in these situations. But ironically, it is just the time when they may be isolated and rejected by past friends who take sides or feel threatened in their own relationships.

Jack, a rather thin looking hotelier came to see me with his second wife, Joan. They had been married 17 years and, after the first year, he had rarely made love to her except when another man had shown her particular interest. Joan was a woman full of feeling, and much as she loved Jack, had come near to despair at their lack of physical lovemaking.

Quite early on Jack stated that he wouldn't 'speak ill of people – it didn't do any good'. Joan tried to prod him into saying what a 'bitch' his first wife had been – having affairs, 'slagging him off' behind his back and finally leaving him for someone else. Jack would only say 'that's all over now'. Though he wanted to make their lovemaking work, Jack consistently failed to make any move other than a quick cuddle. Joan had long since stopped trying to arouse him for fear of rejection. He was a man in a suit of armour, feeling sad but quite unable to express his anger and rage. Rage, not only at his first wife for leading him such a dance, but, it emerged, at his mother before her who had constantly smothered him with 'dos' and 'don'ts' whilst treating him as the apple of her eye. Poor Joan, she is still trying to penetrate the armour!

Sudden loss of relationship, like sudden death, has a far greater shock impact initially. The shock waves reverberate widely, especially in a church community. Usually it is only one partner to whom the ending is sudden, however, and that is part of the pain. For that partner and others who are friends there may be the inevitable 'what-if's' and guilt at not taking seriously signs which, with hindsight, they now see as amber lights flashing. Having not been aware of danger, the partner who is left can feel especially vulnerable to the same thing happening again. They may feel a great loss of confidence in *any* relationship, consequently. These feelings can be echoed for years in the church communities. Lack of trust, hidden anger, guilt and depression express themselves in diverse ways if they are not given a voice. If the person who leaves is the minister (and sadly this is not rare) there may be no obvious pastoral leader to handle the situation and the feelings may remain buried for years.

When the attractive, charismatic and gifted minister of a small village church suddenly announced that he was leaving his wife and daughter for another (married) woman, the church was devastated. Gossip was rife in the area and those who disliked the church made much of what they saw as hypocrisy. Some years later, recognizing that the damage was still going on despite the devoted pastoring of a loving new minister and his wife, the church elders called for a night of prayer, confession and repentance in the church.

Life stages

Pregnancy

Pregnancy is not normally seen as a 'loss' unless something goes wrong. It is usually regarded as the fulfilment of sexuality in many respects. However, few couples make the change from marriage or living together to parenthood without some losses and the resulting effect on their sense of themselves as sexual people.

Many women feel less inclined to make love in the early stages of motherhood. Hormonal turbulence, physical discomfort and an element of post-natal depression may be to blame. If this loss of interest persists, however, it may need help in the form of careful pastoral listening at first and perhaps referral for counselling.

Carole was delighted to be pregnant and she and her young husband, Nick, made love contentedly up to the last few weeks of her pregnancy. When little Joe was born, Carole was absolutely wrapped up in her new role and expected Nick to feel the same. She was not very interested in love-making, saying she was tired with being up at night breast feeding. Nick found himself caught up in a storm of unexpected feelings. He, too, was thrilled with Joe and loved to handle and bath him. But he was unaccountably irritable with Carole and sulked if she spent too long with the baby. He felt like a cross little boy. Ashamed of the ambivalence of his feelings, he withdrew somewhat from their relationship. Carole, angry at the loss of love and support she both expected and needed, felt even less inclined to make love and eventually refused altogether.

With help, Nick realized that his 'small boy' feelings were not something to be ashamed of but to be looked at. He was able to make a connection between Joe's birth and the birth of his younger brother when he was six. Rage and jealousy at his mother's preoccupation with the new baby, suppressed then because of fear of losing her love, had surfaced towards Carole. Seeing this he was gradually able to separate the two events and see Carole as his wife, not his mother. Carole responded with relief and delight and their love-making was soon re-established.

The menopause

Quite apart from the physical symptoms of the menopause, most women feel a passing regret at the loss of child-bearing with the cessation of their periods. There is no rite of passage for this – only jokes relating to 'significant birthdays' which suggest that life is going to be downhill from now on! Of course, many women ride 'the change' well and emerge with much more energy and a new lease of life. But for others it is very problematic. For those who have not had children, whether through infertility or singleness, there can be a real need to mourn the loss of expectations and hopes. These may have been buried for a while in a busy life, but can resurface at this time with all their sadness. Such pain needs loving and sensitive listening and even perhaps a gentle open-ended question to enable a person to say more. For other women deeper fears lurk. Sue's mother had severe depression around her menopause and 'was never the same again', according to her daughter. The family suffered from her spells in hospital and her inability to cope at home with the simplest decisions. Nearing 49, Sue became increasingly sad as she looked at the future as if she was near the end of her attractiveness and enjoyment of life. She wanted lovemaking more frequently as if to reassure herself that she could still do it. Slowly she realized that her fear was that what had happened to her mother would inevitably happen to her too. She needed permission and help to see herself as a very different person in very different circumstances from her mother and therefore not liable to respond to the menopause in the same way.

Ageing

In today's society with its emphasis on fitness and health we may be drawn in to the irrational belief that we can defer ageing and even death for ever! But we have seen that, for Christians, the losses of ageing and death may be times of a special nearness to those we love and to God, albeit in the context of pain as well as joy. Sexually, ageing brings inevitable losses – loss of youthful looks, of firm shape and of energy as well as the loss of sexual function in genital arousal. So many people come for help over this, wanting to get back what they have lost. Some will go to the lengths of surgery and implants to get it. For others, and hopefully for many Christians, we may be able to ease the process of acceptance of change by enabling them to give their feelings voice. We can encourage the appropriate mourning of what has gone but also the remembering of it with thankfulness to God for his gifts. We can honour the changed person – not as an 'old wrinkly' as our youngsters are apt to call us, but a person with considerable experience of loving. It has been said that 'no-one is useless whilst he is still able to receive love'. We do not cease to be sexual beings because we are old, and because we no longer get erections or orgasms. The giving and receiving of love and physical touch can go on until death.

A dear friend, Jim, was still a 'sexual' man at 90. Fond of women and loved by nurses and residents in his home for his courtesy and delight in a hand to kiss, he gave his love generously and it was reciprocated. The fact that he was unable to walk alone, was nearly blind and quite deaf was beside the point in terms of his sexuality. I mourn his dying, because he, by his loving openness and enjoyment of me (and others) as a friend and as a woman, enabled me to respond in love from a deeper and different place in my sexuality than had been touched in my relationships with younger people.

Surgery

Jean had needed a mastectomy (removal of a breast) for cancer three years previously. Soon afterwards, her husband, Harold, had said he could not bear to look at the scar. Already devastated by the loss of part of what she saw as her 'womanhood' Jean became deeply depressed. She saw no point in going on living. Unwittingly, but cruelly, Harold had failed her just when she needed his loving affirmation. Even though he later changed and was able to look at her and touch her, that moment went deep and added to the physical scars of the operation. Not surprisingly, the couple's love life never fully recovered, although they did reach a measure of forgiveness and understanding of the other's feelings.

The loss of part of our body, especially a sexual part, needs to be mourned and grieved over. Grieving takes time and attention and may be helped by sensitive pastoral care. Awareness that each person's perception is different, as in any bereavement, is vital. One woman, with a basic confidence and good self-image may grieve quickly and adjust fairly rapidly to living with loss. Another, especially if basic support by loved ones is lacking, will take longer and may never fully complete the work of grieving.

We offer, through the Church, services which acknowledge and mourn the death of people; but there is no similar service as far as I know, which allows a person to acknowledge before God and close friends the loss of a breast or a womb. Not everyone would want such a service, but some might value a time of recognition of the loss and prayer for the future. Possibly hospital chaplains know more of this than I do and offer such services - if so, I am glad. Those ministers who are working with losses such as these might like to think about how a simple service could be offered to those who want it, as well as personal prayer. Structure and liturgy can be part of the healing process, especially in the context of the Eucharist.

Hysterectomy may come largely as a welcome relief to a woman who has had heavy periods and pressing fibroids (benign growths of the muscular wall of the womb). To another it may represent loss of her womanhood leaving an unfillable void within and emptying her of sexual feelings by its physical and emotional absence. For those women, and their partners, whose orgasm is dependent on contact with the cervix (the firm neck of the womb at the top end of the vagina) or on the pressure of an enlarged womb, a hysterectomy may mean a need to re-learn ways of lovemaking and the loss of known pleasure.

Prue Tunnadine (a doctor specializing in psychosexual medicine) quotes a lovely story of Biddy, an Irish midwife and mother of four, who was being examined by a young gynaecologist she knew well, prior to hysterectomy. Fat, jolly and 'pouring like a pig' she lay on the couch. The consultant said to her 'Come on now, Biddy, it's only a useless lump of muscle' (referring to her uterus). Biddy's spirited reply was 'It may be only a useless lump of muscle to you, mate, but it's me womanhood to me!' She had her operation, but as Prue comments: 'In her perception of the meaning of this lump of muscle to many of us, she had a point'.[7]

I wonder how often as pastoral carers and ministers we take the time and the trouble to ask about the meaning of hysterectomy to a woman before or after surgery. It can be very rewarding as well as reassuring to her to know that she is *allowed* to feel grief for the loss of a troublesome organ.

Women, of course, are not the only sufferers. Their partners can also suffer indirectly and through their own surgery. I have sat with couples who are mourning the loss of penile size following a variety of operations, some of which do reduce its size and others which (logically at least) should not. Vasectomy (male sterilization) can, by its emotional effects on a man's sense of his sexuality, reduce his capacity for arousal. One couple were absolutely convinced that a circumcision had shortened his penis. 'They took too much away – it's just *not* the same', they said. I imagined them examining the poor organ which withered under their combined gaze! Obviously after such surgery there is nothing physical that can be done (although in special cases a vasectomy might be reversed, and recently some work has been done on the reversal of circumcision). What is needed is time to mourn the loss – often unexpected – and re-establish physical lovemaking in the context of a real acceptance of the changed partner. When a man's sense of manhood is focused on his penis (as with a woman and her uterus) this may take time and include a period of depression as part of the mourning process. In a Christian context it could be helpful, at the right time, and not prematurely, to encourage the person to see him or herself as God sees us. His complete acceptance of us and his love unchanged by our changes may help towards our self-acceptance.

It is not only loss by surgery of the specifically sexual parts of our bodies that can affect our sexuality. Space does not permit examples of other losses but they would include the deep hurt of loss of limbs, mobility, sight, hearing, looks, hair (in ageing or chemotherapy) as well as disfigurement caused by burns and accidents. All such losses deserve ongoing and patient along-sidedness with the sufferers, for the full impact of the bereavement may hit them long after the original trauma is past.

Bereavement through death

Death of a sexual partner

The Holmes and Rahe Social Re-adjustment Rating Scale published in 1967, and still regarded as a valid assessment tool today, puts 'death of a spouse' at the top of its list of life events requiring re-adjustment. In a very real sense the death of a partner, whether actually married or not, can be like loss of a vital part of the self. Indeed, since the two have become 'one flesh' in the biblical wording, that is not surprising. Bereavement can be prolonged, particularly in the elderly who are more prone to get stuck in depression than young people. Indeed, it is a familiar story to most of us to hear of the surviving partner dying themselves within a short time, as if they could not bear to live alone.

What is perhaps more surprising is the extent of bereavement even when the marriage has not been a particularly happy one. It is as if the 'fit' has become familiar, if uncomfortable, and a partner is still mourned as loss of 'self'.

Ken was a talkative East End Jewish cab driver. 'Fond of women', he was faithful to his wife until she died when he was 58. He went into a deep depression after her death for two to three years. 'I felt so sorry for myself', he said, 'as if life had ended for me. I even pretended to be ill to get attention from the children.' Looking back, Ken said he had 30 years of 'hell'. His wife was critical and never satisfied, putting him down for being a cab driver (a job he loved) and reluctant but compliant sexually. He never had erection problems and in spite of his love of women, never 'strayed'. It was as if he just accepted the status quo. His mother, a 'typical East End Jewish woman', had 'spoiled him rotten' and still did! His father was absolutely under her thumb, he said, passive and compliant like Ken. Ken met Barbara, a loving Jewish widow, who also 'spoiled him rotten'. He so wanted to please her but couldn't keep an erection long enough for intercourse. Desperate for help to 'get it right' he came to my clinic. I offered some insight into his process – sexual potency with a women he could feel angry with but impotency with one for whom he could do no wrong (like mother). He accepted this, but still seemed to expect me, the powerful woman doctor, to make it better. Perhaps when he can dare to be angry with the loving *and demanding* women in his life, he will be able to stand up for himself again – in every way!

Unacknowledged partners

If grief for a husband or wife is so painful, there is the added pain of grief for those who have not been openly able to acknowledge their love – for whatever reason. Perhaps a few close people will be alongside – perhaps none at all will guess at the pain. Homosexual couples may not find the love and pastoral care they need in some churches and that is a tragedy, whatever we believe about homosexual practice.

In her novel *The Bird of Night,* Susan Hill writes from the point of view of an old man whose famous poet lover, Francis, went mad. To protect his friend he has isolated himself in his grief but is pursued by researchers none the less.

'Sometimes a day comes without even a letter and then I can believe we are still in that world which was private to us, that none of them know anything about Francis. I live now for such days. Then I can sit here, or walk as far as I am able, to where the path begins to curve across the marshes. I can look back and see everything clearly, I can remember the truth'. [8]

Inequalities

Lily Pincus, in her marvellous study, *Death and the Family*, published in 1976, points out the inequalities in death between men and women:

What does it mean to be a widow in our time and place? A time in which equality of the sexes, women's liberation, dual-career marriages are major themes for discussion in the media . . . Death takes no notice of these discussions. So far as death is concerned there is no equality of the sexes. Men die at a considerably younger age than women . . . and many more men than women re-marry . . . Many widows feel they are being rejected or avoided, while widowers are made to feel precious, like eligible bachelors. None of the 'touch of death' attitudes with which widows are often tainted seem to affect widowers – here too there is inequality. [9]

Such attitudes make it particularly hard for a woman to re-adjust as a sexual person in her own right after being bereaved. Indeed, it is not unusual for a woman to introduce herself as the widow of her husband when he has been dead for more than 20 years. Such holding on to a precious status and role needs to be quietly respected. It may be that for that woman it is a defence she desperately needs in the face of the 'nakedness' of widowhood.

Re-marriage

Many surviving partners do not wish to re-marry. They may prefer singleness or they may regard themselves, as, in a sense, still married to the loved person. Apparently more men than women re-marry and certainly, in my clinical experience, this is so. It is also far more frequent for men who re-marry to have sexual problems, usually impotence. My impression is that if a woman decides to re-marry she has taken an emotional decision to allow another man first place in her life, whilst not forgetting the late partner. Having made sense of her decision emotionally, her ability to give herself sexually, assuming it was previously easy for her, goes along with her choice. Many men, on the other hand, decide quite quickly that another partner would be good, to end the loneliness and boredom of life alone. They have not made that commitment at such a deep level. In the area of their deepest expression of feelings – genital sexuality – there are problems. It is as if their minds and hearts can transfer love to another woman but their penis says 'no'.

Richard, a man in his early 60s, was devastated when his wife of 35 years died of a stroke. Sara, a widow, who knew them both, offered comfort. They decided after a year to marry. 'Rationally' Richard said, 'I know I had to make a new life and that Sara was good for me'. But his penis expressed his conflict and he was unable to make love. One day he recounted his fantasy of walking down the road in heaven, meeting his first wife and then (here he broke down and sobbed) asking 'Whose husband would I be?' Four years after his wife's death, he was still considering her 'wishes' in the daily decisions he made. The process of letting go was a complex one, full of ambivalences and very hard for both partners in the new marriage.

Death of a child

It is a rare couple who can handle their individual mourning of a child, whilst giving each other the love and support that they need. The differences of perception will be inevitable, however loving the family unit. The unpredictability of grieving – the one predictable thing in grief – means that whilst one is in the depths of despair, the other might be bright and buoyant. The sheer emotional energy required for grief leaves little to spare for the other partner, sexually or otherwise. It may add to the difficulties that a husband may want the comfort of genital closeness in bereavement and the wife be quite unable to give it. She may need emotional closeness and he is unable to give that. So in such tragic circumstances it is not unusual for a couple to drift apart in their grieving and either to break up or to bury the feelings deep with a mutual (unspoken) agreement 'never to talk about it'.

Lily Pincus described a couple whose third child had died at the age of nine. They were in marital difficulties and she only knew of the boy's death from the referral letter. In the first two sessions he was not mentioned, even by name. Finally, Lily Pincus asked whether the older boys missed their younger brother very much. With tears and tenderness, after six years, their grief was expressed. Their son had died when left at home the day before his birthday. Angry at being left, he had found some fireworks meant for his party, lit them and set a sofa on fire. He had been killed by the fumes.[10]

Sharing their grief in a safe place with trusted helpers removed a huge obstacle in this couple's communication. I have often found it necessary to help people to mourn the death of a child, whether through abortion, stillbirth, cot-death or later on. Years afterwards they are amazed that their grief is so 'raw' and that they *both* feel it.

Cot death

One couple's sexual difficulties dated back seven years to the cot death of a son at three months. They had other children but the wife remained frigid. Exploring her feelings, she discovered her deep anger at her husband who checked the baby at bedtime the night he died. She wondered whether he had actually done so. Underneath was anger at herself for being ill and not doing it as she usually did. She needed to forgive both her husband and herself before she could respond lovingly again.

Abortion and miscarriage

In a training group of Christian Listeners studying loss one evening, it emerged that four women in the group of twelve, including a GP, had suffered miscarriages. Acknowledging their grief together in the group and being allowed to weep for their unborn children was therapeutic – not only for them but for the rest of the group who shared the experience. More often, the very mixed feelings of loss surrounding abortion and miscarriage are quickly set aside in an attempt to get on with life. A woman may be encouraged, if appropriate, to get pregnant again to 'get over it'. But parents, particularly mothers, cannot forget a child so easily. Consciously or not, that child has become a part of the family and of her.

> Can a mother forget the baby at her breast
> And have no compassion on the child she has borne? (Isaiah 49:15)

One woman told me that she had a miscarriage 17 years ago. 'It would be his 18th birthday this month'. She had 'carried' her son with her for 18 years, not in a neurotic way but as part of her life story. In her moving and compelling novel *Family*, Susan Hill tells the story of her experiences of childbirth. The birth of her first daughter was followed by three miscarriages, a premature baby girl who died after five weeks of life and, finally, another full-term healthy daughter. After her first miscarriage she writes of the trauma of the experience for her:

> Reason was irrelevant, it was not the head that was reacting with such violence but the heart. When you lose a baby, however early, you suffer a bereavement, and you have to mourn and grieve, and give yourself time to get over it. And the emotions affect the body, which in any case has suffered a hormonal upheaval.[11]

Denial of relationship with a baby miscarried or aborted is denial of a part of a parent's sexuality – in its capacity to create, possibly to damage, and to love. As with any denial, the buried feelings deplete the living ones in some way. In his book, *Requiem Healing*, written with Michael Mitton, Russ Parker tells how he, and later his wife Carole, came to a healing recognition of their two 'lost' children who had miscarried. Coming from the perspective of evangelicals with a deep scepticism of 'prayers for the dead' both Russ and Mike realized the healing potential of such recognition before God of unborn children as loved family members.

Russ recounts how he and Carole had buried their feelings about the two miscarriages (before and after their two living children were born) and got on with life. In 1975 Russ was listening to Dr Ken McCall talking about praying for children aborted or miscarried. He says:

As an evangelical I found I was objecting to what I was hearing. However, in my heart, I simply started to cry. Whatever questions I was raising in my mind, I suddenly realized that the two children lost years earlier through miscarriage were real human beings.

I went to my room as soon as I could and in the presence of God I recognized our two children and gave thanks to God for them and said that I would be looking forward to meeting them when I go home to be with my heavenly Father. I also said to God that I was sorry for not recognizing them as real people belonging to our family. I felt a deep peace inside and the pain and depression which had daunted me for a number of years was gone. Also I felt a sense of being a complete father.[12]

In addition to other forms of 'Requiem' (a service for the dead) Russ and Mike encourage ministers to make available a service in which parents can name their unborn child before God, thank him for that child and entrust him or her to him. Even if they do not know the sex, intuition may be given and if so, followed. Healing and peace has come frequently from such a service, usually in the context of Eucharist. I would warmly recommend this book to all in pastoral care.

Death of a sibling

Since Cain and Abel, Jacob and Esau, sibling rivalry has been recognized as a 'fact of life'. Many, if not most of us, are shaped to some extent in our personalities as men or women by our relationships with our siblings. Competitiveness, jealousy and comparison are taken into our adult lives, consciously or unconsciously. They affect us as sexual people. The death of a brother or sister, especially in childhood, can have profound effects on the developing sexuality of others in the family.

Anna was 20 when her 15-year-old brother was killed in a road accident. Just emerging as a young adult at college with a life of her own, she felt bound to go home and 'hold her parents together'. Their son had been their pride and joy for they had always wanted a boy and Anna had felt second best. Now she had to be the son they had lost. What could have been healthy independence turned into a sense of inordinate responsibility towards her parents – the need to make everything right for them. Not surprisingly her emerging sense of self as a woman was affected and she later struggled with her sexual orientation. In a situation such as this there might be a place for restored relationships if a Requiem Eucharist could be offered as part of pastoral care.

Perhaps more commonly the death of a younger sibling may be seen by the older child as fulfilment of a 'death wish'. The need to be 'good' in order to keep parental love, while feeling jealousy towards the young baby who is getting more attention creates the fanciful wish that he or she would go away – or even die. When the sibling does die, the older child may think he has killed him. Instead of growing up learning to handle the inevitable love/hate feelings involved in a close relationship the child is left with an unsolvable dilemma. The dead brother or sister may then be idealized and the relationship then viewed as 'perfect' to cover the hatred felt and its awful results. No sexual partner can hope to come close to such perfection and sexual difficulties may well follow. Exploring the mixture of feelings surrounding the sibling's death and owning them may help an adult to relate more freely sexually, but sometimes such defences are deeply rooted and hard to change. So much meaning is invested in them.

Death of a parent

Christine's father died when she was six. Her mother never remarried, devoting herself to her four children. As soon as she could, Christine left home and soon married a man 20 years her senior. The 'father figure' element was obvious, even to her. She had her own four children. No real problems occurred until at 45, with a husband facing retirement and occasional gradual impotence, Christine found that she was the breadwinner and emotionally and sexually she needed to grow up. This she achieved, though not without pain and with counselling help.

Liz's father did not die, but divorced her mother when she and her sister were very young. He stayed abroad, they returned to England. To Liz it felt as if he had died as she did not see or hear from him again. She was an attractive girl and had several boyfriends but felt unable to commit herself to any of them because 'you can't trust men, can you? They go away and leave you just as you start to love them'. Rather like a self-fulfilling prophecy, Liz drove her boyfriends away just as she began to feel close to them, until she made the connection with her feelings about her father's 'betrayal'.

The principle of a 'life for a life' is found often in family work as a recurring theme. When a parent dies as their child marries or gives birth, there can be deep guilt and depression arising from the unconscious feeling that the child's sexual emergence has 'despatched' the parent.

Bill and Fiona had married late. Four days after the wedding,

Fiona's much-loved father had died. For a over a year she could not allow Bill to make love to her - though they had done so with great pleasure before the wedding. Fiona said, 'I feel as though by marrying Bill I have killed my father'. In fact, her father had been delighted at the wedding but that was no help to Fiona until her grieving was over and she could dare to give herself permission to love Bill again.

Birth, sex, death

These three themes are constantly interlinked in people's stories and struggles, as we have seen. In the story of the Fall, when death was introduced into Eden, it brought with it painful birth and shameful nakedness. Part of good pastoral care is bereavement care. But to help in bereavement, particularly in the process of 'stuck' grief is to encounter the great themes and day-to-day practicalities of birth and sexuality. It is also to encounter denial and hatred – both of which, when owned and forgiven, release a person to love more freely again.

So we come back to the concept that loss can also be gain, in the hands of a loving God and with the help of loving people. Lily Pincus puts it this way:

There is no growth without pain and conflict: there is no loss that cannot lead to gain. Although this inter-connection is what life is all about, it is difficult for the newly bereaved to accept. Only slowly may he, who has been in touch with death through the loss of a significant person, regain touch with life. A life which may bring new growth through the accept-ance of death and pain and loss, and thus become truly a new life, a re-birth.[13]

HOMOSEXUALITY AND
SAME-SEX FRIENDSHIPS

> Truly, to write of the healing of the homosexual is to write
> of the healing of all men everywhere. We are all fallen, and
> until we find ourselves in Him (God the Creator), we thrust
> about for identity in the creature, the created. [1]

Recently, at a workshop I was leading, a man whose name I do not
know gave me an insight into homosexuality which encapsulated,
in a new and fresh way, something I had felt for a long time. I cannot
ask his permission to share this, but I am going to pass on his 'gift'
to me, knowing that only he would be able to identify its source
and trusting that he, too, might want others to see this perspective.
Struggling with the knowledge of his son's homosexual partnership
this loving Christian man took it to his Lord in prayer. 'How do
you see him?' he asked Jesus. 'I see love that is genuine' came the
response.

> Man looks at the outward appearance, but the Lord looks at
> the heart. (1 Samuel 16:7)

So often, because of our own sexual blind spots and because of
our prejudices, we get caught up in discussion and debate about
the outward appearances of homosexuality and take only a cursory
glance at the *person*, barely considering his or her 'heart'. Whilst
not condoning behaviour which is outside God's plan for his

Kingdom, we need his help to see from his perspective and with his priorities any individual whom we try to help pastorally - or ourselves if this is our struggle also.

As we shall see later, the needs which underline a homosexual orientation, to whatever degree, are basic human ones, common to us all: for love, acceptance, and a sense of worth and 'being'. Their expression and direction may have become distorted for a whole variety of reasons, but their core is the common ground of our humanity and the place to which Christ's gospel speaks most deeply and profoundly to us all, if we will listen.

Some definitions, patterns and misconceptions

Before going further it might be useful to give an indication of ways in which the word 'homosexual' is defined and understood today. The most general meaning is 'emotional and sexual attraction to a person of the same sex'. We will review that definition when we look at causes of homosexuality, but it will serve for the present. Many writers suggest a broad spectrum in the range of human sexuality from the exclusively heterosexual to the exclusively homosexual. My clinical experience would agree with this, allowing for some denial and repression of homosexual attraction when it is felt to be unacceptable on moral or religious grounds. Obviously not all such attraction is expressed outwardly, either emotionally or genitally. Some of it remains purely within the imaginary and fantasy life of an individual.

Incidence

Figures from the National Survey of Sexual Attitudes and Lifestyles published in January 1994[2] suggest that 6.1 per cent of men and 3.4 per cent of women report some kind of homosexual experience. Those who have had genital contact with a person of the same sex are 3.6 per cent and 1.7 per cent respectively. These figures are consistent with other non-British surveys in countries such as the US, France and Norway. The climate of acceptability found in some American cities and in parts of Europe allows social taboos to be dropped more easily. Some people with a predominantly heterosexual orientation may also be drawn in. Their desire to experiment with the unusual, illicit or illegal may override their preferred sexual orientation.

Some misconceptions

Whilst we are dealing with definitions, it could be helpful to clear away some misconceptions. 'Homosexual men are all paedophiles' (sexually attracted to children). This is not true. Paedophiles are no more likely to be homosexual than heterosexual. 'Homosexuals usually cross-dress'. Again this is not true. Cross-dressing (in the clothes of the opposite sex) is more usually linked with transsexualism (a belief that he or she is more truly a person of the opposite sex) or transvestism (usually a man whose heterosexual drive relates to female clothing, often underwear). Transsexualism is at the extreme end of the homosexual spectrum. The difference can be said to be one of degree not of kind. In terms of the same-sex deficit in parental love which we shall come to later on, the deficit for the transsexual can be said to be so severe as to cause 'gender dislocation'. He (or she) does not feel himself to be of his own anatomical sex.

Traditionally homosexual men are thought to be feminine in their mannerisms, and lesbians rather 'macho'. Again, these are fairly rare stereotypes, similar to the heterosexual 'Rambo' and 'Bimbo', with underlying reasons for their presentation. They are not necessarily part of the usual range. Possibly it is the thought of these more bizarre manifestations of sexual disorder and their links with homosexuality that has caused many Christians to step backwards from defending and understanding their homosexually orientated Christian brothers and sisters.

Roots of homosexuality

The debate over the causes of homosexuality has been long and weighty, but no final conclusions have been reached. Biological (hormonal, genetic or neurological), psychological and sociological explanations have all been suggested. Perhaps more important than the theories are their implications with regard to the possibility (or otherwise) of change in a person's orientation. A paper in the *British Journal of Psychiatry* (March 1992) looking at the work of Michael King and Elizabeth McDonald, entitled 'Homosexuals who are twins: a study of 46 probands', finds that 'genetic factors are insufficient explanation of the development of sexual orientation'. And a study from the *American Journal of Psychiatry* (December 1980) entitled 'Religiously Mediated Change in Homosexuals' by Dr E. Mansell Pattison and Dr Myrna Loy Pattison concludes with these words: 'When homosexuality is defined as an immutable and fixed condition that must be accepted, the potential for change seems slim. In our study, however, when homosexuality was defined as a changeable condition, it appears that change was possible.'

Some attempts to look at a biblical perspective on homosexuality, at least within the more conservative churches, have come to the conclusion that we must 'hate the sin but love the sinner'. The Gay Christian Movement and others in favour of homosexual practice would take exception to the use of the word 'sin' in this context. A personal tension, for me, in this whole area has been my awareness of the fact that I often find myself drawn to homosexuals as *people*, whether they are male or female, practising or non-practising. There is, almost always, an attractiveness about them which is above average. I don't mean an outward attractiveness but one which has to do with qualities of vulnerability (at times not immediately apparent), gentleness, sensitivity and an ability to be both in need of love and willing to offer it generously. Obviously there are exceptions. But this has been my experience so regularly that I mention it here because it has given me cause to believe that I am probably not alone in this response – and to reflect on the reasons for it. It makes the 'hate the sin and love the sinner' approach rather too black and white.

Whilst we cannot be categorical about the causes of homosexuality, I have found the work of Dr Elizabeth Moberly, drawing on the psychoanalytical perspective, to be particularly helpful.[3] It adds an important dimension to our biblical understanding and its implications for pastoral care. Elizabeth Moberly says that:

> From amidst a welter of details, one constant underlying principle suggests itself: that the homosexual - whether man or woman - has suffered from some deficit in the relationship with the parent of the same sex; . . . there is a corresponding drive to make good this deficit - through . . . same sex, or 'homosexual' relationships.[4]

She stresses that homosexuality is a complex and multi-faceted phenomenon in its *expression* but this underlying principle holds. By 'deficit' is not meant necessarily a wilful or deliberate maltreatment by a parent:

> But in every case, it is postulated, something of a traumatic nature, whether ill-treatment, neglect or sheer absence, has in these particular instances led to disruption in the normal attachment . . . The psychological needs that are normally met through the child's attachment to the parent are left unfulfilled, and still require fulfilment.[5]

This is not to say that the causation of homosexuality is a simple matter. It is not a case of direct 'cause and effect'. Similar emotional trauma will affect individuals differently, and not everyone who suffers separation from a parent of the same sex will be homosexually orientated. The deficit is on an intra-psychic and possibly unconscious level and may, in part, be contributed to by the particular combination of temperaments between parent and child.

The discovery by American scientists in the summer of 1993 of a possible 'gay gene' does not necessarily discount this theory. We do not know how such a gene might affect a person, but it could be linked in some way with a child's response to any disruption in the relationship with the same-sex parent. Perhaps it might make for increased vulnerability here. What it does *not* mean is that there is no possibility for change, if that is desired. Certainly genetic 'links' should not be taken to be genetic determinism; those who seek change should not be abandoned by psychology and psychiatry.

Elizabeth Moberly goes on to point out that when an individual experiences this particular form of psychological damage, in addition to disruption of attachment and the corresponding drive for a new attachment, there is also a 'defensive detachment' from the source of pain. This leads to same-sex ambivalence (not necessarily overt) rather than simply same-sex love. This requires an addition to our definition of homosexuality to include the defensive detachment element which may show itself in hostility to the same sex.

> The attraction involved in the need for attachment has to contend with the aversion involved in the defensive detachment ... depending on whichever side of the ambivalence is the more prominent, the homosexual may ... experience authority problems (one manifestation of the defensive detachment) or dependency problems (one manifestation of the drive for attachment).[6]

I have summarized this particular theory in some detail because I have found it enormously helpful to me in bringing together some of the puzzling facets of homosexuality and because of its implications. In the light of this it seems to me unsurprising that homosexuals are attractive people, by and large. They frequently give out much of the love they seek for themselves. They will have a strong pull to relationship which more 'fulfilled' people may not have. In addition the 'unfulfilled child' within them may draw out the 'caring parent' in others, whether homosexual or heterosexual.

From a Christian point of view, the most important implication would seem to be that the unmet or insufficiently met needs of a homosexual for love and intimacy from the parent of the same sex are, in themselves, right and God-given needs. What is more, they spring from childhood relationships which are affective but not genital in their expression. Not surprisingly, in the search for a same-sex adult as a partner such needs may be expressed in both dimensions. Very often, as I have come to know homosexual people, I have been struck by the greater longing for affective intimacy, in men as well as women, than for genital satisfaction. Sometimes with deepening understanding even quite promiscuous male homosexuals will reach this insight, though their defensive detachment from parents of both sexes may have reduced their affective capacity greatly.

Bill and Gillian illustrate, in their stories, two differing responses to the disruption of parental attachment. Bill – an only child of elderly parents – felt keenly the absence of a father to play with and relate to. Both his parents were sober and somewhat withdrawn. Bill lived largely in a world of his own imagination. He followed his father into teaching (perhaps an attempt at closer identification) and found himself strongly sexually attracted to his male colleagues during his training and later during his work as a lecturer in a residential college. In fact, though he formed intimate friendships, Bill never translated his feelings into genital activity. He was able to be close to women, too, and eventually he married. Understanding some of the roots of his feelings of repressed sexuality enabled him to enjoy love-making with his wife. Bill had to 'embrace' his homosexual orientation, understand it and integrate it rather than banish it with guilt and shame as he had tried to do for years.

Gillian's story was of a little girl crying out for her mother's presence but often left with an elderly aunt whilst her mother, a headmistress, went to work. When she cried and screamed for mother, her aunt would lock her in the bathroom until she was quiet. This made her pain all the worse. It created a deep ambivalence towards the mother she both longed for and hated –

for leaving her. In later years Gilllian was drawn into a succession of lesbian relationships with older women in an attempt to repair the broken bond.

Same-sex friendships

I have listened to Christians who are troubled by a degree of sexual arousal within close same-sex friendships which have no actual genital expression of any kind. Some are anxious that they may be homosexual and back away from such intimacy in fear.

If we take Elizabeth Moberly's insights as a guide-line, it is likely that because of our humanity we all experience some degree of deficit in parenting. There is probably therefore, a sense in which close same-sex friendships are likely to have some element within them of a wish to 'repair' such a deficit as well as the sheer enjoyment of adult to adult relating. The 'homosexual' element, in Dr Moberly's terms, could be a small – or significant – part of that. Pastorally, such discernment could be very important and reassuring. Richard Foster comments on this area in *Money, Sex and Power*.

> A person who has experienced same sex arousal need not be frightened that he or she is destined for a life of homosexuality. The experience is quite common and needs to be responded to firmly . . . A theological, sociological, and psychological framework is needed to help channel sexuality. That framework can be used to say a firm 'no' to homosexual activity in much the same way that a married person uses a Christian framework to say . . . 'no' to extra-marital sexual activity.[7]

Some biblical guide-lines

Much current theological debate revolves around the issue of the genital expression of homosexuality between committed, loving partners. Most Christians would, I think, agree that promiscuity is sinful. Some, such as the Gay Christian Movement, would want to make a strong case for homosexuality as a 'natural' variant in God's creation, with its own right to emotional and genital fulfilment. From what has gone before it will be clear that my view is that the emotional needs of a homosexual person are God given and a basic human right. But what does the Bible have to say about the rightness or otherwise of their physical expression? *Does* it offer celibacy as the only Christian option for a person who is attracted solely to a same-sex partner?

Those who make a case for homosexual 'marriage' or its equivalent, argue persuasively from Scripture that the bans on homosexual behaviour relate to assault (Genesis 19 and Judges 19) rather than to homosexuality as such. Equally the references to it as 'abomination' in Leviticus 18 and 20 are interpreted in their religious context as idolatry and not seen to be related to the loving bonds of a committed relationship. David Field asks whether the Old Testament has nothing to say against physical love-making between two homosexuals without any hint of idolatrous worship. I quote part of his conclusion for its straightness and its compassion.

> The context of the law against homosexual behaviour in Leviticus includes condemnation of intercourse with blood relations and adultery, as well as prostitution and bestiality. Either of the former can, as we know, be the consummation of a relationship which is every bit as tender . . . as the love bond between two men or two women. The biblical ban extends to all four sets of circumstances, despite the immense heartache involved for all concerned in abstaining from the full physical expression of their feelings. [8]

What of the New Testament? What does it have to say? As far as we can tell, Jesus never addressed the subject of homosexuality publicly. He did, however, have much to say about sins such as selfishness, greed and hypocrisy. He condemned adultery (of thought as well as deed) and gave a clear place of importance to marriage with its complementary roles for husband and wife. He was particularly concerned for the vulnerable and for orphans and widows – those without parents or partners. He laid strong emphasis on the coming of God's Kingdom, where the Creator's will is fulfilled, in its present incomplete form and in its fulness when he comes again.

David Field looks very helpfully at the theological context of Paul's teaching on homosexuality in Romans 1, 1 Corinthians 6:9 and 1 Timothy 1. In the Romans passage, the theological context is creation. What is described as 'natural' or 'unnatural' relates, therefore, not to what is humanly 'natural' but to what is natural to men and women as God made them. In this context, therefore, homosexuality may now be seen to be a part of humanity. It has to be seen as an aspect of fallenness since, even in its most loving forms, it does not mirror the completeness of male and female *together* made in God's image. It is 'incomplete'. David Field goes on to look at the theological context of the other two passages. The context for these, he says, is the ten commandments which are deeply rooted theologically and ethically in the creation teaching. I recommend his booklet and its references for further study.

These may well be seen as hard and unloving conclusions to reach – unacceptable to many Christians and incompatible with a God of compassion. If we take sexual expression and gratification, on a genital level, to be a legitimate end in itself, that may be so. But as we have seen in the previous chapters there is far more to the expression and fulfilment of our sexuality and our personhood in Christ than that.

I can see two particular biblical grounds for hope in the pastoral care of homosexual people. Firstly, God is our Redeemer as well as our Creator. He is working constantly for our good and by his Holy Spirit can bring about a change in all aspects of our sexuality as we open it to him. As the Rev Christopher Guinness, co-ordinator of Living Waters UK, has commented:

If the church offers a framework in which the issues of homosexual struggles can be addressed, the healing work of Christ on the cross related specifically to the hurting areas of people's lives and His healing given, then the apparent harshness [of the above postion] is set against the healing hinted at in 1 Corinthians 6:9 'such *were* some of you'.

This is not to say that we should expect all homosexuals to become heterosexuals if we pray enough. That would be naive and unrealistic. Some are very loving people with their 'wounds'; perhaps because of them. It does mean that we can ask for and expect a measure of healing this side of heaven. What is needed may be the strength to cope with a celibate lifestyle *if* that is God's will for a person. However, it could be that God is less concerned about the rights and wrongs of homosexual practice than some of his followers. His priorities for healing of an individual at a given time might be far more to do with the quality of loving relationship than with the specifics of genital practice. We must not fall into the trap of deciding for God on the conditions for redemption – or its starting point. Writing in the *Tablet* in January 1988, Jack Dominian says:

Homosexual men and women, created in the image of God, are as much in need of stable and loving relationships as their heterosexual counterparts, and the principal aim of society and Christianity should be to ... assist in this rather than condemning. Within stable and exclusive relationships which make possible sustaining, healing and growth, abstinence can be encouraged for those who accept the scriptural inter-pretation.[9]

Secondly, I was greatly struck by the thought offered by the German theologian Jürgen Moltmann that God's judgement is the penultimate event in the coming of his Kingdom.[10] The ultimate event is the 'making of all things new' (Revelation 21:5). At that point, stripped by God's judgement of all that is unacceptable and unholy, our true selves will be made whole and new in his eternal presence. (Although this was not said specifically in the context of sexuality, I am sure that 'all things' will include this aspect of our personhood in so far as it applies eternally.) The present hope that Christ brings us is that some of that 'making new' is already open to us – all of us – in our sexual fallenness.

Some expressions of homosexual orientation

A need to cling hysterically within same-sex attraction

Sometimes the separation 'deficit' is a very early one and such wounds go deep. A baby experiencing this kind of separation from its mother in the early weeks and months of life may be left with an experience of unbearable dread, a sense of 'non-being'. This is the 'schizoid position' described by Dr Frank Lake, a Psychiatrist and founder of Clinical Theology.[11] Severe or prolonged separation from mother, the source of being, leads to this sense of non-existence. This is one of the hardest forms of suffering I know – leading to severe psychiatric problems such as deep and recurrent depression and sometimes to homosexuality. Because the schizoid position is held by the baby in relation to the mother, the psychodynamics are different for boys and girls. It is only in women that their lesbian orientation can be said to be an attempt to repair the bond with mother. Then, with this depth of woundedness, there is often strongly hysterical clinging to mother figures, sometimes interspersed with withdrawal into the schizoid place. If the schizoid position is held by a man, he may well transfer his need to a wife to whom he, too, will cling hysterically.

Mary had a mother who was very severely ill with depression bordering on psychosis. She was never able to give her daughter a secure sense of 'being' because she had no such sense in herself. She would be erratic in her feeding, handling and touching of Mary who responded by reaching out in a desperate way to other women she knew. This could be appealing as she was a pretty child and always wanting to please. In later life, although she married and had children, she lived with a deep sense of unhappiness. She searched for her 'mother' in a number of women friends, often mothering them in the reversal of her own needs. These relationships were far more satisfying and important to her than her marriage – something about which, as a Christian, she felt deep shame. Mary never became sexually involved in an overt way with her 'mother figures' but was driven by her need for intimacy into clinging to them dependently and showing terror if they moved away, either emotionally or physically. Although she was deeply unhappy, she did not really want to explore the terror of abandonment which lay beneath her behaviour. For some people it is enough to be received and understood – they cannot bear more change in this life. They need to go on with their unsatisfactory but defensive patterns of 'being' and be respected in that.

Mary was relatively easy to help pastorally, provided the help was given by several people and did not depend on one woman alone. Even so, she presented an 'unfillable void' behind her own outgoing kindness.

Some people with a 'hysterical' need for same-sex intimacy (in Frank Lake's terms), and these are frequently women, present a far greater problem than Mary. They can cause pain, disruption and chaos in a pastoral care setting. They can be highly manipulative and need to be handled with the greatest of care as to clear messages and boundaries of availability, since they will misreport, mishear and distort what is said to them. Their helpers, friends and family may end up fearing that *they* are going mad! Many warm hearted and well-intentioned pastors have had their fingers (and more, their self-respect and reputations) badly burned by such people.

In this kind of situation there is a crucial need for skilled supervision, probably by a psychiatrist or clinical psychologist; for strong supportive prayer and for a defined plan of action for all concerned. Even then, the best that can be done may be a form of loving containment of a person who is doing everything possible to avoid staring into their terrifying abyss of 'non-being'. I mention this, not because I have no faith in a healing God, but because I have less faith in the capacity of well-intentioned Christians to work within their capabilities and within the limited capacity for change that is normally possible in a person with a severely wounded sense of self.

Strong emotional attachment to the parent of the opposite sex

It has been postulated that a dominant parent of the opposite sex and a weak same-sex parent can tend towards a homosexual orientation. In the light of what has gone before, a strong attachment to the parent of the opposite sex is more likely to be an effect of defensive detachment - especially in a male homosexual. Attachment to mother is normal. If there is a deficit in the bond with father then one outcome may be a lack of emotional separation from mother, the so-called 'mother fixation'. It seems to be rather more evident in male homosexuals, probably because the bond with mother is the first emotional attachment for both sexes. If that is intact it is easier for a young boy to retreat to it than for a young girl to forge a strong primary bond with her father - though this can happen.

Matthew was the younger son of a northern tradesman. His rather 'macho' father loved sport and was 'one of the boys' at the local pub. A self-made man, he despised 'book-learning'. His elder son was very like him. Matthew was quite different - gentle, sensitive and artistic, he never came 'up to scratch' in his father's estimation. Lacking his father's affirmation, Matthew formed a particularly close bond with his mother. He liked to help her cook and could be very creative in the kitchen. They would read stories together. In adolescent and adult life Matthew struggled with his emerging attraction to men and recognized his homosexual orientation. He would sometimes have masturbatory fantasies about his male friends but his far greater 'pull' was to emotional intimacy with them, especially a need to be held and cuddled. He had many good and close female friends also.

Matthew's path to healing was not, perhaps surprisingly, through the deepening of his opposite sex attachments. He needed the strong loving friendship of Ted who was not homosexually orientated but could accept Matthew as he was and offer him intimacy without abusing the friendship by making it sexual in a genital sense. As trust deepened between them, Matthew was able to make a greater separation from his mother, though retaining his love and affection for her. He could, in a sense, remodel himself as a man on Ted and on other men he admired and respected. This was not an easy path to tread, and it continues as a journey. Breaking deep childhood patterns, re-forming bonds of intimacy and, in time, letting them go too, is a very hard process – but under God it *can* be done.

Ambivalence about dependency needs

Another manifestation of the ambivalence within the homosexual is demonstrated by a person's response to dependency needs, their own or those of others. This was shown by Juliana.

When she was a small girl, Juliana's parents divorced. She never saw her father again. Her bond with her mother was also disrupted by that event – mother becoming dependent on her for love and therefore binding her in a relationship more of duty than freedom. Yet they needed each other, clung together and became, in Juliana's words, 'too close'. To escape, and thinking a substitute father would be the answer, Juliana married an older man and set about having her own large family. It was only in middle life, following her mother's increasing dependency and eventual death, that she started to own her homosexual feelings. Juliana had not coped well with her mother's dependency, wanting to push her away. She hated the thought of her husband becoming dependent and found his sexual approaches increasingly repulsive. She turned to same-sex fantasies for the comfort and intimacy she so needed, but which her mother had failed to give. As she was a strongly religious person, these worried her greatly until she could see something of their source and begin to address her deeper needs.

It is a very frequent finding that masturbation is strongly linked with a homosexual orientation. Indeed it may be there that such an orientation first shows itself. For Christians and others this can provoke great guilt and distress. The principles I mentioned in chapter 7 apply equally here. I think that one of the more common mistakes in pastoral care and counselling of people with this difficulty is to ask them to attempt - by prayer and willpower - to stamp out the habit without first examining the accompanying fantasies in an objectifying way to understand their meaning. Without this there is little hope of breaking a compulsive cycle and finding more satisfying ways forward.

A degree of gender confusion

Apart from the severe 'gender dislocation' of transsexualism which may occur when psychological damage is severe and early, other degrees of confusion may contribute to homosexuality. For example, parents may be deeply disappointed that a child is not of the opposite sex. They may even treat a boy as a girl or vice versa, to the point of dressing them accordingly in some cases. Even the disappointment expressed may be enough to make the young child try their best to be the sex their parent wanted - putting a condition on his or her acceptability that is fundamentally unattainable.

Christine was not the son her parents wanted as their first child. She tried her best to be like a son to them. Deep down she felt unacceptable because of her biological sex and grew to hate her femininity. Despite that, her need for acceptance drew her into lesbian relationships which both attracted and revolted her. Christine's conflict was a particularly difficult one for her to handle as an adult Christian because in this case her deepest need, for acceptance, was inextricably linked with her sexual identity.

John was rather like Matthew in having a 'macho' and sporty father who condemned his son's more sensitive and caring temperament. His mother both valued and needed him as, after her divorce, she became quite severely disabled. John became trapped in a caring role with his more feminine characteristics valued highly and little encouragement to find out what kind of man he really was. Having split up with a girl friend he became increasingly attracted to other men. Fearing that this meant he would turn out to be 'gay' (in his terms, homosexually promiscuous) he trapped himself further and felt unable to leave his mother at all. In a sense John's 'father deficit' was increased and intensified by his mother's need of him in a rather typically feminine role. He had to do a lot of work, over a long period of time, to dare to leave the security of his mother's need/love and begin to explore his sexuality in the masculine world of his peers.

Searching for missing qualities

Some homosexual people are clearly searching in their same-sex partners for aspects of their sexuality or personality which are felt to be missing or diminished. For some men, for example, this can be a very male physique; perhaps with large genitals. It could be qualities of attractiveness to women or academic ability. For a woman it could be physical beauty, femininity or a capacity to care and mother. By forming an intimate (and often genital) relationship, the unconscious hope is that these qualities will become a part of themselves and they will then be the acceptable man or woman they long to be. The danger is that this search can so easily progress to narcissism, envy and idolatry. The truth is that *no* other human being can ever make us whole – only God can do that.

> They exchanged the truth of God for a lie, and worshipped and served created things rather than the Creator. (Romans 1:25)

A hope for healing – some implications for pastoral care

Healing in pastoral care is never something to be imposed on a person but is, to quote Bishop Morris Maddocks, 'Jesus Christ meeting us at the point of our need'. Healing for a homosexually orientated person is essentially about fulfilment of unmet needs. In this sense there is no real difference between homosexual and heterosexual for we will all have unmet needs this side of heaven. There may be a difference, however, in a homosexual in the perceived 'deficit' and the need for reparation. Such a person may come for pastoral help with a deep desire and need for healing. Even though there might be a genetically linked vulnerability involved, I believe that it is always right to open the heart's longings to God in prayer and obedience and trust him for what he will give. We cannot predict the answer given but there *will* be answered prayer. Of that I am convinced.

Relationships and prayer together are necessary for healing. Sexual abstinence may be necessary, but it is not an answer in itself. Only the meeting of same-sex emotional needs will provide that. We should not pray that God will 'cure' a person of legitimate needs! For some a decision will be made to give up a homosexual partner if the relationship is preventing the healing work of Christ. This may well lead to a process of mourning with the normal stages of *denial* (that the relationship needs to be broken), *anger* at God that this should be necessary, *bargaining* to be allowed to keep it, *depression*, and finally *acceptance* of the loss and a renewed sense of self as a separate individual.

A prime factor in healing will be one or more same-sex relationships which are 'reparative'. These can provide real loving acceptance and affirmation, including some non-genital physical touch if appropriate, whilst firmly holding the sexual and personal boundaries. They could be offered by a Christian with a homosexual orientation who has experienced a fair degree of healing already and is able to minister to another without being seduced by his or her own needs. They could also be provided by a person who is predominantly heterosexual, but with a real understanding of the homosexual condition. Either way, that person has to be a trustworthy 'parent' or they will do more damage by their involvement. Sadly it is not uncommon for counsellors, including Christians, to abuse such a relationship and to trap the counsellee far more firmly in their homosexual condition as a result.

In view of this, the question arises as to whether a homosexual can be helped, pastorally, by someone of the opposite sex. I think the answer is a qualified 'yes' – they can be helped in understanding and insight. However, the reparative work must also be going on at the same time. Ideally this work can best be done by a same-sex counsellor. Such a relationship will need real perseverance and commitment. It will have to 'ride' ambivalence and detachment at times, as well as strong attachment and possible dependency. If offered more within the context of Christian friendship rather than professional psychotherapy, this may well call for experienced supervision by a psychotherapist or a psychologist. Such help (with the permission of the person involved) could prove to be invaluable.

The wider Christian family also has a vital part to play in the pastoral care of homosexuals. True, they need acceptance and understanding. But they also, like all of us, need a range of real friendships in which they can feel at home, not needing to hide their sexual orientation but not having it seen as their primary identity either. In some churches home groups provide a safe place in which to share struggles and concerns about sexual issues. Many of our churches still have a long way to go in achieving this aim but without such a context of care, even a strongly reparative relationship can still leave a homosexual person feeling a deep and general loneliness.

Prayer for healing

Listening prayer

Leanne Payne says that 'Listening to God is the most effective tool we have in our "healing kit", for by it we know how to collaborate with his Spirit'.[12] We listen to God's voice through the Scriptures as he shows his love and compassion and his holiness. We listen specifically for his will and his word on such issues as homosexual practice and the priorities for healing for any given person. And he speaks in many other ways also as we open ourselves to him. Elizabeth Moberly puts it this way:

> It is God who heals, and so our dependency on God is all important. Listening is vital to the ministry of healing, and it should be two-fold: listening to the other person, and listening to God, in a continuing and deepening sensitivity to the guidance of the Holy Spirit ... Our part is to pray, and to allow God to work as he wills. [13]

Forgiveness

There may well come a right time to ask for God's help in forgiving a parent who has hurt the young child, wilfully or otherwise, and to heal the deep sense of hurt and resentment. The healing which can result from forgiveness is so profound that this step should not be forced or hurried but allowed to take its place when the true nature of the hurt felt has come to light. [14] Christopher Guinness, commenting on forgiveness in this context, says:

> Forgiveness at this depth is, of course, the central work of Christ on the cross. It is God, by His Spirit, who enables the forgiveness to be very specific. Not just a general 'I forgive you', but a specific 'I forgive you for ...' The depth of forgiveness needed is seen as the person forgiving is enabled to see how they in turn reacted sinfully to the sin committed against them, and the convoluted results of that.

Healing of memories

Sometimes a specific memory or series of memories comes to light in connection with a defensive detachment taking place and prayer can be made for Christ to come into that memory and bring his healing and his light. Sometimes there may be no specific memory, but the effects of such a relational deficit will have persisted into the present and are accessible here and now to prayer for healing.

The healing of empty spaces in our hearts is completed by the filling of that emptiness with God's love. Though a person may feel this 'infilling' in great depth during prayer ministry, it will also need to be continued and confirmed through human channels as Christ the Healer uses his body, the Church, to minister his love.

This kind of healing process takes time: the deeper the hurt and the greater the defensive processes, the greater the time and care that will be needed – even though prayer may somewhat accelerate the process. Generally speaking, God does not 'zap' a person to a totally healed state. If he did the shock might kill them! He brings his healing step by step in such a way that the individual grows, like a healthy child at his own pace, into maturity and wholeness. Like the growth of a child, there are changes in the pace of growth and vital and crucial turning points of awareness. So it is in the healing of an adult.

Prevention – prayer in separation

Some Christians have been given a special concern for children as they grow up. Parents and godparents have specific children to pray for while others have a more general care for this group. There is a real place for prayer for children and parents who are at points of vulnerability due to separation during childhood – at around birth or later on. To pray for God's holding of them in that separation could be vital and life-giving. One couple I know with a grown-up family of their own had a special ministry, both of prayer and practical 'presence' to the younger children of neighbours whose elder son had a serious accident. During the parents' enforced absence, this couple took extra care to be available to and to listen to the younger ones.

Love

The implications for those concerned in the pastoral care of homosexuals are great. The implications for those who are excluded or stigmatized are devastating. I quote Elizabeth

Moberly's moving conclusion here as I cannot put it better:

> Love, both in prayer and in relationships, is the basic therapy
> . . . Love is the basic problem, the great need, and the only
> true solution. If we are willing to seek and to mediate the
> healing and redeeming love of Christ, then healing for the
> homosexual will become a great and glorious reality.[15]

Personal postscript

I have struggled in the writing of this chapter more than any other
in this book. The struggle has been about writing from a place of
personal integrity, which is true to what I believe about our holy
and compassionate God and about biblical teaching. That place of
integrity may change, but I have to write in the present. Struggle
implies conflict and conflict can be creative – if it is not avoided.

Many Christians have agonized over the tensions between their
sexuality and beliefs before coming to what, for them, was a
considered choice of behaviour and practice. It has been said that
the most interesting things in life happen on the boundaries. Those
who have had to wrestle with the boundaries of their sexuality –
especially the celibate and the homosexual – have much to offer
to others. Jim Cotter uses a phrase drawn from American Indian
tribes to describe homosexual people – 'threshold people'. 'They
were "threshold" people, and were to be found as teachers, helping
people over the threshold from childhood to adult life, as healers,
on the boundaries of illness and health, and as . . . priests, at home
on the boundaries of death and life.'[16]

I have been helped by those with a homosexual orientation to
cross some of my own thresholds – of fear, of prejudice and of
ignorance. I have also had to face some of my scepticism and lack
of faith. There are more thresholds to cross, no doubt, and I know
that as we journey together any healing that God brings will be
mutual.

SEXUAL ABUSE

My God, my God, why have you forsaken me?
Why are you so far from saving me,
So far from the words of my groaning?

. . . he has not despised or disdained the suffering
of the afflicted one;
he has not hidden his face from him
but has listened to his cry for help. (Psalm 22:1,24)

Sexual abuse, particularly of children, has the power to generate a cry of dereliction in the sufferer that echoes the cry of Christ himself on the cross. 'My God, *why* have you forsaken me? Why are you so far from my groaning?' I think that it finds an echo, too, in the response which must come from the very heart of God – a roar of righteous anger and a deep groan of anguish as he views this aspect of his created world. And an even deeper anguish as he looks at his Church and sees that it is far from exempt from this most penetrating of sins against the person. Child sexual abuse has been described by one survivor as 'soul murder'[1]

Jesus knew what it was to be abused – not sexually as such – but to be the victim of violent men. He was, literally, 'pierced' for us, in his body but also in his mind and spirit. Separated for a time from his father, the one who gave his life meaning, he knew the darkness of abandonment. From that place he listens to those who have been abused, as no one else can.

If we, as Christians, find ourselves caring for the sexually abused, we too, may feel a roar of anger erupting in us at the violence and injustice of it. We may experience deep anguish also. Such feelings are right and God-given. Indifference would be intolerable – and immoral. *But* – if we give vent to such feelings indiscriminately we could end up roaring like bulls in a china shop and possibly adding to the suffering of the abused. We need the energy of such feelings. But we need to use some of that energy to create the space and availability to be quietly alongside, to wait and listen and learn. We need to hear, for each individual, the answer to the question 'How was it for *you?*' Such alongsidedness does take energy – and patience, persistence, hope and deep compassion. It is very hard work and not to be undertaken lightly. So let these qualities spring from the God-given angry 'roars' inside us in response to abuse, of any kind.

The subject of sexual abuse is a huge one. Much has been written about it from both a secular and Christian perspective. I am not aiming, therefore, to be comprehensive in this chapter. I will try to offer those insights which I have discovered by sitting alongside people who have been sexually abused (and some abusers) and in discussion with other carers and counsellors. Apart from the specific sections on child sexual abuse and rape, much of what I say will apply to the sexual abuse of both adults and children.

In talking about sexual abuse we are talking about an 'iceberg'. Although the last decade has uncovered so much, it is still only the tip we can see and examine. Much is kept hidden as guilty secrets especially within the family. Statistics from the 1985 MORI survey for the BBC found that twelve per cent of women and eight per cent of men acknowledged sexual abuse as children. The likelihood is that because of under-reporting the actual incidence is higher. Peter Gibbs, in his very helpful Grove Booklet, quotes some research by Finkelhor (a recognized authority on the subject) which shows that abuse in children is widely distributed across social, ethnic and religious groups. He comments: 'The children who had been victimized did not come disproportionately from any identifiably social, class, ethnic, religious or racial background. It seemed as though sexual victimization was widely and broadly distributed.[2]

Given such widespread occurrence and ongoing debate, it is amazing that in many churches the subject of child sexual abuse never seems to arise at all. Yet possibly around one in ten of the congregation will have had personal experience of it! In a damning indictment of the churchs' blindness to the problem, Dr Anne Townsend, writing in *Healing and Wholeness*, quotes Isaiah 42:19-20:

> Who is blind but my servant . . .
> who is blind as my dedicated one, or blind as the
> servant of the Lord? He sees many things but does not
> observe them; his ears are open but he does not
> hear.[3]

She goes on to suggest two reasons for such blindness. The challenge to the existing abuse of power in churches where male dominance is the accepted order of things and the taboo on talking about sexual matters.

Sexual abuse is a pastoral concern for Christians whether we like it or not. Taking up the challenge may mean facing into some of our personal and corporate assumptions and fears about power and sexuality. In neglecting this area we risk behaving like the blind disciple or worse still the monkey who 'hears no evil, sees no evil and speaks no evil' and whose very silence allows the evil to continue.

Abuse as violation -- breaking of boundaries

Many of us who are involved in pastoral care will not have suffered sexual abuse as such, but we may have experienced some kind of abuse which can help us to empathize with sufferers to some degree. How many people when burgled, for example, say 'I feel violated - as though all my belongings are dirty'. One person told me that the first thing she did, after finding her underwear had been rifled through, was to put it all into the washing machine. We can feel indignant and helpless all at once, not to mention the shock that it could happen to us. When burglary occurs at a time of increased vulnerability (in old age or bereavement) it is particularly hard and unjust.

I was staying in London with a friend some weeks after her father's death. We had gone to the home of another friend for the night as we had a meeting in the area next day. We parked my friend's car in a side road as there was no drive or garage available. Next morning we went to collect it. I still remember the shock of seeing the car with its door swinging slightly open and all the glass of the passenger sidelight over the floor and seats. What little there was inside it had gone. The worst loss was not the window or the cassette tapes, nor even the camera in the glove box, but the film inside it which contained the last photos of my friend's father. We stood speechless and numb whilst our host became helpfully comforting and practical. 'Why?' I was asking myself in helpless rage. 'Why should it happen now, to my dear friend in her bereavement?' I even wished in vain it could have been my car.

Boundaries broken - in this case the fragile physical security of door locks and a glove box - can feel like violation. They represent deeper boundaries which, having seemed secure, then seem equally fragile. We can no longer rely on protection for the vulnerable and the innocent. What we have taken to be safe is now seen to be far from safe and the 'knock-on' effects can be great. For months after my friend's burglary, I kept all my cassette tapes in my boot and consequently deprived myself of any music apart from the radio!

I have found the following diagram helpful in understanding sexual abuse in terms of the violation of personal boundaries:

SEXUAL ABUSE AS VIOLATION – BREAKING OF BOUNDARIES:

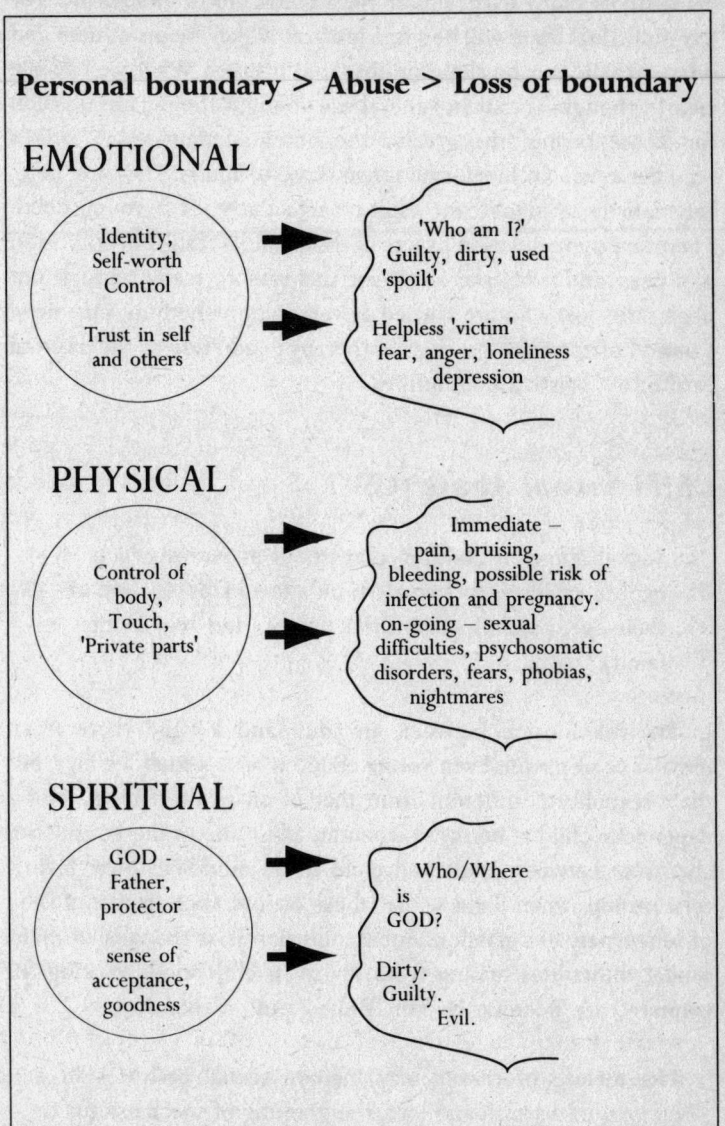

Personal boundary > Abuse > Loss of boundary

EMOTIONAL

Identity,
Self-worth
Control

Trust in self
and others

'Who am I?'
Guilty, dirty, used
'spoilt'

Helpless 'victim'
fear, anger, loneliness
depression

PHYSICAL

Control of
body,
Touch,
'Private parts'

Immediate –
pain, bruising,
bleeding, possible risk of
infection and pregnancy.
on-going – sexual
difficulties, psychosomatic
disorders, fears, phobias,
nightmares

SPIRITUAL

GOD -
Father,
protector

sense of
acceptance,
goodness

Who/Where
is
GOD?

Dirty.
Guilty.
Evil.

This diagram is a bit like those offered as a guide to bereavement, made up of many experiences but a guide, not a 'blue-print'. For any individual there will be some features which are prominent and others which may be slight or absent altogether. What we can see clearly, though, is that in general the younger the person is when the abuse begins, the greater the potential damage. A child's boundaries are far less formed than those of adults. They are 'held' very largely by significant adults, particularly for a young child. Therefore their violation by one of those adults results in confusion at a deep and profound level. For this reason, many (though not necessarily all) who are abused as very young children, may need a period of specialist psychiatric therapy in addition to the pastoral care of a Christian community.

Child Sexual Abuse (CSA)

> Sexual abuse of children consists of activities which expose children to sexual stimulation inappropriate to their age, psychological development, and role in the family. [4]

In any relationship between an adult and a child there is an imbalance of power. Even young children have sexual feelings, but their sexuality is different from that of an adult. The trust of a dependent child is betrayed when an adult allows the boundaries and roles between adult and child to be muddled. In a 'loving' relationship, when child sexual abuse occurs, there is a confusion of tenderness and passion. Such confusion is at the root of many sexual difficulties arising from abuse in childhood. Writing for primary care doctors, Dr Gill Wakley puts it this way:

> The misuse of power may include sexual activities in a context of warmth and love, the granting of special status or privileges, bribery, and frequently extreme secrecy, but it continues to be a misuse of the power of the adult over the

dependent child ... rape has many parallels with this situation of power imbalance.[5]

Some expressions of CSA in the adult

Such distortions of roles between adult and child are bound to express themselves in a whole variety of ways in the sexuality of the adult who has been abused as a child, as well as in more general psychosomatic symptoms. There is a very wide range of response, from deep woundedness and inability to form adult sexual relationships at all, to apparently normal functioning until a 'trigger event' is reached. The trigger may bring back the memories of abuse. Such points could be the beginning of sexual intercourse, where there are flashbacks of the abuser in the place of the partner, or the birth of a child – often of the same sex as the abused – with the consequent fears for *their* safety. The effect of child sexual abuse on the adult's sexuality can be to push the person towards promiscuity or invisibility.

Promiscuity

Suzie always came to see me looking as though she should be on a street corner giving men the 'come-on' in no uncertain terms! Deep cleavage showing up top and a generous expanse of stockinged leg, combined with beautiful make-up and carefully piled up curls spelt available sexuality all over! She told me she could not bear to go out looking other than 'immaculate' in her terms. Underneath was a very different story. Suzie had been abused from the age of six by an uncle in his late teens. Stripped naked on the bed, when he was baby-sitting her, she remembered closing her eyes as he looked at her, unable to bear his gaze. She remembered no more. Even talking about a vaginal examination – for a cervical smear for example – caused her to crumple into tears of terror, her immaculate make-up making tracks down her cheeks. Suzie could attract men like a magnet but she rarely enjoyed lovemaking - unless she closed her eyes and was a bit drunk. She frequently acted out her feelings of childhood impotence and rage by hitting out verbally and physically at the men she 'ensnared'. She called herself, rather aptly, a 'spider'.

Some easing of Suzie's situation came from the knowledge that her terror could be accepted and understood. Her mother had simply refused to listen to her hints of abuse. She also gained insight into her need to punish men if they came too close. She did manage to come to see me looking a little less 'immaculate' and a little more gentle before we finished our sessions.

Invisibility

Karen was the kind of person who is very easily overlooked. Thin, drably dressed and likely to run off at any moment she did all in her power to remain invisible. Though gifted in administration and very willing to be helpful, she constantly underplayed both her gifts and herself. Her tale of abuse by her father was an intensely private and personal area to her. Full of guilt and shame and feeling utterly degraded by it all, she still clung to the edge of a Christian community which offered her the only hope of 'family' she had known. It was through deep depression that Karen's needs finally became known to a trusted few women friends and she started on her slow journey to healing. It was significant, I think, that for both Suzie and Karen their initial healing came through women. Both had mothers who could not or would not respond to their need for care and protection.

'Mice' can be men also

Henry was a broken man when I first met him. He had grown up unable to say 'boo to a goose', as his wife put it in her scorn for him as a husband. Henry carried a great load of guilt and confusion unknown to his wife. At seven years old he had been dressed up as a girl and abused by a lodger. The awful thing, to him, was that he had both hated and enjoyed it. Eventually he found loving acceptance from his eldest daughter but went too far. He tried to meet his sexual as well as his emotional needs through their relationship. Reluctantly, she told her mother and 'all hell broke loose' as Henry said. When we met he was about to go to court and lose all contact with his family.

In that first meeting, I felt all I could do was to listen to Henry's brokenness and cry to the Lord for him as his anguish touched my heart deeply. Perhaps he had never been prayed for before - I do not know. Later, he made a long journey back from another part of the country whilst on parole in order to discuss the options for further help.

Life as a victim

The feeling of helplessness in an abused child to do anything about his or her situation may continue into adulthood in inappropriate but very real ways.

Lesley had been abused as an 11 year old by her father. It went on until she was 15. She had felt his need of her and, as sometimes happens, found a role in meeting it, though she knew it was not right. Trapped in this role, Lesley became a self-styled 'carer' within and outside her family. She felt unable to say 'no' and to stand up for herself in any way. In one sense she extended her father's abuse of her by inviting abuse of her willingness to care. Until she understood something of these links, Lesley resented her victim role but was quite unable to climb out of it.

Another expression of helplessness may be the 'nothing good ever happens to me' script. A man whose father abused him physically and verbally for years said 'I feel as though round the next corner there is always a man with a big plank waiting to knock me down'. Such people are often trying their best to please others (especially in a Christian context). They do seem to invite a degree of abuse by their insistence in being a doormat. An important part of pastoral care will involve giving help in seeing where that feeling of helplessness comes from - and alongsidedness as they take the enormous risk of saying 'no'. To do this is to do, in the present, what terror prevented them from doing in the past – saying 'no' to their abuser. Hence it is a major step in their healing. Because of the roots of the problem the 'no' may come out rather violently at first and this needs understanding within the Christian community.

'Secrets'

Denial is one of the most frequent features of child sexual abuse. Abusers tell a child 'This is our secret' and even threaten dire consequences if it ever comes out. Faced with exposure, they may well deny it all as a figment of the child's imagination. Mothers, aunts, and other responsible adults, such as teachers, brush aside signs of sexual precocity or withdrawal in previously normal children. There is a conspiracy of denial in many families (including Christian ones) to keep the truth at bay. If we, who have not been abused, are tempted to think 'how awful' – imagine how we might react if one of our family began to hint that it was happening close to home.

'Secrets' are a very heavy load to bear at any time – the more so when linked to such a social taboo. Yet many of the survivors of incest, for example, keep those secrets to the grave out of choice and a sense of loyalty. Some make a considered adult decision not to reveal details of the abuser and that is to be respected. Amongst other things, it may be part of a much needed sense of being in control.

Here, though, I want to highlight another side of the secrets conspiracy. Because of the breaking of boundaries which should be held and the vulnerability that creates, there is a 'flip-side' in some people. They feel that what should be private and personal is, in a way that is irrational but deeply felt, available for all to see. They have an awful secret, *and* they are 'skinless' and exposed. It is almost as if they feel as though anyone can see it if they looked hard enough. They have lost the sense of being in control of who knows or sees things about them. After listening to one young girl talking of her rape, I said 'It's as if you feel it's printed on your

T-shirt'. 'Yes', she said, 'that's exactly how I feel'. Such a person may present as very prickly indeed to hide their 'skinlessness'. No wonder they do not readily let others get close to them!

Abuse as a way of getting attention

Because it is of such current concern, some people may find that their experience of abuse is a good attention-getter and use it that way rather than because they really want to find help. A good clue here is a readiness to share the experience in detail with lots of people in a rather rehearsed way. Sometimes the abuse is quite marginal to the person's present problem but is a useful 'way in'. To talk of the trauma of being flashed at as a child may be easier than to talk of shyness and inhibition as a sexual adult. Pastorally we need skill and discernment here, not to dismiss the person as playing games but to look beyond the story of abuse to the present needs.

It could be helpful to use the following questions in such a case:
- What do you think is the most important need you have in the present?
- How do you think your experience of abuse may have contributed to this?
- Are there any other factors or life events which may be significant?

Responses in the counsellor

I have already hinted at the beginning of this chapter that our responses to abuse as carers and counsellors are likely to be powerful. We may find ourselves wanting to pull back, but also drawn by a sense of horror and excitement, if we are honest. Abuse produces acute emotional distress and we need to be aware of our own reactions and defences if we are to stay with that distress in others. More than anything, this calls for *a good supervisory relationship* in which we have the space to plumb some of the depths of our true reactions in honesty and integrity. In a research seminar on child sexual abuse by experienced psychosexual doctors, for example, we found to our dismay that a common response was one of dislike or disbelief in the victim at first. Normally a pretty compassionate group, we studied what this meant. We found that we were usually picking up a person's own self-loathing and expectation of not being heard and understood.

As listeners we may well be shocked by what we hear, though we will not show that to the person sharing. We may also find ourselves feeling guilty and dirty and even having unhelpful sexual fantasies afterwards. It can help to put on the 'armour of God' (Ephesians 6) prayerfully, piece by piece, before we meet to counsel, or afterwards if we are taken by surprise.

Ambivalent feelings in the abused

For those new to counselling the abused it may come as a real surprise to hear that there were aspects of the experience which were both 'good' and exciting. This is much more common where the abuser is known, but sexual arousal and excitement *can* be a feature, even of rape. This is a very difficult response to own without feeling responsible in some way for having 'asked for it'.

For a child, a special relationship with an adult is often a great gift in their growing years. Even if that specialness is distorted by sexual abuse, by secrets and by threats, it remains special. To a child deprived of other strong loving relationships it may be all that they have. Helping a person to separate out their legitimate needs to be loved and feel special and their (false) guilt at the sexual abuse is an essential step in the healing process.

Disclosure of sexual enjoyment in abuse requires time and trust. Conscious awareness of enjoyment is not a part of everyone's experience and such disclosure should never be forced in any way. However, it can be carefully listened for and a moment found to indicate that it is alright to acknowledge and own it. This can bring deep healing as a person is put back in touch with their potential for good sexual feelings when they had repressed them along with the horror of the abuse. Gill Wakley gives a superb example of a doctor enabling a patient to talk about her sexual arousal in this way.

> Mrs M was talking again about the events of her childhood. In an astonished tone of voice she said, 'When I was sitting on top of him and going up and down, I remember feeling warm, no hot, right up my body to the neck and face, and afterwards I would snuggle that warm feeling to myself right inside me and it kept me from minding when he was shouting and hitting me when I had done something he thought was wrong. I had forgotten about that' . . . The doctor said quietly, so as not to disturb the atmosphere of excited complicity, 'It's a very powerful feeling isn't it', and Mrs M looked relieved.[6]

Ritual abuse

Child sexual abuse taking place in the context of powerful and terrifying rituals, whether clearly satanic or not, is obviously an even more harmful manifestation of this particular evil. The evidence for its occurrence is clear. Dealing with it is even more costly than other forms of abuse. As Hilary Cashman writes in her informative (and intensely painful) chapter on the subject: 'Professionals helping ritually abused children are vulnerable to depression, fear and burn-out. They carry, with the children, the brunt of a concerted and calculated attack designed to isolate the child and scare off the helper.'[7]

Anyone involved in the pastoral care of the ritually abused should be working *only* with the close supervision of those who can give professional oversight from experience, both of the rituals and their effects and of the satanic dimensions.

Who are the abusers?

It is beyond the scope of this chapter to give more than a few guide-lines on the help needed by abusers. I recommend Peter Gibb's Grove Booklet for initial reading here and have drawn on some of his insights and experience.

The majority of abusers are male. One study showed that 95 per cent of abusers of girls, and 80 per cent of abusers of boys are male. The exception is in ritual abuse when women are far more frequently involved. Most are known to their victims; something which makes it much harder for the abused child (or adult) to get help – or even to be believed.

In spite of the popularity of the theory that abusers have been themselves abused, it would appear to be less often the case than is supposed. Much evidence for it is based on prison populations who are not typical of the population as a whole. If the theory were true, women abusers would outnumber men, whereas, in fact men outnumber women by about nine to one. Perhaps the most significant reason for challenging the theory is that it can lead to despair in victims who are trying to build a very different lifestyle for their children. Hilary Cashman says: 'The implications that victims become abusers is offensive and destructive to victims struggling to survive and rebuild their lives. It undermines their own parenting skills and their fragile self-esteem.'[8]

It is generally agreed by those who have studied abusers that they are not seedy old men in raincoats but apparently 'normal' men. There is no 'typical abuser' in terms of class or occupation. Some may be authoritarian, rigid and controlled personalities – not infrequently found amongst the police, clergy or armed forces. Such men may be pillars of the church or community.

As we have already seen, secrecy and denial of abuse is very common. If it is admitted, it is likely that the abuser will deny most of the responsibility for it – changing and distorting the reality so as to appear innocent. The fact is that, although he may be full of remorse after the act and promise never to do it again, child sexual abuse is compulsive behaviour akin to addiction to alcohol and 'abusers rarely give up abusing'.[9] This is a grim truth, but one which it is necessary to hear if we as Christians are to be realistic about an abuser's intentions to stop and about the safety of his family or other children, should he not get skilled help. Of course we must pray for abusers but we need to be alert to these facts lest children suffer more.

Some comments from 'Colin' (an abuser quoted by Hancock and Mains) warn the church leaders and community against soft options here:

> One thing that has to be understood about the incest offender – you can't let him off the hook, not for one instant. The sex offender wants to take the easy road ... But you can't feel sorry for him ... If they had let me off the hook, I would have continued. That is why the discipline has to be hard line.

> And it is very hard to be disciplined, to go through therapy, to go through a gaol sentence. Yet this is what had to be done to be able to start straightening out. I say that ... because I have been there.[10]

Some legal implications of working with abusers

If it becomes clear in counselling that the person may have been involved in child sexual abuse, then it is important to warn him that as a counsellor or as a church leader there is no immunity or privilege. If the counsellor is questioned by the police he will have to disclose what he has been told. Obviously this is very different from a counsellor or clergyman going off on his own initiative to a police station.

For this reason, if a client seems to be about to disclose child abuse, it would be advisable to suggest that he sees a solicitor with understanding of the problem for advice rather than going on with the disclosure to the counsellor. Obviously, if the abuser requests help in going to the local social services department to make a confession and ask for help, it might be appropriate to accompany him, at least initially.

Careful and detailed making of notes under these circumstances is particularly important. Advice given, whether taken or not, should be noted and dated, with reasons. Above all, when there is doubt as to how to proceed, it is vital to get advice from a supervisor and legal adviser as soon as possible, rather than letting the situation continue.

Rape

A sexual assault of any nature, on a person without their consent.[11]

In these days there is much discussion in the media about the nature of rape. 'Date rape' is a current term being bandied about to include forced sexual intercourse after a few drinks and an evening out. One man, recently convicted of raping a colleague after a ball, said, 'I spent several hundred pounds on her, why shouldn't I do what I like?'

'Date rape' may reflect something of our materialistic society in its need for rapid satisfaction. When things fail to satisfy, people become things too, to be used for a 'quick fix'. Power, outside of a genuine relationship, is always dangerous and liable to misuse. Sexual harassment is another form of the abuse of power – often by an employer – stopping short of actual sexual intercourse.

Many of the effects of rape are similar to those of child abuse, apart from the confusion of roles when the victim is adult. Disbelief of the victim's story and a tendency in society to think that 'women ask for it' have militated against justice and understanding for years. The work of rape crisis centres has done much to mitigate that recently. Judy Hanson makes the point in her Grove Booklet on *Rape as Bereavement* that: 'Rape is aggression that is acted out sexually, not sex that is acted out aggressively.'[12]

At a very deep level the roots of rape, like those of child sexual abuse, are linked to the power struggles between men and women. The Christian gospel surely has much to say about this, if we will only begin to open ourselves to the issues involved as Anne Townsend suggests. The present agonies over the ordination of women as priests speak volumes for the Church's need to address areas such as what true equality before God really means in practice.

Space does not permit me to say a great deal on this very important subject of rape. But again, much has been written about it and a few suggestions for further reading are available in the references. I will end with Tracey's story – which, like many others, illustrates the confusion and guilt which can arise from this form of sexual abuse.

Tracey was a likeable and friendly barmaid. Generally she did not accept lifts, but felt she had got to know and like Geoff well enough over a few evenings to accept his offer to drive her home on a dark, cold night. Geoff was a teacher. He said he needed to call in at the school to collect some books. He invited Tracey to come in with him. Suddenly a door banged behind her and most of the lights went out. Geoff threw her to the floor and proceeded to rape her, not only with his fingers and penis, but with the stem of a bottle. Horrified and in great pain, Tracey lay not moving a muscle. Afterwards, in silence, he drove her home.

Because of her inability to resist, Tracey did not tell anyone what had happened, or go to the police. She felt that she had 'asked for it' in accepting Geoff's lift and going with him into the school. Only when I met her, some years later, did she recall for the first time the agony of the pain and her terror that the bottle would break inside her. It was a revelation to her and relief beyond bounds to be told that her action in staying still had possibly saved her life. She had felt that it was weak to the point of saying 'yes' to what had happened.

Tracey is far from being alone in her story. Commenting on different responses to rape, Ray Wyre, founder Director of the Gracewell Clinic for Sexual Offenders in Birmingham, says:

Whatever they may feel at the time of rape, survivors are often
left with a tangle of self-destructive emotions and may be
plagued years after the event by feelings of guilt about not
having fought harder . . . The very fact of their survival can
be evidence that they acted in exactly the right way.

It must be valuable to know that there are different types of
sex attacker and that some are likely to take flight if
challenged verbally. You do not need to risk repelling them
physically to drive them off.[13]

A medical friend of mine was 'jumped on' by a young man as she
locked up her clinic one winter night. With great presence of mind
(and perhaps an instinctual guess as to the type of attacker he was)
she said, 'Don't be silly, I'm old enough to be your mother!' He
fled! Sadly not all attackers are so easily repelled.

Some guide-lines for the pastoral care of the abused

We have seen already that to enter this area of sexual abuse requires
great care and respect or we may add to the abuse unwittingly.
Having said that, we need to be careful not to 'take over' in any
sense - either in a counselling or protective parent role. We need
to enable and model a relationship of equality, not of dominance
- on both sides.

An abused person needs to feel in control of the processes of
disclosure and change. This means a respect for the fact that they
are in the 'driving seat' when it comes to what is shared and how
far to progress. But the counsellor is also there in a definite role
of enabler and facilitator. Some counsellors, in bending over
backwards not to 'push', fail to challenge when necessary. Some
people who have been abused try, often in subtle ways, to
manipulate the counsellor - a kind of abuse in itself. This may be
by inconsistency about appointments or by wanting extra time out

of hours. It could be by constantly challenging any suggestions made or insights offered. In wise hands, this is all grist to the mill in the process of gaining understanding and growth, provided it can be looked at as something to learn from without blame or judgement.

Whilst disclosure, in the right context, can be healing, that does not mean that explicit details of the abuse need necessarily be disclosed. It may even be harmful to go over these and such sharing should *never* be insisted on. When the abuse occurred in a very young child, the details may be vague or deeply unconscious. However, at the right time, the *feelings* surrounding the abuse and the person's perception of it will need to be heard and explored. Particular sensitivity is needed with touch in the care of the abused. Touch which should have been tender, in a child, has become 'sexualised'. This can make it very difficult for the adult not to interpret any touch, however meant, as sexual. A kindly hand on the shoulder may be misread as a sexual advance and therefore, in a sense, as abuse. Until the abused person has developed deep trust in the counsellor, sufficient for such an encounter to be discussed freely between them, I would suggest that physical touch is generally avoided. Much affirmation and warmth can be given in other ways, such as use of eyes and voice.

Stages in the healing process

These may well include:

- Sharing the aspects of the abuse that seem important.

- Expressing protest and rage at the abuser and others (e.g., mother if abused as a child). This is part of the regaining of control out of a feeling of helpless impotence.

- Expressing guilt and shame (sometimes to do with a feeling of having 'asked for it' or enjoyed it). This is a necessary prelude to handing back the responsibility of the abuse to the abuser.

- Restoring a sense of self-worth. To 'freeze' in terror and 'allow' the abuse is a natural self defence, not a sign of complicity.

- Restoring a sense of being in control – not needing to live as a victim. This may include learning to parent the 'inner child'.

- Forgiving the abuser, others and self. This must not be forced prematurely – it is not easy. It is often an act of will first. God may change the feelings by his grace later. At the right time it can bring great relief and release.

- Renewing the relationship with God the Father – especially difficult when the earthly father (or step-father) was the abuser. Sometimes it is helpful for a person to tell God how she feels at his allowing such a thing to happen. Sometimes the more motherly aspects of God's nature need stressing (Psalm 139, Isaiah 49:15 following). Above all he is a deeply compassionate God who *never misuses his power*

- Establishing enjoyable sexual relating. For some this may come – in time; for others it may never be a realistic goal. A couple may need skilled help in this specific area.

For some these stages may all come within one-to-one sessions with the skilled helper – a counsellor, pastoral leader, psychotherapist, psychiatrist or social worker. For others a mixture of 'ways in' contribute to their healing over a long period of time. Like bereavement, the healing of sexual abuse can feel like walking up a mountain of scree – two steps up and one back. Only when we look back do we realize that we are on a different bit of scree! Work in groups of adults who have been abused can have real value. Hearing each other's stories can minimize the sense of isolation felt and bring mutual support and comfort. For specifically Christian help many churches have started such groups. 'Safety Net' has been set up in conjunction with the Chaplaincy of St George's Hospital, London, to address common issues affecting 'survivors', who meet together three times a year.[14]

The place of prayer and liturgy

There is a sense in which all care of victims of abuse - whether in childhood or adulthood - needs to be bathed in prayer. We invite the God who has not turned away his face and who has listened to their cry for help to make himself known - both directly, and through the carers, to the sufferer. The work of the Holy Spirit is central and goes to places which, humanly, we cannot touch, bringing his light and gentle persistent healing.

Specific prayer may well be needed, but never as a bludgeon to push a person on or as something to do if we are stuck! We may need to ask God to break the chains of persistent patterns of fear, of flashbacks or of unhelpful sexual practices resulting from the abuse. For some this might also include homosexual orientation.

Prayer for healing of memories can be a very important part of healing, sometimes over a period of time. It needs skilled handling, but can bring great relief as memories of the dark places of abuse are uncovered and acknowledged and the Holy Spirit invited to come and cleanse them, bathing the place with his light. Memories of abuse are frequently linked with specific rooms or other places such as sheds or cars, which after such prayer, are felt to be accessible once more to the abused person.

Deeply buried memories of abuse may surface *slowly* in prayer as the Holy Spirit brings to light what can now be dealt with. He is always gentle, in my experience, and very patient with a person's resistance. This process may take years as a little of the memory is revealed and integrated each time it is faced into.

Hilary Cashman mentions what she calls 'rites of passage' for abuse survivors.

> The abused person's journey from victimization to survival should be supported and celebrated by his faith community.

> Probably the most moving contributions to such liturgical 'celebrations' are those written and offered by survivors themselves. They could be part of a formal service or informal

one with a small group of supporters. They mark and offer to God, a stage in the healing process. In their chapter 'Litanies, Psalms and Songs' Mary Pellauer and others have collected some of these moving resources together.

We need them to express and transform the anguish and the hope.
We need them to connect these experiences with all that is or could be. We need them to make us weep, to rejoice, to act ... we need them to bless us as we struggle.[15]

A healing community

Those who have personal experience of abuse may well, in time, have a special ministry to others. Care should be taken that this does not happen too soon, as they could become over-involved, with confusion between their own experience and that of others. Good listeners also have an important part to play as Peter Gibbs puts it:

Loving acceptance and honest prayer with the fragile victim can be offered by many others who are not counsellors but who have been chosen by the victims as listeners. Those who have come to terms with their own experience of abuse often have a special ministry in this field.

Healing is not only personal, but corporate. Our churches may also need to be healed. If we as Christians are willing to recognize the problems of abuse as real and to re-assess our assumptions about the use of power and about Christian sexuality, if necessary, then the way is open for us to become, for victims and abusers, a 'healing community'.[16]

Any involvement as a church in caring for the sexually abused will be costly. We will need all our resources in Christ and in each other. More than anything this ministry needs to be supported and backed by prayer. Most of us feel inadequate - and in a very real sense we are. But the Christian community is one very important way in which God's face *can* be turned towards the victim and his ear *can* listen to their cry for help.

BOUNDARIES, REFERRALS
AND FURTHER RESOURCES

Centuries of easy-going churchmanship have stereotyped pastoral care-givers as providers of 'Tender Loving Care', a non-confronting client-centredness which invites the counsellor to collude in a moral [*and emotional*] muddle.[1]

A link in a chain

If we are to incarnate Christ in our pastoral care, should there be *any* boundaries to our willingness to spend time with people? What is the right balance between unconditional acceptance and confrontation? How do we equate the biblical demands on us 'to lay down our lives' for another – the challenges of self-giving – with our need, at times, to 'pull up the draw bridge' for the health of ourselves and our family and friends? When and how do we recognize the limits of our strength and competence and seek further help for the other person or for ourselves? These are some of the important questions in Christian care and counselling and I will look at them first in a general way and then as they relate to some specific sexual difficulties.

When pastoral care feels heavy and especially when people seem to be looking to us to provide them with answers and a sense of well-being, it is good to remember that it is not any one individual who incarnates Christ on earth, but his body, the Church. I am only a part of that body, called to give what I can, to do my part faithfully. But I am interdependent with others in care and counselling as in other respects. As Cardinal Newman puts it in one of his meditations: 'I am a link in a chain, a bond of connection between persons.' Pastoral care can be lonely work. Living with our own expectations and those of others can isolate us unhelpfully from the body of Christ. Without breaking confidence, we may need to reach out and ask others to support us in prayer as we counsel. We need good supervision. We may need the skill and the time that others can give to 'our' clients and parishioners. Sometimes it is our pride or our fear of being thought weak that stops us from asking for what we need. We can impoverish ourselves and others in this way.

Unconditional acceptance

Unconditional acceptance is a vital starting point in pastoral care. It undergirds our attitude to the other person and fosters respect, as we saw in chapter 3. But it is not a static quality – by its very reflection of Christ's love for us, it has about it a 'drawing' quality of momentum and forward movement. Our response to Christ's covenant love for us is to long to be more like him and a willingness to be challenged and changed in the process. So it is with the unconditional acceptance offered by Christians in the power of God.

Frank Lake illustrates this well: 'God in Christ permits us to come to him whatever our state, indeed, he calls us to come and from that point he takes upon himself the task of putting us right. We cannot be less than this to others. In this sense we are, or hope to be, permissive with no limits to our acceptance.'[2]

Acceptance cannot be conditional upon change, or it ceases to be unconditional! Change is a free response to acceptance. Part of effective counselling is to know when to point out discrepancies in a person's story or when to confront sensitively, in order to enable change to take place. Just as a river flows faster between firm banks and loses energy if it floods the fields, so part of our role in enabling a person to change is to attend to and hold the banks or boundaries - both moral and emotional.

Self-giving

To be fully available to another does *not* mean suspending our judgement, squandering our time ineffectually, or becoming a doormat. Christ's pattern was to seek to say and do what his Father required of him, often leaving unmet needs in the process (see Mark 1:37-38). He did not always entrust himself to others if he sensed a shallowness or unreliability in their response.

> Now while he was in Jerusalem at the Passover many people saw the miraculous signs he was doing and believed in his name. But Jesus would not entrust himself to them, for he knew all men. He did not need man's testimony about man, for he knew what was in a man. (John 2:23-25.)

Commenting on this passage in *The Bible and Counselling*, Roger Hurding says:

> Jesus had the measure of human nature and where he sensed the shallowness or suggestibility of people's responses to him, he could withhold his trust in them. Carers and counsellors also need this wisdom for gauging the right level of transparency in their encounters with others.[3]

This gauging of how much to offer of what is in us also applies to the selection and timing of such things as confrontation and the use of biblical texts and teaching. To quote Frank Lake again: 'There is a time to be silent, a time to be selective, and a time to declare the whole counsel of God . . . Here we need the conjunction of personal intuition, sound knowledge, training and experience, with that humility which overrides all these and enables us to listen afresh to the Holy Spirit.'[4]

Sometimes we need caution about offering our money or possessions too. Some clergy families I know have a policy of never giving money to callers at the vicarage, but always offering a drink and a sandwich. Sometimes this is an even more costly ministry! In parts of London where abuse of alcohol is common amongst those who sleep rough, vouchers for meals are given instead of money as they cannot be exchanged for anything else.

We can take heart, as we make mistakes in our discernment and timing of self-giving (as we all do); if we are working on the basis of covenant love and commitment to the other person, we do not have to 'get everything right'. God can honour and work with our imperfect attempts in surprising ways.

Defining our boundaries

Boundaries are much easier to define, in one sense, at the counselling end of the pastoral care spectrum. A counselling 'contract' can be agreed in terms of length of sessions and duration of counselling, as well as its aims in respect of limited change. In terms of pastoral care within the Christian community, boundaries are far harder to delineate and the edges are often blurred between friendship and care. When there is strain or abuse of boundaries, then they need to be re-evaluated, possibly by a meeting of all concerned. Every Christian community will have its share of very needy people who test its resources to the limit and beyond. A hard look at the boundaries of acceptance and self-giving in the terms already defined can free church members to give generously what they *can* give and not resentfully what they can't.

Janet was a busy wife and mother with a part-time professional job. Maureen, an attractive and vivacious young mum in the same church, became friendly with her and wanted some informal counselling. Gradually Maureen's demands on Janet increased and she realized she was avoiding her phone calls and evading her in church. When Maureen asked Janet to spend an afternoon each week with her as part of their friendship, she had to say she could not give that much time so regularly. Maureen was upset and angry, accusing Janet of leading her to expect real friendship (in her terms) and then letting her down. She had deep underlying needs for mothering and had unconsciously transferred onto Janet her longings for someone to be always there for her and constantly available. The friendship lapsed and it was only later that Janet learned that Maureen had followed the same pattern with several other women in the church. Earlier consultation about her neediness might have allowed for a more realistic attempt to help Maureen to feel loved and cared for without being a drain on any one individual. Unfortunately she moved away and left the church, possibly to repeat her pattern of need elsewhere.

Emotional needs of those who care

If Janet had given in to Maureen's demands a very dependent relationship might have developed which would have been even harder to break. If, as counsellors, we are meeting our own emotional needs more through our counselling than through our intimate relationships with family and friends, then we may be in danger of colluding with the dependency needs of others. Such collusion will mean that the work towards inter-dependence which a person needs to do for their healing and growth will be avoided. It threatens not only the counsellee but the counsellor. Yet, if we are honest, most of us are tempted at times to enjoy and prolong the sense of being vital to the well-being of another. Writing about this in the context of listening, Anne Long says:

> It can be all too easy to substitute the intimacy we should experience with those in our closest circle, by the intimacy experienced as listeners where we are, often temporarily, admitted to some of the personal details of someone else's life . . . If we are giving out to those we listen to at the expense of our growth in relationship then there is something wrong. And using phrases like . . . 'Christian availability', 'sacrificial

ministry', is no excuse for not making times to foster the quality of relationship that each of us needs in our journey to maturity.[5]

Here, as always, a good supervisor or senior partner can help us to see what is going on and take appropriate action. However, a supervisor can only comment on what they are told! A question worth asking ourselves is 'Are there any counselling relationships which I am reluctant to discuss fully with my supervisor? If so, what might that be about?' In the area of sexuality and sexual difficulties, as we have seen in earlier chapters, the way is wide open for collusion and meeting of emotional needs of the carers if we do not ask ourselves this kind of question fairly regularly.

Finding ourselves out of our depth

In any pastoral care or counselling relationship we may reach (or think we have reached) the boundaries of our competence and skill. But as Anne Long says: 'It is not failure to know when our own level of competence is reached or when we suddenly feel out of depth.'[6]

She suggests some useful questions to ask ourselves to check this out. I have adapted the following from them with her permission.

- Is X making progress with my help, or going round in circles? Does he make use between sessions of what we discover together, or ignore it? (Mutual evaluation of progress can be a great help from time to time).

- Are there other resources that could help X at present e.g., medical, psychological or spiritual?

- What are my feelings as I listen to X? Do they tell me anything? (e.g., am I feeling bored? Dreading our next meeting? Resentful?)

- Is X meeting certain needs in me as I listen to him (or

her)? Is there any inappropriate sexual feeling around on either side?

- Do I have the feeling that I could not refer X on to anyone else, even if no progress has been made, because we have such a 'special' relationship? (A good indication that transference and counter-transference is in operation).

Clarification in supervision may help in a decision as to whether to refer a person or not. Sometimes we may be enabled to continue with a difficult client rather than passing them on as we had intended.

Sukie was a competent and very bright young woman, always on top of her work as a librarian and a quick thinker. As a child she had suffered sexual abuse and was having help for that elsewhere. Her pastor's wife, Jill, gave her occasional times in which she could explore her spiritual journey and relationships. In these sessions, Jill always ended up feeling hopeless, slow and ineffectual. She wondered about the usefulness of going on, thinking that Sukie might be better off with a 'real' spiritual director – one who would 'know what to do'. At a supervision group, Jill explored her feelings. The group helped her to see that Sukie's defence against her childhood abuse was to be confident and coping. Underneath was a deep fear of helplessness. This she projected onto Jill in their times together. Understanding this helped Jill to go on helping Sukie rather than seeking 'expert' help as she had intended doing and also to explore with her something of the dynamics between them.

Making a referral

If a referral is made, the way it is discussed and arranged can make a great difference to a person in need of further help. If it is done badly, the message given can be 'You are far too disturbed for me to cope with, you need a *real* expert'. This can lead to despair lest even a 'real expert' cannot cope either!

Properly made, a referral can leave a person with a sense of self respect and control of the situation. The role of the pastoral carer or counsellor can then change to that of someone who supports and prays from a position of understanding and shared pain. This role can be of very real value as long as it does not revert to counselling again and conflict with work being done elsewhere.

The steps in referral might be:

1. An explanation by a pastor or counsellor as to why they think referral could be helpful.
2. Time for response by the counsellee, including feelings about the change suggested. (It may be necessary to come back to this in another session if it is a hard thing for them to accept at first.)
3. Discussion of possible avenues of referral.
4. Exploration of these possible avenues by the counsellor or counsellee or both.
5. Identifying the best route of referral and the role of each in making the change. (Only in exceptional circumstances would it be advisable for the counsellor or pastor to make the actual appointment for someone, although they might well make sure that they could be seen and possibly write a referral letter with permission.)

Any relationship of pastoral care, however brief, is personal and intimate to some degree. To hand a person over like a parcel will not do (however relieved we may be to do so at times!). Love and respect for the person in need demands care and thoughtfulness in the search for the right help. Having said that, a number of pastoral care relationships, formal or informal, simply stop at the instigation of the client without a satisfactory conclusion being reached or a referral being made. Whilst we would want to minimize these, all of us in pastoral care have to live with the dissatisfaction of untied ends at times and the frustration of not knowing whether our work was of any value. This is part of the reality of care and counselling work and no amount of training or experience can remove it entirely. It is a person's right to walk away without comment if they wish to do so. Just occasionally we may have a chance to see, much later, our place as a link in the chain.

Eleanor, whom I mentioned in chapter 2, recently returned after about three years, with her husband. Her search for a more active approach in her need for an orgasm had failed and she was, at last, ready to look at the reality of her situation. As a couple they are making some real progress at last, though they have both had to make big adjustments to meet each other sexually.

Rare exceptions

Most of those with experience in pastoral work will have one or two people who by all the 'rules' they should not continue working with. Even though the pastoral counselling is technically out of their depth the person continues to grow and change. Someone said to me recently that 'the Holy Spirit does not like rules and regulations'. I think that this is only a partial truth. The Holy Spirit can readily work within the disciplines of listening and counselling, and frequently does. To abandon such disciplines and think we can float free with the Holy Spirit alone as our supervisor is not only irresponsible and arrogant, but can make his task hard if not impossible at times. God gives us guide-lines, training and experience to learn from and use, not to cast aside. However, the Holy Spirit is not *bound* by rules and regulations and neither, in a sense, are we. Sometimes he works outside them against all the odds and we see God's hand in it all in a new and fresh way.

Claire was referred to me by her GP after her first child was born. Her sexual difficulty was only a small part of her disturbance which was a very severe post-natal depression. I feared for her and for her relationship with her baby and suggested to her GP a referral to a psychiatrist. He wrote back saying that Claire seemed to be more helped by coming to me; he would be willing to prescribe antidepressants as necessary and we could review the situation together in time.

Claire's problems were, theoretically, out of my depth. Working with her over several years stretched and challenged me to my limits. I learnt as much from her (or more) as she received from me. We went on because slowly but surely she was changing. We worked through dependency, transference and the birth of her twins together. She worked hard and with great integrity and grew as a person far beyond my initial expectations. Perhaps our Christian context for pastoral care is what gives us (occasionally) the freedom to cross boundaries that more secular training and ways of working see as rigid. However, we still need good supervisory relationships in which to discern when we really are in step with the Holy Spirit and when we are simply indulging our 'Messiah' fantasies!

Sexually related disorders which may need referral

In addition to such conditions as clinical depression and the psychoses (mental and emotional disorders in which there is a degree of loss of contact with reality) which affect a person's sexuality but which require medical treatment primarily; there are some aspects of sexual difficulties which may need another skilled helper or further training in a particular field. We have already covered homosexuality and sexual abuse, both of which may demand help beyond the scope of pastoral care or counselling. We now turn to difficulties in genital functioning, to physical and emotional disabilities and to AIDS.

Difficulties with genital function

Whilst no one is ever a 'set of genitals' but a human being with feelings and perceptions relating to the genital aspects of his or her sexuality, some difficulties present themselves as having a specifically genital focus. Examples would be vaginismus (a tightening of the muscles to the entrance of the vagina making penetration painful or impossible), impotence (insufficient erection for penetration) and premature ejaculation. Non-consummation (inability to have penetrative sexual intercourse) could arise from a combination of these factors or from one alone.

There are many helpful and effective approaches to these difficulties which do not involve physical examination. These include the Sensate Focus approach based on the work of Masters and Johnson in the USA, cognitive behaviour techniques and various adaptations of psychotherapy. However, the approach used by the Institute of Psychosexual Medicine in training doctors and some nurses in psychosexual work does make use of the genital examination where appropriate. It has particular value in these kinds of difficulties as it allows for examination of the unconscious dimensions of a person's perceptions of his or her genitals. The relevance of this to their sexual responding and functioning can be explored as the physical examination is undertaken. Sometimes this offers a much faster route to the understanding of a problem than can be achieved by listening and counselling alone.

Obviously such a way of working is open only to the medically trained and otherwise would require referral. However, I would stress that referral to a doctor for such an examination needs to be to one trained in this use of brief focused psychotherapy and not to someone who would examine only for physical abnormality. For further reading on this approach I would warmly recommend Dr Prue Tunnadine's readable and lively book *Insights into Troubled Sexuality - A Case Profile Anthology.*[7]

Vaginismus

The tightening of the muscles which form a ring about three-quarters of an inch inside the vaginal entrance, when severe enough to interfere with penetration, is a response to fear which is frequently unconscious in its nature. The muscles can be consciously controlled but they also have an involuntary component which can act independently. Only very rarely is there a physical block to penetration - such as a very thick hymen or a vaginal septum (dividing wall). Exploration of a woman's fears of penetration whilst examining her vaginally can be very revealing and helpful. Fantasies about the vagina abound, mainly because it is hidden from view, unlike the penis. Common ones are: that it is very small, fragile and tears easily; or that it leads directly to other organs such as the gut or bladder. In the latter case, penetration can be thought to be an invasion of the whole of her 'insides' both physical and emotional with all their private 'dirt'. Men, too, have their vaginal fantasies, one of which is that it has teeth and can castrate them - an understandable cause for impotence! It is only when a person is able to give voice to these 'irrational' fantasies that they can begin to dare to explore how the vagina really feels and replace the fantasy with the reality.

Impotence

In addition to the kind of exploration of fantasies described above, (but in this case focused on the penis), some physical causes of impotence require medical diagnosis and treatment. The erectile tissue in the penis fills with blood when a man is sexually aroused and the blood is trapped there by valves in the veins. Both blockages in the inflow (especially due to disease of the small arteries) and damage to the valves holding the outflow steady can cause impotence. Diabetes can affect a man's potency by damaging arteries and nerves, but the link is not inevitable and can be hard to prove conclusively. A variety of medications and other rarer medical conditions can be causes of temporary or permanent difficulties with erections. Because of the complex interplay between the physical and psychological aspects of impotence it is most helpful if both can be evaluated before an approach to treatment is decided upon.

Moshi was a bright young man in his late thirties. Married with two children, he complained of diminishing erections for the past year, with almost complete impotence now. His relationship with his wife was fine and he seemed to have no obvious emotional or psychological causes for his difficulties. Some hormonal and chemical blood tests showed an abnormally high level of prolactin – a chemical secreted by the pituitary gland at the base of the brain which, in large amounts, inhibits erection. This was the first sign of an over-growth of the pituitary gland – a non-cancerous tumour which, if not removed, can damage local brain tissue by pressure as it grows. Removal of the tumour resulted in the return of Moshi's erections to normal.

Ejaculatory difficulties

Unlike impotence, which can have a variety of physical causes, premature ejaculation and delayed ejaculation are almost never physical in origin. They have a variety of emotional causes, among them performance anxiety in premature ejaculation and unconscious anger at or fear of women in delayed ejaculation. They respond to a range of counselling approaches. Generally speaking they require referral except in the case of performance anxiety in a young man, which may be better handled by sympathetic listening and encouragement in the context of good pastoral care. The treatment of delayed or retarded ejaculation is often a difficult process, even for the psychosexually trained, especially if the reason for referral is that the partner wants a baby rather than the man wants change for himself.

To refer or not to refer?

With these pointers to referral, we might wonder whether, as pastors and counsellors, we have anything to offer if a person presents with such a difficulty. I would always want to encourage careful and leisurely listening before referral, if it seems appropriate. Listening not only to what is being shared and its feeling content but also to what effect it is having on the listener. We might ask ourselves such questions as:

- How am I feeling as I listen to this person?

- Am I comfortable, anxious, sexually excited? Angry or depressed? What might that be telling me about him or her?

- Have I 'space' in myself to listen further? Do I feel out of my depth or preoccupied with my own sexual agenda?

It could well be that in a number of cases referral would not be needed after faithful listening.

Gavin was a dapper, middle-aged man with premature ejaculation and a very low sense of self-worth. In the course of telling his story he shared how, as a child, he had watched as a boy in his nursery school was stripped of his pants and laughed at for masturbating. He had not laughed, but had felt outrage on his behalf. Later he told me of a Clinical Psychologist he had seen who invited him to lie on a couch and talk. Minutes later, he heard him snoring. 'I wasn't paying good money to let him sleep!' he said indignantly. (I felt my eyelids go rigid in case he should interpret a blink as doziness.)

Gavin was too scared to get close to any women at present in case he should fail sexually. Listening carefully, I heard in his story his fear of getting close to me, in case I laughed at him or simply dozed off in boredom. It was not necessary to examine him (it might have felt like humiliation at this stage) to hear the nature of his fears and to share my understanding and acceptance of them with him. There was no revolutionary cure as far as I know. He thanked me for the relief of being able to talk freely and went on his way. Such help could well be given by good listening in the context of pastoral care, provided the listener is at ease with the sexually explicit content.

Sexual difficulties and disability

In a sense, listening to anyone in difficulties with their genital functioning is listening to someone who is disabled. Where there is other disablement too, the problems may be compounded. Probably the greatest barrier to listening to a handicapped person talking about their sexuality is our own attitude - often partially denied - that such a person should not have sexual feelings or needs. Dr Wendy Greengross challenges society's view in her book *Entitled to Love*.

> Sexual success, being beautiful and loved and cared for, is one of society's ideals. And in this rat-race of relationships, the deformed and the incomplete are not even in the running. Society by and large, just cannot cope with the idea of the disabled having the same emotional needs and desires as the rest of the population. [8]

In Christ, whose identification with the poor and marginalized began with his birth in a stable, we surely have something to say about the dismissal of disabled people from the arena of sexuality. Listening honestly to our own reactions to disablement and possibly discussing them with a trusted friend, is the first step towards being free to hear more clearly the cries of the handicapped to be valued as sexual people.

Whilst a specific referral for help may be necessary - either because of the nature of the disablement or of the sexual difficulty - much can be done in pastoral care by attending to the whole person. Indeed much that is shared may not relate directly to the disablement at all and could apply to any of us.

Jack is an example of a person whose sexual needs and difficulties related to his disablement, but were not caused by it. I include his story by way of encouragement to listen in depth, if we are able, to the *person* before hurrying to get expert help.

Jack had severe rheumatoid arthritis. He had to retire from his work as a bus driver, which he loved, on medical grounds. Then he had an operation to remove some constricting tissue from his penis. This had left his penis shorter, he felt. Jack's wife was blind following diabetic complications. She came only once, with her guide dog, to tell me that there was 'nothing wrong with *her*', but please would I get Jack functioning again so that she could have some sexual pleasure!

Disability was such an obvious feature with this couple that it took some time for me to hear Jack's true feelings. His unexpressed resentment at his wife's demands and criticism of his short penis had, in effect, caused him to 'down tools' completely. He had become impotent. It was only slowly, as he was able to share and own his anger, and later some sexual excitement, that he began to change. Despite his severe physical handicaps, he and his wife found a position in which intercourse was again possible and enjoyable. Jack had become 'a man' again despite his disability.

From a different perspective, Dr Elizabeth Forsythe writes of the healing power of being listened to by a priest. She herself suffers from multiple sclerosis.

> One of my helpers has been a wise old priest with whom I have been totally honest and able to talk freely about the unspeakable. He can, in his radiance and utter humility help me to understand a little about God's love and about human love ... He was able to throw the first rope across my personal chasm between the horrors of the needy and the security and safe position of the needed. Out of his love and humility ... I began to understand the power of love which can accept all things not necessarily with human approval but with understanding.[9]

Sexuality and AIDS

A vast amount is being written at present about HIV and AIDS from Christian and secular, medical and social perspectives. It is not hard to find further training in this area now for anyone who needs it. Health Trusts, Social Work Units and church-based counselling agencies run courses which are both factual and experiential. All I want to do here is to point out some of the possible blocks to effective pastoral care of those who are HIV positive (or think they may be) and offer suggestions for further reading and training.

The first barrier for all of us is the 'unknown' aspect of HIV/AIDS. We may be able to glean facts about the disease – such as the nature of its spread, the symptoms of AIDS, about HIV testing and counselling, but what is it like to meet with and talk to a person with AIDS? How will we handle it?

The pioneering work of the Mildmay Hospital in Shoreditch (East London) in providing terminal care for AIDS patients and their families has yielded much in the way of new understanding and models of care. In *A Place of Growth* Shirley Lunn, Senior Counsellor at Mildmay, writes of her initial fears of encounter with AIDS patients. Her fears were of not knowing how to react, of what others might think, of catching the virus and so on. She found that it was impossible to maintain these kinds of fears: 'It was impossible to be frightened of them; they made it all so easy for me. I was so impressed with the love and loyalty shown by their families and partners that . . . I realized that any fears I might have experienced initially were gone.'[10]

The unusual or unknown can prevent us, in the first instance, from meeting and receiving the person within it all. Honest listening to ourselves with the help of a supervisor or senior partner will clarify some of these barriers and fears and free us to hear more clearly. Other barriers we may need to attend to might be our prejudices about the groups who most frequently present with HIV and AIDS – homosexuals and drug abusers. We may catch ourselves in some moral indignation thinking 'it is their fault' – and in measure so it may be, but is not for us to be their judge. God's judgement, unlike ours, is primarily for creative renewal rather than condemnation, for it comes from his immeasurable compassion. I strongly recommend *A Place of Growth* for further reading on this subject and Mildmay's training and information days for those within reach of London.

Not all of us will be called to be involved in AIDS or with disability as part of our pastoral care, and that is no failure. For those of us who are, we too may find a place of growth.

Some conclusions

I began this chapter with a look at boundaries and at the Christian expectations we may have of ourselves and others in pastoral care. I moved on to areas which may cross our personal boundaries and challenge our competence and experience. The outcome of that challenge might be to make a referral or to extend our own skills through supervision and further training.

The late Dr Tom Main, a wise psychoanalyst who led training seminars in psychosexual medicine, used to find that his doctors frequently suggested referral of the patient who was proving too much for them. 'This patient needs to be seen by an expert,' would go the doctor's refrain. 'Ah yes, Dr A,' Tom would say, 'which *particular* expert did you have in mind then?'

We need to consider carefully our reasons for referral and whether they are valid. Then we have to find an appropriate source of help and enable a person to find the right kind of bridge towards making the change. Some of us tend to refer too quickly, underestimating what we can do; others too slowly, rather overestimating our usefulness. As in any aspect of pastoral counselling, each encounter is unique. All we can ask of ourselves is that we note prayerfully what is happening with any given person and then 'think, think, and think again'!

SEXUALITY AND SPIRITUALITY

There is a sense in which this whole book has been about sexuality and spirituality. Spirituality has been described as 'theology on two feet'.[1] Richard Rohr has said that 'at its core, sexuality is a constant expression of the spirit'.[2] The two are inextricably linked for: 'God has forever made human flesh the privileged place of the divine encounter.'[3] Yet like magnetic poles they do have a tendency to spring apart! The Church has much to account for in its attempts, over the centuries, to separate what God has joined together. Body and soul seem to be so much more manageable without each other! Yet the Christian gospel loses its true power when it becomes 'disembodied'. A frequent complaint about church teaching is that it does not connect with our everyday human experience. That experience is located in our bodies and expressed, in large part, through our sexuality. The holding together of sexuality and spirituality is an ongoing demanding process, challenging us constantly. We will certainly be tempted, at times, to let go of one or the other part. When we do so there may be relief, but there is also a loss of tension. Like an elastic band in use, there is strength and energy in that tension - whereas a flaccid elastic band has neither!

Risk and paradox

> The word became flesh and lived for a while among us.
> We have seen his glory . . . full of grace and truth. (John 1:14)

These are such familiar words. To communicate grace and truth the creator of the world chose to use a human body. Not an adult body, but that of a vulnerable baby. And the baby grew in a human womb and was cared for by human parents. Grace and truth were fleshed out in bodily form - seen, heard, touched. Jesus was no disembodied spirit or angelic messenger but in every sense flesh and blood. How amazing that God should risk his whole self-revelation by putting it into such a fragile container. Yet he trusts his creation, in spite of its evident weaknesses, with his very self. Such is part of the paradox of our Christian belief.

If God can take such risks, can we not begin to trust our bodies as containers of the incarnate God and as temples of the Holy Spirit? We can demonstrate something of God's grace and truth in our bodily sexuality *or* we can tell lies with it. What we cannot do is keep it silent, however much we might like to think we can.

Sexuality and dying

It seems to me that if sexuality and spirituality are linked in Christ's birth and life then they will also be evident in his dying, and, by implication, in ours also. Most of us will not have to die publicly. Because Christ's death was witnessed by so many we can see evidence of his sexuality - his relational energy - in the 'then and there' of his dying as well as in its spiritual and theological implications.

Stripped naked, exposed physically and emotionally, and in great pain; Jesus still retained his awareness of others and his care for their needs. He was able to promise the thief who pleaded with him that 'today you will be with me in paradise'. He looked down at his grieving mother - still faithfully alongside - and his dear friend John. Knowing their needs he 'gave' them to each other to be mother and son after his death (John 19:26,27). Amazingly he could still nurture those he loved from the cross.

The bond which had sustained Jesus throughout his life on earth – the love relationship with his Father – was broken at his point of complete identification with our sin. His cry of dereliction and forsakenness must draw into it echoes of all broken human relationships. At that moment he stood where we stand: outside the intimacy of the Trinity, as it were, looking in. And he did so that we might have access to that place that he knew as home.

It is not only in Jesus' words on the cross that we can see evidence of sexual and spiritual links. As the whole event is played out there is surely more than an accidental similarity in the parallels between Christ's death and resurrection and human sexual relating. Self-giving, physical piercing and complete surrender give way, in the resurrection, to the wonder of new life: life which is gift for others and which spreads outwards in ever increasing circles. This greatest act in history is surely an act of sexuality, in its deepest sense, as well as of spirituality. At its best sexuality unites and reconciles. It brings peace. Christ's death on the cross brought the deepest reconciliation of all time – for individuals, but also for nations and for society.

> For he himself is our peace, who has made the two one and has destroyed the barrier, the dividing wall of hostility . . . His purpose was to create in himself one new man out of the two, thus making peace, and in this body to reconcile both of them to God through the cross, by which he put to death their hostility. (Ephesians 2:14-16)

I suspect that there is much more sexuality expressed at the time of a person's dying than is commonly acknowledged. We know only a little of what passes between lovers, friends and family as death approaches. But with the intensity and focus that dying brings, social and personal taboos may become less important. Through word and touch reconciliation and peace may be brought in ways not previously open.

One man told of how he brushed his wife's teeth as she lay dying. He knew she liked her mouth to be fresh and he offered her this intimate and loving gift. Others have said how the physical care of a partner or friend – or perhaps a parent – has involved handling their bodies, including their genitals, in a way that has something both sexual and sacramental about it. There is a depth of truth and a profound and intimate beauty in such caring. For other people their pain is that the barriers are *not* broken down and they experience the intensity of isolation rather than intimacy. There is truth in both experiences.

From isolation to integration

In chapter 1 I touched on the deep loneliness that many, if not most of us, feel alongside our pull to relatedness. That emptiness is part of our need for fulfilment – it is a creative part of our sexuality. If we rush to fill its place with human encounters we may dull the ache for a time, but it will return like a hunger only partly satisfied. There is a sense in which we need to embrace the emptiness in order to be fulfilled. Only in that way will we truly encounter the welcome that is at the heart of God. In *Reaching Out* Henri Nouwen describes this as moving from 'loneliness to solitude'.[4] In the place of solitude we can at last stand alone without needing to rush to others for comfort. Then we can meet God and others with a new reality.

At a recent personal growth group led by a Gestalt counsellor I did some work on a dream. Having recounted part of the dream, I was invited to explore it further in my imagination. I was swimming in the sea with a breathing mask on. It was safe, light and warm in the shallows but I felt drawn towards the deeper water and was afraid. Slowly, breathing in oxygen from a line and sending a trail of bubbles to the surface, I allowed myself to descend. I was not sure what was there – death or life – in that dark place. My hands touched the sandy bottom and I wriggled forward, sensing now that I was approaching not death, but the heart of God himself. Something was being said to me, but I didn't know what. My facilitator told me to take my time and find out. One word came as I lay there on the sea bed: 'Welcome'. Never before had that word spoken so directly to me with all its warmth and light. I felt it connect, physically, with my heart. I wept with gratitude as I received it. After a time I swam back to the surface, only this time my oxygen line was feeding me from below – I was breathing in God's 'welcome'. That was oxygen indeed!

The following poem was written some years ago on the same theme.

Let Love Disturb You

Smooth surfaced sea, you promise much
and in your tranquil moods reflect the sun of love.
Blue shallowness hiding the deep
and unknown darkness; primitive
with life forms
sparse and elemental in their timelessness.

Lord in your beauty I can see and feel you.
Deeper, I begin to fear. Currents draw me;
pulling me away from the familiar.
Who is pulling? Is it myself – or can it be your
loving hands saying 'come with me,
I want you here; and deeper still I lead you'.

Drowning, lost in darkness and deep disturbing longings
I am trying to cling with my own hands,
to struggle, to survive, to love *my* way.
Yet in the dark eternal silence you are calling;
quietly, strongly.

Can love be present when there is no light?
Can I be rocked and pulled apart from what I know
and – separated from my very self – lie like some

poor wreck in time upon the sand
amongst those timeless elemental forms;
and find love there?

If I go deep, will you go deeper still
calling me on? Will your strength crush – or hold me?
I am afraid; but if my fragile love, like surface sunshine,
must be broken up and storms rage
through it to know more of you,
then take me Lord and 'deep calling to deep'
submit me to you.

I am all darkness, Lord, all storm and tears.
I offer them, and crying to you find
you have been there before me, drawing me on.
Beyond the deepest darkness and the roughest storm
you are unbroken in your light and peace; preparing for
  me.
My longing matched by yours I meet its source, my
  jealous loving God,
And rest content awhile.

As Christians we worship a God who is Trinity – three persons in intimate relationship. Intimacy is at the very heart of God – not exclusive intimacy but inclusive welcome. In a beautiful and well-known icon painted in 1425 by Andrei Rublev, the three persons of the Trinity are depicted sitting at a table. The icon is based on the story of Abraham's hospitality given to the three travellers at Mamre (Genesis 18:1-5). There is great beauty in the loving attentiveness of Father, Son and Holy Spirit to each other. In the centre of the table is a chalice – the symbol of Eucharist. And there is a space at the table for another – for us. It is as we deepen our encounter with the intimate heart of God – with its welcome, its passion and its faithfulness – that we can deepen our encounter with our neighbour and our friends. For we have been to the place where sexuality and spirituality meet. As Richard Rohr puts it:

'God's way of loving is the only licensed teacher of human sexuality. God's passion created ours. Our deep desiring is a relentless returning to that place where all things are one. If we are afraid of our sexuality we are afraid of God.'[5]

Sexuality in prayer and worship

> To deny our earthiness is to bottle up deep and divine energies of creativity and imagination.[6]

Growth in our sexuality will bring with it the potential for growth in prayer. Part of good pastoral care will be to enable that growth to take root and develop. We owe much to the traditions of contemplative prayer as well as to the charismatic movement for widening our horizons in the Evangelical church to the dimensions of creativity that they offer. Weaving together the mind, body and emotions in expressions of adoration, praise, listening and intercession is an exciting experience. Sadly, like sexual experience, it sometimes fails to be earth-moving – but we can still reach for the stars!

Creativity

Sometimes I have spent time in prayer which has felt so sterile as to be useless. I do not think it *was* useless – in one sense it is not my feelings that count, but God's response. However my feelings prevented me from receiving clearly anything God wanted to say to me. At times I have gone outside and found one flower or some leaves, maybe a twig or two of blossom. Arranging them on my table I have knelt just looking at their beauty. Gradually I have found that God can speak to me through them. His creativity enfolds mine. My spirit is nurtured and begins to open itself freshly to his word.

On one occasion, at a conference, I had spent time counselling a disturbed and paranoid woman in the room in which I was sleeping. When I went back to the room later it felt contaminated by the hatred she had spilled out. I had only ten minutes before others were due to join me. I put on a tape of a Mozart adagio and danced out before God my need to free myself and my room from those feelings. This form of prayer brought a deep sense of release and peacefulness.

A clergyman I know has a gift of tapestry work. He designs and works beautiful expressions of truth that he has discovered in prayer and in life. Many are given as gifts to others on special occasions and have brought real blessing. Music, poetry, journalling, drawing, painting, gardening . . . the list of ways in which we can use our creativity in prayer can be endless. All we need is the freedom to realize the rightness of making the connection between this part of our sexuality and its spiritual expression.

The use of our bodies

I have already given an example of dance used in private prayer, expressing easily what would have been clumsy in words. There are many variations on this - for example silent expression, with our hands or our whole body, of thoughts and feelings which are difficult to speak out. Our bodies can sometimes be more articulate than our voices.

Even if liturgical dance has not come to our church fellowship, many churches now encourage physical involvement in songs and choruses as part of worship. Being both an introvert and an individualist I confess I often find the actions to choruses more of a chore than an aid to worship! I can see that for others they are a delight. What I *can* take pleasure in is the freedom to use my arms and hands in a personal response to more meditative worship songs in an atmosphere focused on the Lord rather than on the chorus leader. We need to find our own way of expressing ourselves through our physicality and sexuality. For some there may be no outward involvement but there can be great joy in identification with good liturgical dance. By 'good' I do not mean technically brilliant, but dance which, in simplicity and clarity serves to communicate spiritual truth. In her book *Praise Him in the Dance* Anne Long describes it this way: 'This is no gimmick but, properly used, is part of that living flexibility which the Spirit is bringing to some of our liturgical forms and traditions.[7]

Imagery in prayer

With the care and caveats on the use and abuse of the imagination discussed in chapter 7 in mind, we still have a rich meeting place here between our sexuality and spirituality in prayer. The dream work I mentioned earlier was a combination of unconscious imagery (arising in the dream) and its exploration in conscious imagination. Sometimes, as we enter into a gospel story in our imagination, the Holy Spirit gives us new and surprising insights through what we see. Sitting in prayer in a convent chapel one day I was struck by the beauty in a carving of one of the Stations of the Cross. A woman was tenderly reaching out to Christ as he fell under the weight of his cross-pole. Entering into the scene imaginatively, I became the woman – bringing what comfort I could to my suffering Lord. I reached out to him with the whole of my femininity in a precious and intimate expression of love. Later, as I stood at the foot of the cross, the picture reversed itself. His love poured itself out to me. The pouring was both seen and felt in my imagination. Slowly I realized that some of that outpouring was coming from the Lord's breasts. The image surprised me a little at first, but then became a new and deep truth. I saw in this vivid way something more of the feminine as well as the masculine in the person of Jesus.

Genitality in prayer

The subject of genital arousal during prayer is not discussed very much, in my experience. This may well be another example of the persistence of dualism (separation of the body from soul and spirit). Equally, it could also be a fear of being misunderstood or of spoiling an intimate and private experience. However, the writer Susan Howatch has no such inhibitions in including the subject in her recent novel *Glamorous Powers*. The Abbot of Granchester, Jon Darrow, has a vision of a chapel in a dell. He knows it as a vision of the future and a call from God to leave the religious life. As the vision fades, he finds himself kneeling by his bed trembling and with an erection. Later he goes to see his Abbot-General, Francis Ingram. Jon insists that his erection was quite normal in a state of psychic arousal. Francis is not so sure and pursues the subject at some length:

> 'After the vision had ended, what sort of state were you in?'
> 'I was trembling and sweating. The amount of psychic energy required
> to generate a vision always produces a powerful physical reaction.'
> 'Were you sexually excited?'
> Silence . . . Several seconds elapsed before I could say:
> 'Yes, but that doesn't mean anything'.
> 'That's not for you to decide.' Francis wrote on his fresh sheet of foolscap: 'Possible evidence of sexual trouble'.[8]

It is not surprising if as sexual beings we experience genital arousal in prayer from time to time. What matters is its focus and direction. If we are distracted from prayer by other images and need to follow those and masturbate to obtain relief then we do need to look further into areas of sexual frustration or difficulty. However, genital arousal *can* be part of the general arousal of a love relationship with the Lord in prayer. If the focus and direction remain towards him and are honouring to him, then it is simply a part of our worship of the one in whom we 'live and move and have our being' (Acts 17:28). I mention this because as pastors and counsellors it may arise and we need to listen carefully and to use discernment in giving direction or advice.

An interesting and different emphasis on male genitality in prayer is suggested by Adrian Thatcher: '[Men] are too readily obsessed with achievement, performance orientation and anxiety about impotence. They should value the penis more when flaccid and the phallus less.' Quoting James Nelson he goes on: ' "Sinking, emptying is a way of spirituality. It means trusting God that we do not need to *do*, that our being is enough". . . . having a penis is just as much about resting and quietude as it is about power and control.'[9]

Eucharist

In the chapel at Launde Abbey one day I attended an early morning Eucharist. Sitting a few rows back, I was startled to find that as the priest poured out the wine I could smell it as if it were under my nose. The rich aroma drew my senses in anticipation – rather like smells from the kitchen before a good meal. Only once, since, have I had the same experience. The memorial of himself instituted by Jesus was intensely physical. Set in the context of the Last Supper, he linked the bread and wine with the words 'This is my body' and 'This is my blood'. The sensual nature of Communion is often masked by the use of wafers for bread and even by non-alcoholic wine (however good the reasons for upholding temperance may be!). But it *is* sensual – and there are parallels, if we look for them, with human love-making. Both are life-creating and life-enhancing.

> They engage all our senses, especially the less prominent ones of touch, taste and smell. They are both intensely joyful celebrations, each deeply satisfying. Yet both may also be covenanted pledges of love, richly symbolic, festive and liberating.[10]

> Communion is interpenetration . . . The prayer that we may dwell in Christ and Christ in us includes the dimension of the sexual. We are in the process of becoming body-words of God.[11]

After several days together in conference a group of us planned an informal communion service. We had to go out to the local shops for bread and wine. One of us, a priest, celebrated. He gave the chalices to others to pass around. As a friend passed the chalice to me I saw that she had just refilled it from the small wine bottle. It was fizzing! We had bought carbonated red wine in our haste at the shops. As we collapsed in laughter I thought how much more appropriate to our celebration was this 'sparkling' chalice than the more usual still one!

A spirituality of touch -- prayer in sexuality

Our bodily communications can be fun, informal, sensual and creative - and they can also be a form of prayer. I have touched on something of this in describing the care of the dying by their loved ones. I want to explore some further dimensions here.

A baby in the womb

> As soon as the sound of your greeting reached my ears, the baby in my womb leaped for joy. (Luke 1:41)

I am indebted to Elaine Storkey in her book *Mary's Story, Mary's Song* for bringing this particular text freshly to my attention. Mary, pregnant with Jesus, had come to visit her cousin Elizabeth, also pregnant. Babies 'leaping' in the womb are a common occurrence in pregnancy - but this leap was of a different order. 'The movement of this baby is a leap of joy. It is the recognition that although his eyes cannot yet see, nor his lungs breathe this baby knows that he is in the very presence of God.'[12] What a gift to his mother Elizabeth this gesture of praise and adoration must have been. Her own unborn child, John, greeting the Messiah in Mary's womb. Sometimes we just *know* that what seems ordinary in the realm of sexuality and touch is shining with an extraordinariness which speaks of God himself.

Children

Some friends told of the amazing gift to them of being welcomed by African children in a nursery school in the Cape Town township of Khayelitsha.

> 'Busy Bee', a pre-school . . . was like an oasis in a desert. It is housed in two wooden huts on the edge of Khayelitsha township, where sand from the Cape flats creeps in through every floorboard. When the children first go there as three to four year olds, they are often very fearful and cower in the corners. The carers concentrate on giving them love, holding them, stroking and affirming them, telling them how beautiful they are. Gradually the children move out of their fear and begin to mix. But more than that, the children give similar treatment to visitors who come to see the project. We too were stroked, held, kissed and smothered with love – wonderful cross-cultural communication!

Healing touch

The use of touch in the ministry of healing must go back to the beginning of time. In some churches today a rather sanitized and standardized form of touch is used in healing prayer which is very different from Christ's own use of it. A somewhat stylized way of using the hands to 'hover' near a person rather than touching them directly, for example, is in use in a lot of churches. Whilst heavy or embarrassing touch during prayer is obviously inappropriate, this speaks to me of over-cautiousness sometimes.

Jesus' use of touch in healing was never standardized. It varied according to the person he was with. In Luke 5:13 he heals a man of leprosy. We are told simply 'he reached out his hand and touched the man'. Direct touch for a man with leprosy – an outcast and 'untouchable' – was healing in itself no doubt. In Mark 7:31ff. Jesus heals a deaf and dumb man. Here again his touch is direct and suited to the man's need – though today we might well be hesitant about the use of saliva! 'Jesus put his fingers into the man's ears, spat and touched his tongue'. The touch comes before the prayer for the man's ears and mouth to 'be opened'. The physical contact seems to be part of the healing process. Obviously we need to be sensitive to the Holy Spirit and to the needs of others in our use of touch in prayer – but at times we can fail to use ordinary physical contact with another as an opportunity to hold them to God silently or aloud as appropriate.

Sometimes in my medical work I am able to use a genital examination as a vehicle for silent prayer. Awareness of pain or trauma affecting a woman's deepest self, for example, has prompted me to pray for her healing as I do a vaginal examination. Occasionally a new insight has come to us as we have discussed her response to my touch. Even a handshake or a hand on the shoulder can be a prompt to offer the other's needs to God as we make contact. Needless to say there are times when holding, stroking or massaging a partner or close friend in distress can be a form of prayer as well as a great comfort. In bereavement, loss or depression, or in acute anxiety, it may be the 'one thing necessary' – to be held prayerfully in loving arms and be allowed to feel distress in a safe place.

Genital touch

It would be strange indeed if at the height of human love-making there did not come, sometimes, an acute sense of God's presence. The most beautiful expression I have found of this is in an immensely moving novel by William Horwood – *Skallagrigg*. A cerebral-palsied man, Arthur, communicates something of the nature of God's presence to all around him – particularly to those other disabled people living with him in a grim 1930s institution. Their name for the being who could bring them love and life way beyond their severe physical limitations was the Skallagrigg. Arthur falls in love with Linnie, a helper, and they go to a glen to make love.

> 'Skyagree', says Arthur.
>
> 'Why do you always say him?', says Linnie grinning.
>
> 'Me', says Arthur in his way.
>
> 'You?', says Linnie cuddling his face to her breasts.
>
> 'Skyagree', says Arthur, breathlessly, and grinning.
>
> 'I'll love both of you then', says Linnie.
>
> Arthur's gentle eyes are full of tears. Arthur's cheek is wet as he speaks
>
> beyond her, to the Skallagrigg, and Linnie knows how he speaks with love.
>
> Love beyond even their new love. Arthur wants the Skallagrigg to see his
>
> Linnie. Arthur's proud of her and wants to share. Arthur's tears are clear ... as he
>
> says, 'Look!' and up there, if only she knew how to see, is the Skallagrigg.[13]

An ending and a beginning

Our sexuality begins and ends in God. His vibrant gift to us, formed from the earth's void by his hovering spirit and implanted into our humanity for all time, will have its final unity and fulfilment in him. For that is the deepest pull and direction of our sexuality; drawing others close along the way, but drawing us closer still to God himself. In that day when he wipes all the tears from our eyes, when all our groaning and pain is finished, we will recognize with a cry of delight that our aching loneliness, too, has found its answer.

Maranatha

When the corn is green
    the blackbird singing
My love will come
    swift as a fountain springing,
Will seize me
    hold me
    clasp me to him
    bringing
        infinite gladness.[14]

NOTES, REFERENCES AND FURTHER READING

Chapter 1

1. G. von Rad, *Genesis* (Commentary), SCM Press, 1970.
2. Jim Cotter, *Pleasure, Pain and Passion, Some Perspectives on Sexuality and Spirituality*, Cairns Publications, 1988, p. 104.
3. Ibid., with acknowledgement to Sebastian Moore for the original thought behind this reflection, p. 101.
4. Barbara Taylor, *Eve and the New Jerusalem: Socialism and Feminism in the Nineteenth Century*, Virago 1984, p. 146, Quoted in Ann Loades, *Searching for Lost Coins, Explorations in Christianity and Feminism*, SPCK, 1987, p. 8.
5. Margaret Magdalen CSMV, *Transformed by Love*, Darton, Longman and Todd, 1989, p. 14.
6. R. S. Thomas, 'The Word', in *Later Poems, 1972-1982*, Papermac, 1984, p. 50.
7. D. Bonhoeffer, *Creation and Fall*, p. 90, quoted in von Rad *Genesis*.
8. Jim Cotter, *Pleasure, Pain and Passion*, p. 96.
9. *The Letters of Vincent Van Gogh*, ed. Mark Roskill, Flamingo, Fontana Paperbacks, 1983, p. 56.
10. Ibid., p. 207.
11. Jim Cotter, *Pleasure, Pain and Passion*, p. 102.

Chapter 2

1. Macrina Wiederkehr, *A Tree Full of Angels, Seeing the Holy in the Ordinary*, Harper & Row, 1988, p.19.
2. Ibid., p. 9.
3. Roy McCloughry, 'The Last Frontier', *Third Way*, 19 October, 1992.
4. Lillian B. Rubin, *Intimate Strangers*, Fontana, 1985, Chapter 2.
5. Roy McCloughry, op. cit.
6. Lillian B. Rubin, *Intimate Strangers*, p. 54.
7. Pat Collins CM, *Intimacy and the Hungers of the Heart*, Columba Press, 1991, p. 117.
8. Roy McCloughry, op. cit.
9. *Guardian*, 11 January, 1993, p. 4.
10. Roy McCloughry, *Men and Masculinity, From Power to Love*, Hodder & Stoughton, 1992, Chapter 4.
11. Russ Parker, *Failure*, Grove Spirituality Series, no. 23, 1987, p. 24.
12. Henri Nouwen, *In the House of the Lord*, p. 15.
13. Wanda Nash, *Living with God at the Vicarage*, Grove Pastoral Series, No. 42, 1990, p. 4.
14. *Prague Post*, 8-14 September, 1992.
15. For a full and instructive look at this area for caring professionals as a whole, including clergy, see Peter Rutter, *Sex in the Forbidden Zone*, Mandala, 1990.
16. Richard Holloway, *Anger, Sex Doubt & Death*, SPCK, 1992, p. 60.
17. Macrina Wiederkehr, *A Tree Full of Angels*, pp. 2, 3.
18. Ibid., p. 3.

Chapter 3

1. Duncan Buchanan, *The Counselling of Jesus*, The Jesus Library, Hodder & Stoughton 1985, p. 33.
2. Henri Nouwen, *Reaching Out*, quoted by Anne Long in *Listening*, Darton, Longman and Todd, 1990, p. 36.
3. Anne Long, *Listening*, p. 37.

4. Duncan Buchanan, op. cit., p. 159.
5. For further information about Christian Listeners, a training project of the Acorn Christian Healing Trust, write to ACHT, Whitehill Chase, High St, Bordon, Hants, GU35 OAP.
6. The Association of Christian Counsellors, Kings House, 175 Wokingham Road, Reading, Berks, RG6 ILT.
7. Jean Vanier, *Men and Women He made them*, Darton, Longman and Todd 1985, p. 22.

Chapter 4

1. Dennis Brown and Jonathan Pedder, *Introduction to Psychotherapy*, SSP, Tavistock Publications Ltd, 1979, p. 54. (Adapted from Luft 1966.)
2. Albert Mehrabian, *Communication without Words*, Psychology Today, 1968.
3. Martin Seligman, *Helplessness: on depression, development and death*, San Francisco, Freeman Scribners, 1975.
4. Margaret Gill, *Introduction to Psycho-Sexual Medicine*, Defences in the patient, ed. R. L. Skrine, Montana Press, 1989.
5. Myra Chave-Jones, *Listening to your Feelings*, Lion, 1989, pp. 65, 66.
6. Brown and Pedder, op. cit., A very clear account of defence mechanisms is given in Part 1.
7. Richard Holloway, *Anger, Sex, Doubt and Death*, SPCK, 1992, p. 29.
8. Brown and Pedder, op. cit., p. 62.
9. Margaret Gill, op. cit., p. 107. See also Henri Nouwen, *Reaching Out*, Collins, 1976, Chapters 4-6.

Chapter 5

1. Myra Chave-Jones, *Listening to your Feelings*, Lion, 1989, p. 118.
2. Pat Collins CM, *Intimacy and the Hungers of the Heart*, Columba Press, Dublin, 1991, p. 101.

3. John Powell, *Why am I afraid to tell you who I am?* Fontana, 1969, p. 12.

4. C. S. Lewis, *The Four Loves*, Fount Paperbacks, 1960.

5. Roy McCloughry, *Men and Masculinity*, p. 67.

6. Roger Hurding, *Restoring the Image*, Paternoster Press, 1980, p. 85.

7. Richard Foster, *Celebration of Discipline*, Hodder & Stoughton, 1980, p. 102.

8. Ibid., p. 105.

9. Some of these comments on submission draw on material in 'Listening to Marriage', a further unit for Christian Listeners, copyright Acorn Christian Healing Trust.

10. Gilbert Bilezkian, *Beyond Sex Roles*, Baker Book House, 1986, p. 137 and notes.

11. Roger Hurding, op. cit., p. 120.

12. Gilbert Bilezkian, op. cit., p. 161.

13. Roger Hurding, op. cit., Chapter 5.

14. Robert Owen, 1771-1858, when ending his partnership with William Allen.

15. Roger Hurding, op. cit., p. 120.

16. Jack Dominian, *Marital Breakdown*, London, Penguin Books Ltd, 1968, Quoted by Roger Hurding, p. 120.

17. For authoritative and helpful books on this area see John L. Sandford, *Why some Christians Commit Adultery*, USA. Victory House Inc, 1989. Peter Rutter MD, *Sex in the Forbidden Zone*, Mandala, 1990.

18. These principles are taken from 'Listening to Marriage' a further unit from Christian Listeners, Acorn Christian Healing Trust. i and iii are adapted with permission from notes on pastoral care and counselling by Mrs Jan Stafford, All Nations Christian College, Ware.

Chapter 6

1. Donald Goergen, *The Sexual Celibate*, SPCK, 1974, p. 116.

2. Margaret Evening, *Who Walk Alone*, Hodder & Stoughton, 1974, p. 22.
3. David Gillett, in *A Place in the Family*, Grove Pastoral Series No 6, p. 5.
4. Ibid., p. 6.
5. Ibid., p. 9.
6. Michel Quoist, from 'To Love – The Prayer of the Adolescent' in *Prayers of Life*, Gill & Macmillan, Dublin, 1963, p. 38.
7. Anne Long in *A Place in the Family*, p. 16.
8. David Gillett in *A Place in the Family*, p. 7.
9. Audrey Beslow, *Sex and the Single Christian*, Abingdon Press, 1987, p. 29.
10. Richard Foster, *Celebration of Discipline*, Hodder, 1980, p. 6.
11. Donald Goergen, op. cit., p. 112 and p. 220.
12. Norman Autton, *Touch, an Exploration*, Darton, Longman and Todd, 1989, (see chapter 3).
13. Donald Goergen, op. cit., p. 164.
14. Gerald Vann quoted by Donald Goergen, op cit., p. 173.
15. Margaret Evening, op. cit., p. 43.
16. Margaret Evening, op. cit., p. 54.
17. Anne Long in *A Place in the Family*, p. 5.
18. Roger Hurding, *The Bible and Counselling*, Hodder & Stoughton, 1992, pp 135, 136, James Nelson, *The Intimate Connection: Male sexuality, masculine spirituality*, Philadelphia, Westminster Press, 1988, p. 65. Quoted in Roger Hurding, op. cit., p. 136.
19. Donald Goergen, op. cit., p. 141.

Chapter 7

1. Prudence Tunnadine, *Insights into Troubled Sexuality*, Chapman and Hall, revised edition, 1992, p. 14.
2. Ibid., p. 117.
3. Richard J. Foster, *Money, Sex and Power*, Hodder & Stoughton, 1985, p. 123
4. Ibid., p. 126.

5. Russ Parker, *Healing Dreams*, SPCK (revised edition), 1993, p. 7.
6. For a fuller study of differences and similarities between dreams and visions in the Bible and many more examples, see Russ Parker, op. cit., chapter 2.
7. See, for example, Dave Hunt and T. A. McMahon, *The Seduction of Christianity*, Harvest House Publishers, Oregon, 1985.
8. Anthony Storr, *Jung*, Fontana, 1973, p. 110.
9. Russ Parker, op. cit., p. 33.

Chapter 8

1. William Shakespeare, *Macbeth* iv.iii, 209.
2. Richard Holloway, *Anger, Sex, Doubt and Death*, SPCK, 1992, p.87.
3. Ibid., p. 95.
4. Jenny Francis, *Belief Beyond Pain*, SPCK, 1992, p. 47.
5. Ibid., p. 48.
6. J. Moltmann, *Experiences of God*, SPCK, 1980.
7. Prue Tunnadine, *Insights into Troubled Sexuality*, p. 183.
8. Susan Hill, *The Bird of Night*, Penguin, 1972.
9. Lily Pincus, *Death and the Family, The Importance of Mourning*, Faber and Faber, 1976, p. 176.
10. Ibid., chapter 7.
11. Susan Hill, *Family*, Penguin Books, 1987, p. 112.
12. Michael Mitton and Russ Parker, *Requiem Healing – A Christian Understanding of the Dead*, Daybreak, Darton, Longman and Todd, 1991, pp. 7-8.
13. Lily Pincus, op. cit., p. 278.

For further reading on the pastoral care of the bereaved:

Lily Pincus, op. cit., chapter 7.
Elizabeth Kübler-Ross, *On Death and Dying*, Tavistock Pubs.
Ian Ainsworth-Smith, *Letting Go – Caring for the Dying and Bereaved*, SPCK.

Jean Grigor, *Loss - An Invitation to Grow*, Arthur James.

Sheila Cassidy, *Sharing the Darkness*, Darton, Longman and Todd.

C. S. Lewis, *A Grief Observed*, Faber.

Colin Murray-Parkes, *Bereavement - Studies of Grief in Adult Life*, Pelican.

Althea Pearson, *Growing Through Loss and Grief*, HarperCollins, 1994.

Chapter 9

1. Leanne Payne, *The Broken Image*, Crossway Books, 1981, p. 139.

2. Wellings, Field, Johnson & Wadsworth, *Sexual Behaviour in Britain: The National Survey of Sexual Attitudes and Lifestyles*, Penguin, 1994, p. 118.

3. Elizabeth R. Moberly, *Homosexuality: A New Christian Ethic*, James Clarke & Co. Cambridge, 1983. See also for further reading Elizabeth Moberly, *Psychogenesis: The Early Development of Gender Identity*, Routledge & Kegan Paul Ltd.

4. Ibid, p. 2.

5. Ibid, p. 2.

6. Ibid, p. 6.

7. Richard Foster, *Money, Sex and Power*, p. 109.

8. David Field, *The Homosexual Way, a Christian Option?*, Grove Booklets on Ethics No. 9, p. 11.

9. Jack Dominian, quoted in Jim Cotter, *Good Fruits*, Cairns Publications, 1988, p. 85.

10. Jürgen Moltmann, in a lecture in Guildford Cathedral entitled 'An invitation to God's Future', October, 1993.

11. See Frank Lake, *Clinical Theology*, Abridged by Martin H. Teomans, Darton, Longman and Todd, 1986.

12. Leanne Payne, op. cit., p. 148.

13. Elizabeth Moberly, op. cit., p. 43.

14. For further reading on this subject, see Russ Parker, *Forgiveness is Healing*, Darton, Longman and Todd, 1993.

15. Elizabeth Moberly, op. cit., p. 52.

16. Jim Cotter, *Good Fruits*, Cairns Publications, 1988, p. 91.

Some resources for those struggling with issues of homosexuality:

True Freedom Trust, P O Box 3, Upton, Wirral, Merseyside. Offers Christian counselling and help.

'*Living Waters*' *UK*, P.O. Box 1530, London SW1W 0QW. Runs a 30 week discipleship programme in London, recommends and supplies books and runs an annual conference.

Chapter 10

1. Hilary Cashman, *Christianity and Sexual Abuse*, SPCK, 1993, p. 1.
2. Peter Gibbs, *Child Sexual Abuse - A Concern for the Church?* Grove Pastoral Series No 49, p.4. (reference to D. Finkelhor, Child Sexual Abuse: new Theory and Research, Collier and MacMillan, New York, 1984).
3. Dr Anne Townsend, 'When Sexually Abused Children Grow Up', in *Healing and Wholeness*, October/December, 1992.
4. Maxine Hancock and Karen Burton Mains, *Child Sexual Abuse: A Hope for Healing*, Highland Books, 1988, p. 6.
5. Gill Wakley, *Sexual Abuse and the Primary Care Doctor*, Psychosexual Medicine Series 3, Chapman and Hall, 1991, p. 3.
6. Ibid, p. 43.
7. Hilary Cashman, op. cit., p. 103.
8. Hilary Cashman, op. cit., p. 37.
9. Hilary Cashman, op. cit., p. 42.
10. Hancock and Mains, op. cit., p. 130.
11. Judy Hanson, *Rape as Bereavement*, Grove Pastoral Series No 50, 1992, p. 4.
12. Ibid, p. 6.
13. Ray Wyre and Anthony Swift, *Women, Men and Rape*, Headway, Hodder & Stoughton, 1990, p. 7.
14. Safety Net, the Chaplaincy, St George's Hospital, Blackshaw Road, London, SW17 0QT.

15. Pellauer, Chester, Boyajian, (eds.) *Sexual Assault and Abuse, A Handbook for Clergy and Religious Professionals,* Harper, San Francisco, 1987, p. 224.
16. Peter Gibbs, op. cit., p. 22.

Chapter 11

1. Frank Lake, *Tight Corners in Pastoral Counselling,* Darton, Longman and Todd, 1987, p. 79 (my italics).
2. Ibid, p. 80.
3. Roger Hurding, *The Bible and Counselling,* Hodder & Stoughton, 1992, p. 98.
4. Frank Lake, op. cit., p. 80.
5. Anne Long, *Listening,* Darton, Longman and Todd, 1990, p. 68.
6. Ibid, p. 64.
7. Prudence Tunnadine, *Insights into Troubled Sexuality - A Case Profile Anthology,* Chapman Hall, 1992.
8. Wendy Greengross, *Entitled to Love - the Sexual and Emotional Needs of the Handicapped,* NMGC, 1976, p. 1.
9. Elizabeth Forsythe, *Multiple Sclerosis, Exploring Sickness and Health,* Faber and Faber, 1988.
10. Alvin Marcetti and Shirley Lunn, *A Place of Growth, Counselling and Pastoral Care of People with AIDS,* Darton, Longman and Todd, 1993, p. 8.

FOR FURTHER READING

Sex and Disablement

Jean Vanier, *Men and Women He made them,* Darton, Longman and Todd, 1985.

HIV & AIDS

Patrick Dixon, *The Truth about AIDS,* Kingsway, 1987.
Jack Dominian, *Sexual Integrity: The Answer to AIDS,* Darton, Longman and Todd, 1987.
Vicky Cosstick (Ed.), *AIDS - Meeting the Community,* St Paul's Publications, 1987.

Useful Addresses

For psychosexual help: The Institute of Psychosexual Medicine (list of trained doctors available), 11 Chandos Street, Cavendish Square, London, W1M 9DE Tel. 071 580 0631

Sexual and Marital help: The Association of Sexual and Marital Therapists, P.O. Box 62, Sheffield S10 3TS. Tel. 0742 303901 RELATE, Marriage Guidance. (local addresses in Yellow Pages.) Some branches offer help with sexual difficulties.

Sexuality and Disablement: SPOD (Sexual and Personal Relations of the Disabled), 286 Camden Road, London, N7 0BJ.

AIDS: Mildmay AIDS Hospice, Mildmay Mission Hospital, Hackney Road, London, E2 7NA. Tel: 071 939 2331

Chapter 12

1. Philip Sheldrake, *Images of Holiness*, Darton, Longman and Todd, 1987, p. 2.
2. Richard Rohr, *Near Occasions of Grace*, Orbis Books, Maryknoll, New York, 1993, p. 34.
3. Ibid., p. 23.
4. Henri J. M.Nouwen, *Reaching Out*, Fount Paperbacks, 1980, chs. 1-3.
5. Richard Rohr, op cit., p. 33.
6. Matthew Fox, *Original Blessing*, Bear and Co., 1983, p. 59. Quoted in Margaret Magdalen, CSMV, *Transformed by love*, Darton, Longman and Todd, 1989, p. 9.
7. Anne Long, *Praise Him in the Dance*, Hodder and Stoughton, 1976, p. 120.
8. Susan Howatch, *Glamorous Powers*, William Collins Sons & Co. Ltd., 1988, p. 46.
9. Adrian Thatcher, *Liberating Sex*, SPCK, 1993, p. 43.
10. Ibid., p. 41.
11. Jim Cotter, *Pleasure, Pain and Passion*, p. 85.
12. Elaine Storkey, *Mary's Story, Mary's Song*, Fount Paperbacks, 1993, p. 40.

13. William Horwood, *Skallagrigg*, Penguin Books, pp. 351–352.
14. Ruth Burrows, *Living Love*, Darton, Longman and Todd, 1985, p. 95.